THE
WANDERING
MIND

 What Medieval Monks
Tell Us About Distraction

Jamie Kreiner

LIVERIGHT PUBLISHING CORPORATION

A Division of W. W. Norton & Company

Independent Publishers Since 1923

For information about permission to reproduce selections from this book, write
to Permissions, Liveright Publishing Corporation, a division of
W. W. Norton & Company, Inc., 500 Fifth Avenue, New York, NY 10110

For information about special discounts for bulk purchases, please contact
W. W. Norton Special Sales at specialsales@wwnorton.com or 800-233-4830

Manufacturing by Lakeside Book Company
Book design by Lovedog Studio
Production manager: Lauren Abbate

Library of Congress Cataloging-in-Publication Data

Names: Kreiner, Jamie, 1982– author.
Title: The wandering mind : what medieval monks tell us about distraction /
    Jamie Kreiner.
Description: First edition. | New York, NY : Liveright Publishing Corporation,
    a division of W. W. Norton & Company, Independent Publishers Since 1923,
    [2023] | Includes bibliographical references and index.
Identifiers: LCCN 2022049668 | ISBN 9781631498053
Subjects: LCSH: Distraction (Psychology)—Religious aspects—Christianity—
    History—To 1500. | Monasticism and religious orders—History—Early church,
    ca. 30–600. | Monasticism and religious orders—History—Middle Ages,
    600–1500.
Classification: LCC BR195.D57 K74 2023 | DDC 206/.57—dc23/eng/20221209
LC record available at https://lccn.loc.gov/2022049668

ISBN 978-1-324-09444-9 pbk.

Liveright Publishing Corporation, 500 Fifth Avenue, New York, N.Y. 10110
www.wwnorton.com

W. W. Norton & Company Ltd., 15 Carlisle Street, London W1D 3BS

1 2 3 4 5 6 7 8 9 0

They used to say of a certain saint that he bore witness to his faith during a persecution and was so severely tortured that they sat him on a burning hot seat of bronze. In the meantime the blessed Constantine became emperor and the Christians were set free. When this saint was healed, he returned to his cell. Seeing it from a distance he said: "O dear, I am coming back again to many woes!" He said this meaning the struggles and battles with the demons.

—*Apophthegmata patrum*, Anonymous Collection, N. 469, trans. John Wortley

✳

Routine, repetition, tedium, monotony, ephemeracy, inconsequence, abstraction, disorder, boredom, angst, ennui—these are the true hero's enemies, and make no mistake, they are fearsome indeed. For they are real.

—Substitute teacher of Advanced Tax, in David Foster Wallace, *The Pale King*

CONTENTS

THE WORLD OF EARLY CHRISTIAN MONKS

| 0 | | 790 | | 1,580 | Mi |

| 0 | | 1,250 | | 2,500 | Km |

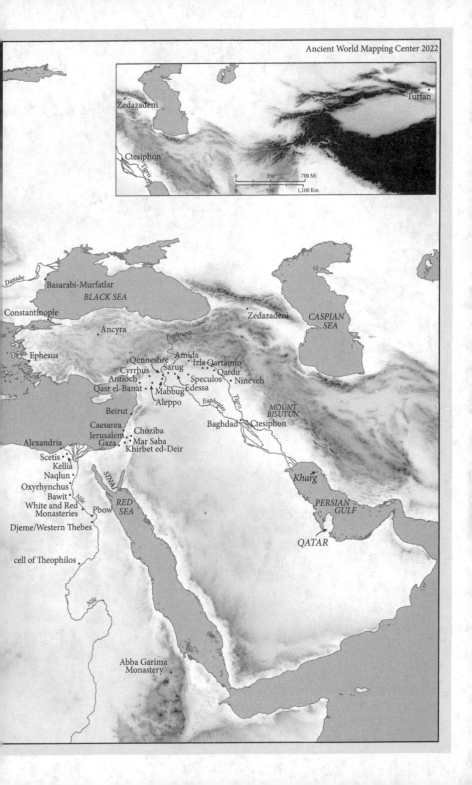

Ancient World Mapping Center 2022

Turfan

Zedazadeni

Ctesiphon

Tigris

0   350   700 Mi
0   550   1,100 Km

Danube

Basarabi-Murfatlar
BLACK SEA

Constantinople

Ancyra

Zedazadeni

CASPIAN SEA

Ephesus

Euphrates

Qenneshre   Amida   Qartāmīn
Cyrrhus   Sarug   Izla
Antioch   Speculos
Qasr el-Banat   Edessa   Nineveh
                Mabbug   Qardu
        Aleppo

Euphrates   *Tigris*

MOUNT BISUTUN

Baghdad   Ctesiphon

Beirut

Caesarea
Jerusalem   Choziba
Gaza   Mar Saba
Khirbet ed-Deir

Alexandria

Scetis
Kellia
Naqlun
Oxyrhynchus
Bawit
White and Red
Monasteries
Pbow

SINAI

Nile

RED SEA

Kharg

PERSIAN GULF

Djeme/Western Thebes

cell of Theophilos

Nile

QATAR

Abba Garima
Monastery

THE WANDERING MIND

INTRODUCTION

Do you feel like you're more distracted today than you were five or ten or fifty years ago? Other people definitely feel that way about themselves. Individuals polled about this problem in 2012 tended to blame stress, major life changes, lack of sleep, and (in fourth place) their phones. In 2019 a team of data scientists and physicists suggested that our collective distraction is growing due to an increasingly overwhelming deluge of information: the more things that call for our attention, the less time we spend talking or thinking about any one of them before moving on. Other observers have suggested that distraction is a growing problem because of increasingly rapid media technologies, the capitalization of labor and time, and our global connectivity—critiques that have been made passionately and continuously since the nineteenth century. And in 2022 the journalist Johann Hari compiled a dozen causes for our chronic distraction; some of them, such as "surveillance capitalism" and overreliance on medication to treat ADHD, are relatively recent phenomena.[1]

Our sense that distraction is getting worse carries ominous implications. Journalists and scientists tell us that distraction has serious consequences, among them unproductivity, chronic boredom, sleep deprivation, bad grades, weak relationships, car crashes, a lack of personal fulfillment, and a loss of civic solidarity. Even in small doses, at a safe distance from heavy machinery, it can still be maddening.[2] At times like ours, when it feels like things are declining rapidly, the distant past can seem especially alluring. Historians know this impulse well: many societies in states of flux have looked to earlier eras in search of a lost and supposedly more stable Golden Age. In the case of distraction, the alarming experiences of modern distraction have prompted nostalgic gestures back to those supposed paragons of concentration, medieval monks. They didn't have these problems, we think wistfully. They had it all figured out.[3]

Modern pundits are not alone in holding up monks as exemplars. Even medieval observers were impressed by how monks seemed never to get sidetracked. But the monks themselves knew better. Although they didn't have Twitter, or YouTube, or text threads full of links from their friends—and even though many monks did actually live in solitude or in monasteries that discouraged casual conversations—they were, in fact, constantly distracted.

Not only that: monks themselves were deeply preoccupied by the problem of distraction. They tried to pinpoint its causes. They developed tactics to combat it. And although they inhabited a very different world from ours, their struggles can offer us new ways to think about distraction and concentration in our own lives. They help us appreciate that distraction is older than our technology. They remind us that our minds are part of larger systems that are inescapably interdependent and variable, and they offer a serious set of practices for cultivating attentiveness in a world in flux. They also give us someone to blame for our predicament: we moralize distraction in part because they did, more than a millennium and a half ago.

These women and men were active in Late Antiquity and the early Middle Ages—or in the centuries from roughly 300 to 900. They thought a lot about thinking because one of the goals that most defined their practice was to connect their minds to God and to achieve a state of attention that was unshakable. In that state, the mind could attain panoramic vistas of the universe that transcended both space and time. It was clear-sighted calm above the chaos.

This ideal is attested throughout these centuries, in Qatar and in Ireland and in the places in between. It appears in monks' hagiographies, handbooks, and treatises, and in the meditational memos that they painted on their walls. But the reason it shows up throughout their writings isn't because monks were *good* at warding off distraction. By their own accounts they were often pretty bad at it. They saw distraction as a primordial struggle—partly the result of demonic antagonism, partly the result of their own misbehaving selves, and primarily the result of the fracturing of the union between God and his creation at the beginning of time. Yet despite their understanding of distraction as common to all human beings, they didn't come to the conclusion that it was morally neutral. Instead they saw themselves as obligated to fight against it. And their struggle became something of a professional identity: stretching the mind out to the things that mattered, against the ethically inferior alternatives, was what made a monk a monk.

The monks' experiences of distraction give us something to commiserate. And even when their lives and perspectives seem startlingly strange to us, their attention to their minds should make us rethink our own.

✳

ONE SIGN THAT concentration mattered so much to Christian monks in Late Antiquity and the early Middle Ages is the proliferation of metaphors that they used to praise it. On a very good day, a monk's mind was stretchy, fiery, clear. It constructed buildings that brushed up against the heavens. It spent time with what it loved. It was a fish swimming in the depths to avoid getting caught, a helmsman steering a ship through a tempest, a potter working on his pot, a cat holding on to a mouse, a hen carefully incubating her eggs.[4]

Observers were impressed by the way that these active inner states translated into seemingly opposite outer states. While monks' minds were at work in concentration, their bodies were as still as statues, quietly setting world records. A monk named Hor was said to have lived in a church for twenty years without ever lifting his eyes to the roof. Sarah reportedly lived next to a river for sixty years without looking at it even once. Martin shared a cave with a snake for three years without letting it faze him. Caluppa prayed in a cave where snakes often fell on him from the ceiling and wound around his neck—but he didn't flinch, either. Landibert stood praying outside until the snow came up to his ankles. James prayed outside for so long that the snow swallowed him entirely, and his neighbors had to shovel him out. And the celebrated monk Pachomius outperformed a parade of demonic visitors who were increasingly desperate to distract him. They turned into naked women and sat with him while he ate. They fell into formation, like soldiers, and marched back and forth, saluting Pachomius by name. They rumbled the walls of his dwelling. They tied a rope around a palm leaf and dragged it around on the ground like they were construction workers moving a boulder, heave-hoing and yelling in the hopes that he would look over and laugh. But Pachomius didn't even glance at his tormentors. In these chronic battles for his attention, the demons always lost, and then they disappeared.[5]

But this is not a book about success stories, because the celebratory accounts of monks' achievements point to a much more interesting history—the dilemma of the majority who did not have perfect concentration. Monks told and retold stories of cognitive feats precisely because most of them were beset by distraction. Even the experts were regularly frustrated by failure. A respected monk and teacher named John of Dalyatha, who lived in the eighth century in what's now northern Iraq, once vented in a letter to his brother and fellow monk that "all I do is eat, sleep, drink, and be negligent."[6] On very good days, John knew what it was like to concentrate completely, and he wrote about the experience with captivating warmth. But his shortcomings still overwhelmed him.

Monks defined distraction in different ways. Most basically it was a mental detour, and sometimes it could be a good thing. For example: an abba (monastic father) named John became so preoccupied by thinking about God while he was weaving a basket that he made twice as much border as was needed. Or a monk named John Colobos got distracted in the middle of a transaction with a camel driver. He went inside his cell to get a rope to bring to the driver, but he became so absorbed in meditation that he totally forgot what he'd been doing and left the driver waiting outside. Eventually the driver knocked on his door, reminded John to get the rope, and John snapped into action—only to get distracted again. He did manage to come through on the third try, by reciting the phrase "rope, camel" to himself until he finally completed the task: the desperate mnemonic of someone whose mind was elsewhere.[7] Monks shared these stories in admiration and amusement.

But usually distraction meant doing something you *didn't* want to do, and being drawn into thoughts you didn't want to have. These were the distractions that monks wanted to dodge, and Gregory the Great offers a famous case in point. Gregory had been a monk before becoming a deacon and then bishop of Rome in 590, and he often felt that the position pulled him away from the contemplative practices he loved. The prologue of his *Dialogues*, a text that was enormously popular in the early Middle Ages, begins with Gregory sneaking away from his job for a few moments of quiet, as a distraction from his distractions. "The ship of my mind is being battered by cyclones," he lamented to the deacon who found him in his hiding spot, and then he launched into a series of stories—for his deacon and for his readers—about holy figures who led better lives than he did.[8]

If Gregory had remained a monk instead of becoming the best-known bishop of the early Middle Ages, however, he probably wouldn't have fared any better. Monks, too, had jobs that forced them to think about things they didn't like. Antony of Choziba (in what's now the West Bank) complained, for instance, that his position as the monastery's cellarer was a distraction.[9] But the more common problem—and the more serious one—was that even when monks created the perfect conditions for concentration, they still found themselves unable to focus on what mattered most to them: namely, on God, on the divine logic that structured the universe from its creation to the Last Judgment, and on their moral obligations within that system. Stretching the mind and the self out to these subjects was a monk's core job requirement, and even more crucially, monks saw it as a matter of eternal life and death. The fate of the soul, even the souls of other people, hung in the balance. Monks were not simply trying to get more work done. These women and men were trying to align themselves with the ethics of salvation. The stakes could not have been more serious.

This was the understanding of distraction and its significance that the early monastic pioneer Basil of Caesarea had in mind. Basil was a shrewd educator. He worked as a bishop in the Roman imperial province of Cappadocia in the 370s; he also spent a decade writing a series of reflections and guidelines in conversation with monastic communities that he supervised, which monks would consult for centuries to come. Basil told his monks that distraction was at play whenever someone was not trying to please God. And he stressed that dealing with distraction was fundamental to all other aspects of his monks' training: "We cannot succeed in keeping any commandment at all," he told them, "if our minds are wandering off in this direction and that."[10]

The dire consequences of distraction became a pervasive motif among Christian monks in Late Antiquity and the early Middle Ages. Once again, an abundance of metaphors attests to the ubiquity of their interest and concern. Distractions were snakeskins that needed to be sloughed off. They were flies that needed to be swatted away. They were smells luring a dog around a meat market. They were "a great dust cloud," a hair poking your eye, an infestation of mice, a dense forest, a treacherous swamp, ruptures in a waterway, bandits. They were storms battering a tree, cargo overloading a ship, usurpers besieging a town, horses breaking out of a stable, thieves breaking into a house. They left a monk gasping like a fish on dry land. They miscarried or aborted his prayers.[11]

Monks' advice for dealing with distractions employed language that was just as vivid. Abba Poemen, an influential teacher at the monastic community of Scetis (today Wadi el-Natrun, west of the Nile Delta), was famous for his analogies. His quips make up a substantial chunk of the *Apophthegmata patrum* or *Sayings of the Elders*, which was a widely circulating and shifting set of stories about early monastic heroes known as the "desert fathers" and "desert mothers"—most of them Egyptians who had lived in the fourth and early fifth centuries. A Syriac version of the *Apophthegmata* cites Poemen as saying that "the chief of all wickednesses is the wandering of the thoughts," a comment that also surfaced in other languages, while in the Greek manuscript tradition known as the Alphabetical Collection, the many aphorisms attributed to him express his determination to help monks deal with distraction. Just as a ruler employs a bodyguard, the mind needs one too, he reportedly said. Likewise monks should organize their thoughts like clothes in a closet, or trap unwanted thoughts in a bottle like a snake or scorpion, or keep good thoughts bubbling away on the fire rather than leaving them to cool like leftovers and attract pests.[12] Failing such inventive imagery, there were always the perennially popular motifs drawn from athletics and the military. Distraction was an opponent in the arena and on the battlefield that had to be vanquished. That combative approach to distraction was one of the reasons that former sports stars and soldiers made such good converts to monasticism. Monks saw themselves as athletes and warriors. This was an endurance sport. This was war.[13]

The proliferation of monastic metaphors for thinking about distraction reflects the relentless efforts that these monks made to capture their cognitive experiences. In that sense they are not so different from us. We are still searching for the right metaphors to describe our brains and how they work.[14] But the monks were savvier than the average modern person when it came to actually dealing with distraction. They were committed to the idea that the mind's tendencies could be transformed. They thought about distraction comprehensively, probing its connections to larger issues beyond their brains, and this led them to develop an array of strategies to concentrate that were remarkably sophisticated. Because they understood distraction to be linked systemically to issues of society, money, culture, and more, they sought to sever themselves from that world and set up new communities and practices based on shared values. They reordered their working days and made themselves accountable to each other. They developed physical regimens to improve the joint functioning of their bodies and minds. They experimented with book technologies, mnemonic devices, meditations, and metacognitive practices, all to improve their attention and dedication to spiritual growth.

Monks disagreed about methods—not to mention metaphors—and they never solved the problem of distraction to their liking. Every strategy had its risks and glitches, as they knew all too well. Their history does not suggest any quick fixes. But their struggles and successes can serve as a warning and a guide down the centuries.

DISTRACTEDNESS IS NOT SPECIFIC to the modern world and the modern experience, and as the monks make clear, neither is our *anxiousness* about distraction. As the neuroscientist Adam Gazzaley and the psychologist Larry D. Rosen have put it, we have "ancient brains": the neurological mechanics that make us so very distractible were bestowed on us and on premodern monks by our shared evolutionary ancestors. But we modern persons are also heirs to a set of cultural values surrounding cognition that are very specifically monastic and, to an extent, specifically Christian. This is not to say that questions of attention and distraction are exclusive to Christian monks. Many spiritual adepts across ancient and medieval Eurasia sought a calm and concentrated mind, and Daoist and Buddhist monks devised an extensive repertory of attention techniques in these same centuries. Some of them treated distraction with indifference, as something to ignore or wait out, while others saw distraction as an evil impediment or as a sign of karmic blockage. Buddhist monks in Central Asia in the fifth to seventh centuries, for example, had a penchant for portraying demons as armed intruders threatening monks in meditation. (The evidence for their views is concentrated in Turfan, a settlement along the Silk Road where, as it happens, many Christian monastic texts would find an enthusiastic reception in the ninth and tenth centuries and possibly much earlier.) In any case, it's clear that early Christian monks were deeply concerned about distraction, sometimes more so than their contemporaries to the east, and thanks to a long afterlife of Christian concerns about distraction, we are still living with that inheritance. Ironically, the popular adoption (and appropriation) of South and East Asian practices in Europe and North America may have obscured our debts to the monastic culture that seeded those concerns in the first place.[15]

Philosophers in the Hellenistic and Roman worlds had emphasized attentiveness—to one's thoughts and actions, to the present, to the divine—as central to the ethics of self-control. But distraction was not much of a concern to them, even though they complained about it sometimes; and they tended to see it as something external to the self. Take the Stoics: philosophers working in this tradition since the fourth century BCE were most distinctive for having rejected the Platonic physics of forms, but they were also deeply interested in logic and ethics, including the ethics of psychology. When they talked about distraction, or *perispasmos*, they were usually thinking about the obligations and odd jobs that kept a person from doing the serious work of philosophy. Distractions stemmed from the demands of other people, and from a failure to prioritize properly. But the Stoics did acknowledge that even unencumbered philosophers could potentially experience a different sort of distraction: the surprise encounter. Humans often found themselves facing things that they had not asked for or anticipated, and the Stoics dubbed these encounters "appearances." Appearances were usually beyond a person's control—whether it was a scene in a play, a sudden sharp awareness of income disparity, the death of a friend, or other such situations—but the Stoics suggested that it *was* possible to control one's reaction to them, which was really what mattered. And they argued that the best sort of reaction to things that were not all that valuable was essentially nonreactive: you should choose *not* to form any sort of judgment or evaluation at all, because it would free you from feeling emotions that were pegged to a particular outcome. The result was a state of calm. Once you treated appearances indifferently, they could not disturb or derail you. In that way, a potential distraction couldn't become an actual distraction.[16]

Christian monks were indebted in many ways to the ancient philosophical traditions of the Mediterranean world, Stoicism included. But they were not nearly so assured about the matter of distraction. It wasn't enough for them to respond appropriately to the surprises and scenarios that made claims on their attention. They thought that distraction could also feel less interactive, that *distractedness* was a kind of preexisting condition—internal, nonconscious, and entangled with the self—that compromised the very commitment to concentrating on things that were important and good. For many Christian monks, distraction wasn't just a potential interference. It had already breached the walls and made itself at home.

This distinctly monastic perspective can be illustrated by comparing two views of nosiness, one of many behaviors that monks associated with distraction. The essayist and philosopher Plutarch wrote a short text in the first century CE dedicated to the subject, *On Nosiness* (*Peri polypragmosynes*), as part of a collection that is known today as the *Moralia*. Plutarch self-identified as a Platonist, but his goal in essays like this one was not to advocate for a particular school of philosophy; instead he was trying to persuade elite readers that philosophy had something to offer them in their day-to-day lives. And his take on nosiness put him squarely in the ancient tradition of thinking about distraction. His main objection to nosiness, like that of so many Greek and Latin writers before him, was that it was inappropriate and unproductive. Canvassing for gossip, peeking into people's houses or vehicles, breathlessly chasing the latest news, reading graffiti on your stroll through town about who is best friends with whom: all of this was a way of distracting yourself from more intellectual pursuits and from the responsibility of tending to your own issues. Nosiness enabled people who were already prone to philosophical inertia to stay that way. As Plutarch pointed out, the effects of a nosy disposition intensified over time. Busybodies who caved to every curiosity eventually became so easily distracted that they couldn't prioritize things that actually mattered.[17]

By contrast, about three hundred years later, a monk named John Cassian also pointed to nosiness as a problematic behavior, but he thought it was symptomatic of something even more serious. Cassian himself was gregarious, curious, and introspective. He spent nearly two decades traveling with his best friend and fellow monk, Germanus, to consult expert monks about how to discipline the self and above all the mind. And when he wrote his own monastic manual in the early fifth century, in light of these many conversations, he concluded that nosiness (*curiositas*, in Cassian's Latin) was a sign of mental instability, more specifically of a condition called *acedia*. A monk afflicted with acedia felt simultaneously dissatisfied and incapacitated. He was so unsure about how to change himself or his situation that he resorted to the maladaptive solution of shuffling over to his fellow monks and poking around in their affairs, like an obnoxious coworker or neighbor.

Cassian attributed this diagnosis to the apostle Paul (who was roughly a generation older than Plutarch), but it betrays the signs of late antique Christian monastic culture. Distraction was still seen as a detour from the commitments that really mattered. But it was not just an externality and an enabler for people who were trying to avoid actual work or introspection. It had also come to signal underlying cognitive conditions that could afflict even people who were determined to think and act ethically. And because it stemmed from inner turmoil, it could not be corrected simply by avoiding certain stimuli, or by resolving to have better intentions or practices. Monks had to tackle distraction systematically, and they saw it as their moral responsibility to do so. If we feel the same way, that's in part thanks to early Christian monasticism.[18]

＊

WHERE DID MONKS' DISTRACTION come from? As we'll see, they identified multiple triggers that will sound familiar, including the business (and busyness) of everyday life, information overload, and other people. These were only proximate causes, however, and monks also proposed metaphysical explanations that took a much longer view. One leading theory was that distractions were demonic. It was already widely believed in the ancient world that cosmic forces exercised influences on human beings. But in early Christian demonology, these vectors became profoundly personalized. In the primeval battle between good and evil, demons deployed intrusive thoughts that were custom-fit to their targets. These weapons seemed so shrewdly designed that, to some monks, it felt like the demons could read their minds. Cassian and Germanus even consulted a monastic elder to verify that this was so. But the abba, Serenus, countered that not even demons had that much power. They were only excellent analysts of human behavior, nothing more.

That didn't make them any less formidable, which is why the monastic literature of Late Antiquity is densely populated with demons, including the posse that antagonized Pachomius. The cantankerous abbot Shenoute, who headed an important federation of monasteries of men and women in Upper Egypt for nearly eighty years until his death in 465, once told an audience that Christ had hacked off all the limbs of the devil, so now the devil's thoughts were the most active thing about him. But unlike Monty Python's Black Knight, *this* figure was no joke. Nor were his powers merely metaphors for a monk's inner struggle to concentrate. Demons were literal opponents and sometimes even physical ones. But although violent assaults were part of their arsenal, their subtle cognitive work was even more sinister. Something as seemingly innocuous as the urge to take a nap might be a demon's doing. This was an argument that Evagrius of Pontus had made in the fourth century. "The bodies of the demons are very cold and like ice," he warned, and so they touch a monk's eyelids and whole head to warm themselves and in the process make monks drowsy—often when they are trying to read.[19]

Evagrius was born in the Black Sea region of Anatolia, and after a winding career that brought him into contact with many luminaries he eventually ended up in Kellia, one of the best-known monastic headquarters in the Nile Delta, where he trained with respected elders and became a teacher himself. When it came to Christian monastic theories and practices of the mind, Evagrius was perhaps the most influential teacher of them all—earning him nicknames including "the illuminator of the mind" and "the examiner of thoughts"—even though his work was also a flash point for controversy. But because monastic culture was as experimental as it was traditional, monks were not afraid to build upon what they learned rather than preserve it unaltered. Cassian was a protégé of Evagrius, for example, and although he also believed in demons, he preferred to point to personal weaknesses or deficiencies (*vitia*) as the more persistent cause of distraction. Cassian suggested that most weaknesses, such as anger and desire and sadness, had originated as forces of good that God had implanted in human bodies to serve as beneficial motivators. But they had gotten twisted for inappropriate uses and become defective. And they kept a monk from concentrating.[20]

Other monks chalked up internal conflicts and their atten-
dant distractions to the will (*thelema*, *voluntas*). The term meant
something like "ego," in the sense that they understood the will
as a force that was both self-preserving and self-dividing. The will
could want contrasting things simultaneously, but it tended to
reach for what was most appealing or expedient or comfortable,
rather than what was most beneficial. And by mixing up a person's
motivations, the will blocked the way to God. Some monks argued
that distraction could be remedied by strengthening the will to
commit to the right course of action, as the Qatari monk Dadishoʻ suggested in the late seventh century. But others proposed
exactly the opposite, that it was a *strong* will, rather than a weak
one, that caused distraction in the first place. This was the view of
a pair of solitary monks named Barsanuphius and John, who in the
sixth century served as spiritual mentors via a voluminous stream
of correspondence with the monastery of Tawatha, outside the city
of Gaza. As far as these two elders saw it, the will had to be shaved
or cut away in bits, by rejecting each distracting desire as it came.[21]

Even as monks blamed demons, personal deficiencies, and the
will with varying degrees of emphasis, they often suggested that
another source of distraction underlay them all. This factor was
not so much personal as it was primordial. Distraction, originally
and quasi-genetically, was the result of humanity's initial separation from God.

At the beginning of creation, so this theory went, the human
condition was characterized by unity and immutability. But when
Adam and Eve disobeyed God and chose instead to focus on themselves, they catalyzed a descent into mental fluctuation and fracture that would afflict the entire species from birth to death. Some
of the earliest monastic texts that survive, letters that the abba
Antony wrote in the 330s and 340s, already explain the monastic
venture as an effort to repair that fissure and reunite with God.
Later in the fourth century, a Syrian homily collection tied the
etiology of distraction even more bluntly to the Fall. "Adam at the

beginning lived in purity. He controlled his thoughts. But from the time that he transgressed the command of God, heavy mountains weighed upon his mind, and evil thoughts mingled with it and became completely a part of the mind, and yet this was not really man's mind by nature since such thoughts are tainted by evil." Distraction was a sign of traumatic division. Failures to concentrate were a repeated reminder of a person's distance from the divine.[22]

Although rooted in the biblical myth of creation, there was also a Neoplatonic tinge to this way of thinking. The Egyptian philosopher Plotinus had suggested in the third century that distraction not only divided the self but also separated it from God. The goal was to subtract those distractions from the soul's field of vision, to create a clear and sublime line of sight upward to the divine. But to the monks who were active a century or more after Plotinus, the mind had plunged so far beneath the heavenly plane that concentration could not simply be a matter of clearing away the brush. It had to stretch itself vertically while fighting off the distractions that attacked it internally and horizontally. It had to mobilize all the tools at its disposal—physical, social, psychological—to work its way back to unification.[23]

In short, Christian monks saw distraction as part of a cosmic drama whose hum was especially audible in the quiet of their cells. It had become imperative to discipline distraction and stretch the mind out to God.

Monks themselves were self-aware of this moral and practical shift. They even commemorated it in an episode in the *Apophthegmata patrum* that circulated in Greek, Latin, and Syriac. A group of non-Christian philosophers set out to test Christian monks in a kind of ascetic evaluation. The first monk they meet is well dressed; he insults them, so they move on. When the philosophers encounter the next monk, an old man they take for a backwater hack, they start beating him up—but the monk doesn't fight back. The philosophers are impressed. They dub him a true monk and wonder how he remains so impassible. They compare notes: He fasts, they fast. He is celibate, so are they. The monk tells them that he trusts in God's grace—and also, he guards his mind. The philosophers ignore his comment about God, but they are shaken by his point about the mind. They decide that *this* is what differentiates them: "We can't do this kind of guarding," they concede. Then they leave.[24]

Although this story was historically astute, it also involved some distortions. It downplays monks' own struggles to concentrate. It chalks up the differences in mental habits to ability rather than to divergent cognitive cultures. And its opposition between monks and philosophers obscures their interactions prior to this one staged sequence. But it does capture the sense that monks' concerns about distraction were unprecedented—and it gets something else right, too. There are two monks in this episode, and one of them does not come off well. It is a subtle nod to the fact that "monasticism" was a variegated and sometimes competitive culture, even in its earliest days. And that diversity also played a crucial role in the history of distraction.

✳

MONASTICISM WAS NOT ONLY EXPERIMENTAL; it was often competitive in Late Antiquity and the early Middle Ages. The fourth through the ninth centuries was not an age of clearly defined monastic orders. It was instead an era of the "monastic laboratory," as one pair of historians has dubbed it. Or as a Christian named Zacchaeus tried to explain it to a philosopher named Apollonius in a fictive dialogue from the early fifth century: monastic practices were manifold (*multiplex*), and there were many kinds of monks (*diversa genera monachorum*).[25]

In this half millennium, monks and the societies that supported them developed so many different practices and perspectives that this book can hardly scratch their surfaces. Even the very definition of monasticism was contested and fluctuating. But the hyperactivity of that laboratory has enriched the history of distraction immeasurably. Monks could agree that distraction was a serious problem, and the solutions they developed to rectify it were breathtaking in their diversity.

To study the history of early Christian monasticism is to be struck by an omnipresent tension between the tremendous differences among monks on the one hand and, on the other, the ideals and debates that bound them together. That tension pervades this book, which spans the continuum of the Middle East, Mediterranean, and Europe while crossing the conventional chronological divisions of post-Nicene and early medieval Christianity (or alternately, the political periods associated with the Roman, Sasanian, "barbarian," Byzantine, Umayyad, and 'Abbasid regimes). That tension also bridges sectarian identities. The monks who insisted on confessional labels called themselves orthodox or catholic, to suggest that their version of Christianity was the universal standard. They called their Christian competitors heretics and developed derogatory terms to flag them as partisans of some misguided leader. But many monks were not particularly invested in this kind of language, and this book avoids it, too, because monastic discourses often cut across doctrinal affiliations and rarely ended in consensus about what was right.

Consequently, I use the term "monk" in a broadly inclusive manner, to refer to women and men who experimented with different forms of monasticism. Christians in Late Antiquity and the early Middle Ages applied many different nouns to monastic practitioners, but their most basic terms could suit either gender: *monachos/monache* in Greek and Coptic, *monachus/monacha* in Latin, *ihidaya* in Syriac, *rahib/rahiba* in Arabic, and *mynecenu/munuc* in Old English.[26] This neutral terminology reflects the widely held conviction that Christian monasticism was a universal option for men and women alike: anyone could be a monk. This is not to say their experiences were identical. As we'll see, women's and men's participation in monasticism was sometimes significantly affected by their gender. And women are underrepresented in our narrative sources—there are far more stories of desert fathers than mothers, for example—even though there are enough incidental references to women monks to indicate that there were a great many of them. In any event, the evidence we have suggests that the cognitive goals and practices that monks set for themselves were similar across gender, and that experimental initiative and influence went in both directions.

Despite its limitations, the body of evidence we have for early Christian monastic culture is still enormously rich. Monks were, frankly, some of the wordiest people in Late Antiquity and the early Middle Ages. And many of their writings were part of their experimental efforts to develop new ways of thinking about monastic life and tackling its challenges.[27] Like all historical evidence, this material comes with interpretive complications, and historians have been careful to note that these sources provide a view of the past that is inescapably incomplete. But they have also discovered that monastic culture was not airtight. Christian monastic communities operated as counseling centers, think tanks, charitable organizations, real-estate developers, financial centers, liturgical hot spots, and festival grounds. Many of them received financial support that ranged from very modest gifts to landed endowments from Christian, Zoroastrian, and Muslim rulers. Some even became destinations for Muslim elites who respected their discipline (and who also enjoyed their books and their wine). Some committed acts of violence as domestic terrorists or as state-sanctioned "shock troops." Others acted as peacemakers.[28]

What this means for our evidence is that although we will never know how many demons Pachomius actually fought, the stories that circulated about him reflect a broader interest in the problem of distraction and its remedies. Combating distraction was necessary to the work that monks performed for the public (as we will see in chapter 1). Even more basically, the cognitive feats of the monks in nearby neighborhoods or on distant mountain crags captivated the imagination of many communities who heard about them. It reassured them to know that men and women were capable of such things, and that a constellated crew of them were stretching their minds in the service of something greater.

The Wandering Mind tracks their approaches from the outside in. It starts with monks' decisions to concentrate on God and follows them into the successive layers of their ideas and practices, moving from the world they abandoned to the communities they joined, the bodies they trained, the books they read, the meditational memories they constructed, the metacognitive monitoring they set up inside their minds, and, finally, the fleeting moments of pure attention that some of them managed to capture. Many of the techniques that monks devised to ward off distraction are still instructive today, and some of them closely resemble modern approaches. Just as fascinating, though, are their views that reveal the gulf between us. Christian monks may have bestowed on us their fixation on distraction and even some of their strategies to fight it—but not everything about them conforms to the present. Their minds sometimes worked in unexpected ways.

CHAPTER 1

THE WORLD

TODAY WHEN WE FEEL HELPLESS AGAINST OUR DIS-tractions, we unplug. We announce on our social media accounts that we're staying off our social media accounts, take digital detoxes, retreat to cabins in the woods. It's a relief while it lasts, a reminder that our minds are still capable of calm—but because such fixes are only temporary, and somewhat privileged, they're not, in the end, all that satisfying.

Our attempts would have made sense to monks in Late Antiquity and the early Middle Ages. They also "unplugged," in their way, as a first step in their campaign to concentrate on God and on their ethical obligations within his cosmos. But that detachment was supposed to be permanent, because they saw distraction as a structural feature of their societies. It was the world itself that had to be abandoned, not some select slice of it.

The concept of monastic separation from the world had multiple birthplaces, and monks themselves had varying accounts of its beginnings. A commentator named Asterius, writing in the early fifth century, identified Adam as the first monk because he had lived in quiet solitude until Eve came along. Other monks liked to trace their roots to Moses, whose obedience to God was defined by the desert. Yet others derived their lineage from the biblical book of Acts, which describes the apostles as having "one heart and soul, and no one claimed private ownership of any possessions, but everything they owned was held in common" (4:32). Today you're likelier to read in nonspecialist accounts that Antony (ca. 251–356 CE) was the first Christian monk and that his fellow Egyptian Pachomius (ca. 292–346)—the undistractible Pachomius we've already met—was the founder of communal monasticism. But there were monks before Antony struck out into the desert and monasteries before Pachomius began agglomerating them in the 320s. The historical simplification is almost as old as monasticism itself. Late antique and early medieval Christians were as drawn to origin stories as we are, and so they tended to focus on a few figures who had become international stars thanks to some very popular texts.[1]

But they relished the origin stories of individual monks, too, because no matter how many times it happened, the choice to abandon the world was an exhilarating tipping point. Moses the Ethiopian gave up a life of banditry to become a monk. The shepherd Apollo murdered a pregnant woman, just to see what a fetus looked like—then fled to a monastery to confess and repent. Bar-Sahde was on a merchant ship to India when it was attacked by pirates, and he swore he'd become a monk if he escaped. And Paul walked in on his wife having sex with someone else, so he turned around and headed straight into the desert to train with the great Antony himself.[2]

Most monks did not have such sensational backstories. But no matter how unrealistic these accounts seemed, they sharply conveyed the rupture that every monk was after.[3] A monk's life began by abandoning "the world" and turning toward a new ethical system. It was a *conversio*: a complete 180.

"The world" itself was not inherently bad. When Christians looked to the Genesis accounts of its beginnings, they usually concluded that everything God had created was good. But "the world" was also a monastic euphemism for entanglement. It was family, friends, property, work, and daily routines. It was legal disputes and endless discussions about farming and livestock. It was gossip, it was news. It was the thrill and trauma and banality of everyday life that overloaded your attention.[4]

So although the world was good, some Christians—and monks especially—saw it as an inherent distraction from the one who had created it. The bishop and monastic theorist Basil of Caesarea insisted that "it is impossible to make progress in such meditation and prayer among the multiplicities which drag the soul about and keep it entangled in worldly engagements." Or as the abbot Hildemar of Civate put it more bluntly nearly half a millennium later, it was impossible to focus on two things at once. Basil and Hildemar would not have been surprised to learn from neuroscientists and psychologists in the twenty-first century that, when it comes to nonreflexive work, the brain cannot multitask. It can only shuffle back and forth between tasks and networks, and soon enough, it starts underperforming.[5] As far as monks were concerned, you couldn't really concentrate if you didn't cut back on all those potential "multiplicities." The world was full of people who were indifferent to spiritual growth, full of habitual interactions and obligations that made one's life hard to change, and full of claims on your attention.

Monks continued to feel this way even as Christianity went from being a minority religion in the fourth century to a majority religion across Europe and the Mediterranean over the next couple of centuries, because religion was only one among many commitments and identities that guided the behavior of most Christians (and Jews and polytheists and Zoroastrians and Manichaeans and Muslims) in Late Antiquity and the early Middle Ages.[6] That multivectored world is what monks wanted to abandon, in favor of the more singular aim of attending to the divine. And although all kinds of people were attracted to the job, they all eventually discovered that the world couldn't be totally quit or quieted. Converting to concentration took a lifetime.

※

THE SIGNS OF THE CHALLENGES that monks faced were there at the start. Most conversions were less spectacular and more complicated than the stories about how Moses, Apollo, Bar-Sahde, or Paul had become monks. Even the preliminary work of "giving up" was hard for most people. Decades before anyone in the Persian Gulf came to think of Mar Yawnan as a holy man, for example, he had felt so much pressure from his parents to pursue a medical career that, rather than tell them he wanted to be a monk, he waited until he was sent on a field study for medicinal botany, then bolted. Likewise a couple thousand miles northwest, in northern Gaul (what's now northeast France), another well-born young man, named Wandregisel, was afraid to tell his parents about his monastic dreams, so he waited until he was already married before taking action: he pitched his wife the idea of becoming monks together, and she was reportedly thrilled about it. That was lucky for him, because the choice to abandon one's spouse without their consent was widely considered to be irresponsible and sometimes even illegal. But his family wasn't the only potential snag. Wandregisel worked in the royal treasury for a king who required high-ranking officials to obtain his permission before leaving the court to become monks—and although the king was Christian himself, he was not always willing to let them go. Wandregisel (like Mar Yawnan) tried to avoid the conversation entirely by quitting without notice. But he was summoned back to court, where he had to defend himself before his king and former colleagues.[7]

On the opposite end of the social scale, some Christians found that the main obstacle in abandoning the world was, ironically, their lack of resources. Although monks were supposed to surrender everything they owned, they still needed to support themselves after their conversions to monasticism. It was a privilege to pursue something single-mindedly, and poorer women in particular found that it was difficult to manage. Women also usually got married at younger ages than men did, so the women who opted out of marriage in favor of the monastic life were likely to be teenagers. Faced with such situations, some women set up pragmatic partnerships with ascetic men and lived together as roommates. These coed arrangements are attested as early as the 300s and continued for centuries. They helped monks share the costs of running a household and probably also ensured some physical protection. Augustine of Hippo—North African bishop, theologian, and monastic supervisor—documented a case in which a North African ascetic living by herself was raped by someone who worked for her landlord, while the monk John Moschos shared a story about a woman ascetic in Alexandria who was harassed by a stalker.[8]

Criminals weren't the only people to follow monks into their new lives. "The world" had nonviolent ways of creeping into monastic life, too. There are examples of servants, slaves, or even entire households accompanying their overseers into monasteries and in the process dissolving their hierarchical relationships. Parents made gifts of their children, known as oblates: the point was not to abandon them, or at least not usually, but rather to forge a close connection with the monks and their saintly allies. Family members joined monasteries together, friends joined together. And monks also arrived with their memories. There *were* ways to keep old memories from intruding on meditations, as we'll see later in this book. But monks didn't always want to let them go. The Irish poet Dígde became a monk when she was old and widowed, and even then she fondly remembered her life as a beautiful and well-dressed woman who had sex with handsome young kings and drank her fill at feasts.[9]

It was impossible to abandon the world and its distractions completely. Total abandonment happened only when you died. Consider a monk named Frange, who ensconced himself in a pharaonic tomb in Djeme in the eighth century, when the Umayyads were governing Egypt. Despite his funereal surroundings, Frange remained connected to the living. He left behind piles of correspondence, documented on shards of pottery that archaeologists have recovered on-site. Frange's letters show that he was in contact with over seventy correspondents, many of them lay men and women. He sent them his greetings, just to keep in touch. He gave blessings to them, their children, and their livestock. He reminded people they owed him payments. (Frange made books and textiles to support himself.) He asked to borrow books. He asked for cardamom. He invited people to visit. But he also sometimes said he wanted to be alone.[10]

Monastic leaders often pointed out that renunciation and conversion were not instantaneous. They were part of an ongoing process of detachment. In the long view, the workload was staggering. Writing in Sinai in the seventh century, the abbot John Climacus supposed that "if people really understood it, no one would renounce the world" in the first place.[11] Even after monks had made their first momentous decision to abandon everything, they had to make continuous efforts to disengage from the possessions, social ties, daily dramas, and other priorities that had consumed their attention up to that point.

✳

THERE WAS NO SINGLE FORMULA for disengagement. Monks detached themselves in different ways, because determining what counted as "the world" and what counted as "abandonment" meant trying to compartmentalize things that were not so obviously suited to compartmentalization. What constituted a distraction from God when he was everywhere? What constituted a distraction from one's ethical obligations when the self was situated within an entire cosmic system?

The imperative to give up one's possessions, for example, took many different forms in practice. Monks loved to share stories about hermits who dispossessed themselves so completely that they even gave up their copies of the gospels. But those cases stood out because they were rare. Augustine of Hippo exhorted the women and men who lived in his monastic communities at the end of the fourth century to surrender their property. And yet, as Augustine's correspondence shows, it could take a while for monks to actually dispense with their assets, usually because they wanted to take time to ensure that their mothers or siblings or other dependents could live comfortably without them. If they lived in the Roman Empire and were members of the municipal administrative class, they would also have to deal with major bureaucratic and tax obligations that would slow the process of renunciation. Because financial arrangements were so sticky, even for monks whose properties weren't so fiscally complicated, some monasteries preferred to treat the act of dispossession as a definitive legal procedure by insisting that before putting on the habit, monks had to cede everything they owned and to document the transactions. They could donate their assets to the monastery, or to anybody they liked: the crucial thing was that they surrender all of it at the outset, definitively.[12]

On the other end of the spectrum many Egyptian monasteries allowed monks to retain personal property, as evidence from as late as the ninth century attests: papyrus contracts and other legal documents show individual monks owning and transacting in land, workshops, enslaved people, and even the real estate of their own cells. And monks around the Mediterranean tried to take on side gigs to earn extra cash—sometimes out of anxiety more than acquisitiveness. John Cassian, ever the perceptive psychologist, knew monks who worried about getting sick or old, for example, and not having the resources to cover their medical expenses. He didn't think this was an adequate reason to earn an income, but others clearly disagreed with him.[13]

These divergent practices reflected a variety of views about whether property and part-time work entailed any mental appurtenances that encumbered a monk along with them. After all, relinquishing material possessions was not an end in itself. It was merely a precondition for a monk to surrender his ultimate asset: "his *secret* possessions, that is, his mind and thoughts" (as a popular collection of fourth-century homilies put it).[14] It was attention, not property, that was the most prized possession at stake, so monks drew different conclusions about how their things affected their thoughts and how they should manage their stuff accordingly. And some of them decided that certain forms of ownership were not detrimental to a monk's mind.

Certain communities of monks instructed their members not to refer to things as "mine," and some expected monks to share clothes. But others assigned sets of garments to individual monks, and one set of Syrian guidelines even allowed monks to write their names in them. In a similar spirit, the women of the Gallic monastery of Hamage engraved messages on their drinking cups after they were kiln-fired, and least one of them wrote her name on hers: *AUGHILDE*.[15]

Bedrooms were tricky, too. Most communities assigned each monk an individual bed. Some had their own cells. But monks could easily come to think of bedrooms or dorms as personal storage areas for "their" things and become preoccupied with possessiveness. So they were frequently told not to put locks on their doors or locks on their cabinets or chests (though the archaeological record suggests that some monks were in fact locking up rooms and furniture). Monks were also prohibited from hiding things under their mattresses.[16]

There were also arrangements to hammer out when it came to *social* renunciation. It was not enough to relocate. Family and friends still posed risks to a monk's attention. A monk might think of his parents' beautiful home and come to see his own "little cell" as "odious." He might picture a loved one while he was praying and in the process split his mind from his voice. Rather than dream about spiritual things, or simply sleep in peace, he might have nightmares about his family members landing in prison, falling into poverty, or dying. Even monks who were related to each other were encouraged to keep their distance if they lived in the same monastery. Although Christian culture drew deeply on Roman family values for its concepts of community, and although preachers who addressed lay congregations preferred to suggest that it was possible to be devoted to family *and* to God, monastic literature tended to present them as polarities. Family was one commitment, the monastic life was another, and they competed for a monk's attention.[17]

This is why most monasteries expected abbots and abbesses to screen their monks' mail, and why some prohibited monks from receiving packages. An inbox didn't have to be stuffed to be a distraction: even infrequent letters and gifts fostered social ties that could compete with a monk's other commitments.[18] For the same reason, monks weren't supposed to accept invitations to dinner parties or weddings or even to festivities that were straightforwardly Christian. They were told not to perform baptisms, or serve as godparents, or attend festivals in honor of the saints that were celebrated at local churches and cemeteries. The problem was not so much busyness; it was the gravitational force of any business at all: at these occasions "the body and mind are drawn back to the life of this world," as the *Rule of the Monastery of Tarn* put it in the sixth century—not only for the few hours a party lasted, but for as long as a monk was energized by her memories of the event.[19]

Visits with family members were problematic for the same reason. Most monks did occasionally see their birth families, but they felt conflicted about it. Frange (the tomb-dwelling, networked monk) kept in regular touch with his sister Tsie, who often worked as his fixer. Tsie had to insist that Frange visit her in person—not just to pick up the clothes that she had procured for him, but to pay her a real visit. Benedict of Nursia's sister Scolastica, who was a monk herself, saw her brother once a year, but when she once asked him to talk with her for longer than usual, it took a miracle to get him to agree. More dramatically, the desert father Piôr did not contact his family for fifty years after becoming a monk. But even his colleagues thought that this was excessive: when Piôr's sister wrote to them inquiring about her brother, they pressured Piôr to go see her. And Jonas of Bobbio once made the trip to visit his parents after not having seen them for nine years, but he got sick the day he arrived, and he took it as a sign that he needed to return to his monastery immediately.[20]

The ambivalence that monks felt in these situations was intensified by their sense that any sort of travel, any kind of excursion into "the world," could sidetrack them. Monks who lived in solitary dwellings encouraged each other not to think of excuses to get up and go outside when they were supposed to be praying. And monks who lived in monasteries usually had to get permission to leave at all (though abbots and abbesses were often on the road for pastoral and political errands, and monks who handled their monasteries' legal affairs also did quite a bit of traveling). Even *talking* about the trips that other people had taken was a way of wandering off. Physical or verbal jaunts just increased the opportunities for mental detours, which could lead to offenses as minor as people-watching or as egregious as soliciting sex workers.[21]

It was best to stay in. But if a trip was absolutely necessary, a monk was supposed to keep his eyes on the prize—sometimes literally. Monks were often recognizable to Christians and non-Christians alike by the fact that they kept their eyes downcast in public. One rule even helpfully suggested that monks should work on memorizing psalms that were written onto travel-tablets. Most importantly, a monk was supposed to "confine your love to your cell," as one set of monastic rules put it in the late 400s. "You should treat it like a paradise."[22]

＊

CONVERSION TO MONASTICISM and abandonment of the world were even more complicated for women and men who did not become hermits or members of monasteries. These individuals were committed to renunciation, discipline, and prayer—but they lived at home, or they did not call any particular place home but instead moved around and subsisted on begging or patronage or both. But despite the challenges, their efforts to disengage from the world make clear that physical isolation was not necessarily the key ingredient to the making of a monk.

A young Cappadocian woman named Macrina, the sister of Basil of Caesarea and Gregory of Nyssa, decided when she was twelve to live "by herself" after her fiancé died unexpectedly. In practice this meant living with her family but never marrying, and taking up work that her wealthy parents normally relegated to the enslaved members of their household. Groups of men and women known in Syriac as the Sons and Daughters of the Covenant also lived at home, with their families or with each other, in the houses or apartments they had inhabited before their conversion to their new life. But they disengaged from business dealings, litigations, and military service. They abstained from meat and wine and marriage. They learned the psalms by heart, cared for the poor, and prayed consistently. Or at least, these are the things that their local bishop, Rabbula of Edessa, expected them to do. By contrast, a ream of legal paperwork in Egypt attests to monks who lived at home but continued to be more engaged in their communities than Rabbula had thought was appropriate in northern Syria: they rented out rooms in their own homes, for example, and continued to participate in lawsuits.[23]

In the fourth century, Egyptian monks who disengaged from the world—whether they joined a monastery or not—called themselves *apotaktikoi* and *apotaktikai*: "renouncers." But this terminology did not last, and monks soon began arguing about who truly deserved to be called "monks." Already in the later fourth century, critics began accusing itinerant monks of failing to support themselves, and they caricatured both wandering and stay-at-home monks as lazy, selfish, and unfocused. The fifth-century abbot Nilus of Ancyra depicted itinerant monks as excellent scam artists with poor impulse control. Two closely related Latin texts—the *Rule of the Master* and the *Rule of Benedict*—rejected domestic monks categorically and accused them of doing "whatever they wanted" rather than following any rules. And Leander of Seville told his sister Florentina in the sixth century that living in town was a form of "private life" that entailed all sorts of constraints on one's attention. "Avoid it!"[24]

The objections went on for centuries because some monks continued to live in domestic setups and others continued to move around. Their detractors stated their philosophical objections, but they also felt threatened by these forms of spiritual prestige, and their complaints were often classist and gendered. Men who had worked their whole lives as farmers could find social mobility as charismatic counselors on the road. Many of their patrons were women. And although anyone could live as an ascetic at home, it seems that the Christians who chose this option were more often women than men. The voluminous caches of papyri that survive from the Egyptian city of Oxyrhynchus, to take a well-documented case, show women *apotaktikai* outnumbering men *apotaktikoi* two to one.

But when the women who had chosen this path were rich and powerful, the critiques were made more carefully. The well-connected and argumentative Jerome (who would later be remembered as a saint and church father) complained about domestic asceticism to friends of his who had chosen precisely this life. One of them, Marcella, had even repurposed her palatial residence on the Aventine to be an ascetic women's center. And yet Jerome—himself a monk who relocated more than once!—did not want to appear to be judging these elite Roman women directly, because they were his friends and also his financial backers. So he dubbed the miscreant monks "Remnuoth," an exoticizing term based on a Coptic slur, which Jerome used to imply that these were aberrant Egyptian practices that had found their way to Rome. He did not say that his friends were bad monks, only that *some* monks who lived this way were doing it poorly.[25]

Not all monks denigrated the Christians who lived as ascetics in their homes. John Rufus, a monk writing at the turn of the fifth/sixth century, praised the ruling family of the kingdom of Iberia in

the Caucasus for "liv[ing] lives of monasticism" even while governing the realm. Likewise John of Ephesus, a monastic hagiographer
writing about half a century later, was immensely impressed by
two brothers and business partners who ran an ascetic household
but also managed to be successful and respected traders, thanks
to their honest dealings and charitable donations. The desert
elder Piamun (not to be confused with the analogy-loving Poemen) told Cassian and Germanus about a religious woman who
lived in a house in Alexandria that she had inherited from her
parents. This woman asked the bishop of Alexandria to send her
an impoverished widow whom she could care for. But this widow
was so well behaved that the ascetic asked the bishop for someone
else. The bishop became irritated about having to deal with the
back-and-forth and handed over an angry and loquacious drunk
who insulted and even assaulted her host. The ascetic took it in
stride, and Piamun told her story to humiliate his fellow monks.
This Alexandrian woman, he said pointedly, had attained a level of
patience and self-abasement that others were able to achieve only
when they fled human society and lived in caves.[26]

Piamun was nodding to two conflicting themes in monastic literature: an obsession with remoteness and an awareness that distance alone did not make a monk. The world—or more precisely,
its distractions—could catch up to you anywhere. But much of the
evidence that we have for domestic or itinerant forms of monasticism was written by its critics rather than its admirers or practitioners. This is the case even though the "alternative" forms of
ascetic life that were so often devalued by other monks were probably more widely practiced than either solitary or communal forms
of monasticism.[27] The people whom *we* picture as quintessential
monks, in other words, seem to have been a vocal minority. But as
Piamun pointed out, it was possible to stay single-minded without physically removing oneself from a demanding environment.
Many monks seem to have resisted the fallacy of multitasking
without resorting to a hideout.

The monks who did leave home for a fixed retreat interpreted the idea of abandonment just as creatively. They described their surroundings as landscapes of desert, cells, and walls, but their habitats embodied this aesthetic in strikingly different ways. Some hermits bunked in caves or tents or the open air in the middle of nowhere. One monk earned the nickname Macedonius "the Pit" (*gouba*, in Syriac) for his preference for living in holes in the ground wherever he went. Others took up residence at the edge of villages, in the towers of churches or monasteries, at the bottom of empty cisterns, or at the top of columns that required a pulley system to supply them with food and water. Monks in this latter category were known as "stylites," a term derived from the Greek word for pillar (*stylos*). In Western Thebes, just across the Nile from Luxor, many monks besides Frange converted pharaonic tombs and other ancient mortuaries into monastic complexes. Sometimes the only modifications they made to these spaces was to give them a fresh coat of paint.[28]

Monasteries, like hermitages, were also situated in "the world" in many different forms. The Great Laura of Saint Sabas featured hermitages carved into the cliffs of a ravine in the Judean desert (fig. 1). On Kharg in the Persian Gulf, off the coast of what's now Iran, monks deliberately chose to build their monastery on the windy and inhospitable side of an island that was otherwise pleasantly habitable. They surrounded their complex with a stone wall and lined at least two sides of it with cells for individual monks (fig. 2). In northern Gaul, a politically powerful widow named Geretrude had the women's monastery of Hamage built in the swampy, sandy, woodsy valley of the river Scarpe. It was bounded by a timber palisade and by ditches filled with water, and the sisters' cells consisted of individual timber huts in close proximity to each other (fig. 3).[29]

Other monasteries were founded in cities, suburbs, and farmlands. The federation of houses that Pachomius assembled in Egypt were located in villages that sat squarely in the fertile plain

FIGURE 1
Hermitage at the
Great Laura of
Saint Sabas.

FIGURE 2
The footprint of
the monastery on
Kharg, facing south.
Seventy multiroom
cells lined the north
and west walls; the
church and other
communal spaces sat
in the center of the
complex, which was
probably built in the
seventh century.

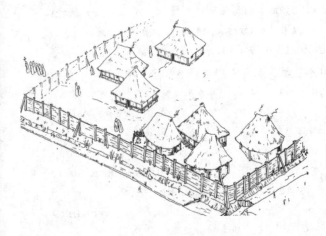

FIGURE 3
A reconstruction
of the southwest
corner of the
women's monas-
tery of Hamage
in the late 600s,
several decades
after it was first
founded.

of the Nile, and monasteries in Syria were often situated in villages or very near to them. And the buildings themselves were constructed in such varied locales, or repurposed from so many different kinds of architectural spaces—tombs, temples, private estates, gymnasia, mansions, and run-down villages, to name only a few options—that they thwart any attempts to define a "typical" monastic structure. This can make it difficult for archaeologists to identify monasteries in the first place. In the sixth or seventh century, for example, a small community of monks retrofitted the bath complex of the city of Argos into a monastery. A lone epitaph is the only surviving clue: it tells tomb raiders to stay away from the monks on the premises.[30]

Even monasteries that seem remote to us today were not necessarily perceived that way fifteen hundred years ago. In western Iran, the monks Yazdin and Pethion set up their cells on the craggy mountain of Bisutun, which was not a backwater at all but rather the most conspicuous landmark in the Sasanian Empire. Far west of them, at the other end of the Mediterranean, the monastic settlements on the island of Cabrera (one of the Balearics) were situated in a bustling corridor of trade and sea traffic, and the monks there imported supplies all the way from the Levant. Likewise in the sixth century, the bishop Justinian of Valencia built the monastery of Punta de l'Illa on Cullera, when it used to be a coastal island: his gravestone boasts that it was both surrounded by waves and encircled by a wall. Archaeologists were actually able to excavate the remains of a large wall on the south side of Cullera, and despite the wall and waves, the monks were still in touch with people beyond their island. Their coins and pottery show contacts around the Mediterranean. They were even importing vials of ointment from Anatolia.[31]

These varied forms of distance and demarcation aren't proof that monks weren't what they claimed to be. Instead they reinforce what monks had already stressed to each other—that, regardless of her surroundings, a monk should *feel* detached from everything that competed with her attention to God. They shared Palladius's story about an angel who praised one monk for her concentration and rebuked another for undermining his own isolation: "She has never separated her heart from God—while you live here, wandering over cities in your mind." Monks likewise remembered the desert mother Amma Syncletica to have said that "there are many who live in the mountains and behave as if they were in the town, and they are wasting their time. It is possible to be solitary in one's mind while living in a crowd, and it is possible for one who is a solitary to live in the crowd of his own thoughts." It was the "cell of the heart" that mattered most.[32]

✳

HISTORIANS IN RECENT DECADES have come to realize that monks' rhetorical emphasis on disengagement from the world was necessary precisely because they continued to be involved in it after their conversions. They labored to construct their cells of the heart in order to be able to provide services to the public that less detached persons could not. And those services constituted a long list. Over the centuries, monks and the communities who patronized them developed significant relationships that made monasticism pivotal rather than marginal to Christian societies—socially, spiritually, economically, and intellectually.

The range of roles that monks came to play in "the world" was vast. In the Levant, particularly in agrarian communities at a distance from the coastal metropolises, monks took up the position of problem-solver. Lay Christians turned to them to fix matters that otherwise seemed intractable, such as exploitative landlords, property disputes, and illnesses. One collection of monastic guidelines in Syriac (the So-Called Canons of Maruta) even expected every town to elect a monk to serve as a liaison to its local jail: the monk was supposed to visit the prisoners, act as their advocate, solicit donations for their legal fees, and more generally ensure that they were properly cared for.[33]

Monks also fielded countless idiosyncratic requests. To take just one example: In his *Life* about the Syrian monk Hilarion, Jerome shared a story about the owner of a horse-racing stable, who approached Hilarion and asked him to break his horses of a spell that a malevolent magician had cast on them. At first Hilarion didn't think it was worth his time. But when the stable owner stressed that he preferred to have a *Christian* solution to his problem rather than seeking magical remedies for it—a savvy argument to make to a monk, because it implied that the only alternatives were pagan—Hilarion agreed to cure his horses. Jerome affirmed that this was a job worth taking, because it turned out that Hilarion's equine services led to a major winning streak at the tracks for the horses he'd healed. That ended up convincing many racing fans to convert to Christianity![34]

Peter Brown, the historian who has done the most to embed the saintly Christian characters of Late Antiquity in their actual human environments, pointed out decades ago that monks were simultaneously distanced and essential to their societies. They couldn't be one without the other: their social disengagement gave them the freedom to hone the insights that their supporters valued; it also established their neutrality as negotiators and advisers. Many Christians believed that monks *owed* their expertise as neutral agents to the communities they had relinquished, even though monks sometimes thought that doing so split their attention. John of Ephesus observed in the sixth century that visitors to Maro the Stylite were offended by his complaints that they were distracting him from God. Nearly a century earlier, the Syriac version of the *Life of Simeon Stylites* had recorded that Simeon—the most famous monk who lived atop a column—had a terrifying vision of an imposing and regal man, surrounded by a large crowd, who berated Simeon for getting sick of his visitors. It was a tough lesson: in the Levant, Christian holy men "grappled with society in society."[35]

In North Africa, the balance between world and abandon-

ment was different. Hermits did not have much of a cult following, unlike their contemporaries in the Levant. Monasteries were
built in out-of-the-way locations only starting in the sixth century. Monks do not even seem to have worn distinctive clothing
until around that time, either. In Egypt, by contrast, monks in the
fourth and fifth centuries represented themselves as self-sufficient
outsiders. They did this to avoid suspicions of being beholden to
anyone else. But they did in fact depend on the supplies and support of other people, as even their hagiographers recognized: the
literature that celebrated Egyptian hermits' version of monastic
disengagement still included many accounts of visitors making
their way to the monks, asking for a word of advice or encouragement. Even women who were told not to visit made the effort to
see them anyway and managed to extract some assistance, despite
the hermits' initial reluctance to help them. These stories made it
into the canon of monastic hagiography, too, alongside accounts of
total withdrawal and autarky: their hagiographers recognized that
the philosophy of abandonment was relative rather than absolute.[36]

In other regions around the Mediterranean, monks developed a
particular set of services that lay Christians enthusiastically patronized: the work of intercessory prayer. Such arrangements evolved
from a widespread and longstanding conviction that monks'
prayers were a conduit to God. John Cassian had compared them
to a cosmic construction project: monks' dedication and training
helped them build a tower of prayer that penetrated the heavens.
And those lines of communication were believed to be socially
beneficial. As early as the mid-fourth century Ephrem the Syrian
was enthusiastically telling solitary monks that "the world which is
buried in sins is being strengthened through your prayers."[37]

Over the centuries, these towers of prayer bore increasingly
heavy loads. The stylite Simeon's prayers were likened to "beams
in a building" that "held up creation." The emperor Justinian confidently stated that when monks live the right way, their prayer
"brings God's favor upon the whole realm"—in the form of suc-

cessful armies, stable cities, and good harvests and hauls from the sea. Christians had also started expecting monks to pray for their souls. "Now that they've all gathered together like a swarm of religious bees," Ferreolus of Uzès said about the monastic community he founded, "I hope they offer the flowers of their prayers on behalf of my many sins and produce a very sweet honey in interceding for me." Other donors got straight to the point. In the eastern Mediterranean they asked monks to remember them constantly in their prayers, to vouchsafe their eternal life; and in Europe many a deed of gift from the seventh century onward states that the benefactor was seeking *remedium animae meae*, "the protection and cure of my soul."

Support came in the form of land; cash; movable assets such as jewelry, textiles, or livestock; children; and tax benefits. The donors who made these gifts saw them as more than transactions. They were *transformations*. Making a donation did not "purchase" salvation. It was a sacrifice of resources that mirrored, in a small way, the more profound sacrifices that monks made when they abandoned the world. The gift allowed a donor to participate in the work of renunciation and divine concentration. One North African hagiographer put it plainly: a donor's support ensured that monks would not be "distracted" by material concerns. All Christians—not just monks—were still expected to pray. But Christians believed that the special metamorphosis of worldly wealth into heavenly treasure could be amplified enormously by professionals who were constantly trying to shut out the world's distractions and reach out to God.[38]

Some monastic churches were closed to visitors, to increase the potency of monks' prayers by sealing them up from outside interference. But other monks welcomed the public to their sacred spaces. The community of Qasr el-Banat situated their church very close to the main road between Antioch and Aleppo so that travelers could easily spot and visit it. To the northwest, in the Suha Reha Valley between the Danube and the Black Sea, pilgrims were welcomed at Basarabi-Murfatlar, a monastery that had been carved out of a chalk mountain—which we know because they scratched graffiti into the chalky walls of the monastery's church.

Monastic communities might offer other services to the public, such as alms and medical care, though they weren't the only ones to do this. They functioned as penitential centers for people who wanted (or were sentenced) to make amends for their transgressions and crimes by living like monks, if not necessarily living *as* monks. Most monks also thought it was important to welcome any guests who showed up on the premises, especially if they were refugees or travelers.[39]

Monks knew that all of this work and care mattered: they saw themselves as morally obligated to provide it. But they still worried that it would set their minds adrift. They might be tempted to rifle through their visitors' bags, or show off in front of guests. Others found themselves bubbling over with questions for the newcomers, or feeling compelled to keep them company. And some just got annoyed. Prominent Carolingian commentators, writing in the ninth century, thought wistfully of Saint Benedict—their monastic icon—and assumed that *he* hadn't been so welcoming to guests in his day, thereby avoiding onerous obligations like the ones later monks faced. But this was nostalgia. Monks had been sharing stories for centuries about the conflicting responsibilities of self-discipline and hospitality. An early medieval ascetic collection in the East Syrian tradition, belonging to Sogdian-speaking Christians in Turfan, offered this consolation: bad thoughts and travelers both move on eventually. The key was not to be ruffled by the interruptions.[40] Century after century, monks felt pinched by the paradox of using their spiritual concentration to benefit a public whose demands could distract them.

✳

TWO OF THE MOST IMPOSING monastic churches to survive from Late Antiquity and the early Middle Ages can be found about two miles away from each other, near the towns of Tahta and Sohag in Upper Egypt. One was built of limestone, the other of brick: today they are known as the churches of the White Monastery and the Red Monastery (figs. 4a/4b). Shenoute—the abbot who had conjured up the image of a limbless devil, moving his thoughts around—built the church of the White Monastery around 450, at a time when monumental architecture was more characteristic of civic structures than monasteries. Despite other monks' reservations about magnificent buildings, Shenoute decided to construct a lavish basilica that expressed his community's ethics of investment in God (in addition to asserting his own authoritative leadership). The monks in the Red Monastery built a new church emulating this model about a century later. Both structures spoke to the double-sided nature of monks' relationship to the world, that relationship of separation and symbiosis. These monumental monastic spaces were funded by an outpouring of donations from lay Christians (fig. 5) who wanted to support the social work that this federation of monastic men and women could perform by virtue of their status as ostensibly disentangled, undistracted outsiders.[41]

To some observers, the generosity of rich patrons was overblown. Gregory the Great shared a story in his *Dialogues* about a Syrian man named Isaac who showed up at a church in Spoleto and prayed there for three days straight. A caretaker of the church got jealous of this highly focused newcomer and became possessed by a demon. When Isaac exorcised him, the elites of Spoleto fell over themselves with offers to build Isaac his own monastery, even though they barely knew him. (He refused all of it, which Gregory very much admired.) A century earlier, around 500, the polytheist historian Zosimos had observed more darkly that monks were highly successful sponges who had renounced everything and yet come into possession of everything.

Zosimos was cynical about the situation, but he had made an accurate observation: as a historian he'd noticed that Christians had changed how they were spending their money. And histori-

FIGURES 4A/4B
The churches of the White Monastery (above), built ca. 450 and measuring 246' × 121'—Shenoute called it his Great House—and the Red Monastery (below), built in the mid-sixth century and about a third the size.

FIGURE 5
A sixth-century portrait of an unnamed donor to the Red Monastery church. He wears elite-grade clothes (including riding boots inspired by Persian fashion), and he holds his arms in a gesture of prayer.

ans in more recent centuries have estimated that over the course of the fourth to eighth centuries—and picking up especially in the 500s—Christians ended up giving about one-third of the real estate within the current and former Roman Empire to monasteries and churches.[42]

With prosperity came scrutiny. Shenoute, who was a master of representation, repeatedly urged his monks to consider the impressions that their business relationships would make on the outside world. They should buy and sell things at reasonable prices. They should pay the going rate for transportation by boat. They should not solicit advance deposits from their customers, and they should pay for things in full themselves. They shouldn't collect an excessive amount of firewood from the commons. Above all, they should not accept things for free: it could make them look like "beggars" and lead the public to "scorn the great and glorious uniform" of the monastic habit. Rabbula of Edessa and Augustine of Hippo voiced similar concerns. The freedom to concentrate on God was not supposed to be mistaken for freeloading.[43]

In any case donors liked to check in. The monastery of St. Gall, in what's now Switzerland, had to indulge more than one emperor who wanted to inspect his investments by trying to distract the monks from their stillness. To the emperors' delight, not even the child monks moved a muscle. We know about this only because a monk named Ekkehard recorded these incidents in the eleventh century. Concentration mattered to the monastery's wider circles of support—not just to the Holy Roman emperors—and Ekkehard retold these stories for the benefit of St. Gall's reputation. Centuries earlier, a set of Syriac monastic policies was similarly pragmatic about donor relations: "The friends, patrons, and teachers of the monastery shall not be despised by [the head of the monastery], but he shall receive them with what he has." It was important to maintain good relationships with the world, but monks did not always like doing it.[44]

Of course they were always entitled to quit, and many of them did. These cases highlight once again the entanglement of monastery and world. Many bishops began their careers as monks and carried their ascetic training with them into their new jobs. It was practically a form of credentialing by the fifth century, because Christians had come to value worldly detachment as a sign of spiritual aptitude (even if some Christians countered that these bishops were getting jobs because of their privileged backgrounds rather than their monastic training per se). Other career trajectories were less auspicious. Many an elite who fell out of favor chose to retire, or was forced to "retire," to a monastery. But these exiles may never have become monks, or at least not monks like the others. They often continued to behave like power brokers. And when the political winds changed, some of them came out of retirement.[45]

Even the more banal cases of monks who returned to lay life show how the sacred and secular spheres were porous rather than inviolate. And monks shared plenty of stories about them, because the monks who came back were reminders that, no matter a monk's reasons for leaving—an affair, a fight, exhaustion—nothing was irreversible. At the monastery of Condat, in the Jura Mountains, a senior monk once complained to his abbot that brothers who were doing a bad job should be kicked out of the monastery. The abbot was horrified: anyone can change and deserves the chance to try. He pointed to a ream of biblical episodes in support of his position. He also pointed to his own monks: he had mourned so many of them for doing disgraceful things. Some of them had even left two or three times. But here they were, again.[46]

In short: as difficult as it was to convert to monasticism in the first place, it was even harder to disconnect from the things, people, and places that relentlessly pulled a monk's mind back to earth. The very services that monks provided out of a sense of moral obligation could threaten their parallel commitment to concentrate on

God. A good renunciation story was aspirational but impossible. The world could not be left behind, not completely. And because abandonment was not a definitive fix, however more effective it was than our own self-imposed shutdowns, monks turned to each other for help, to tackle distraction collectively.

CHAPTER 2

▦ COMMUNITY

P ATERNUS WAS A CHILD WHEN HIS MOTHER GAVE HIM to a monastery, and as with most hagiographical protagonists his spiritual development was precocious. It didn't take long for him to convince his older cellmate to leave the monastery with him, to become co-hermits on the coast of Normandy, on the bay of Mont-Saint-Michel. Three years later, their abbot Generosus tracked them down and found them living in a cave. It wasn't so much their departure that concerned Generosus; it was the fact that Paternus had taken monastic practice to the extreme. He had worn himself ragged from hard work and extreme fasting, and he had refused to see or speak with other human beings besides his roommate for years. The abbot compared Paternus to an unbroken horse that ran off when it was first bridled: he had overreacted to his monastery's rules. So Generosus insisted on some adjustments. He allowed Paternus to stay in his cave, but he told him to moderate his fasting and to make an effort to see and talk to other monks sometimes. It seems to have done the trick. Paternus thrived as a monk in that same spot on the coast until he was seventy.[1]

Paternus never says why he left his monastery and cut off almost all human contact for those three years. Or at least, his hagiographer doesn't offer an explanation. But other monks in Late Antiquity and the early Middle Ages made similar choices, and some of them did speak their minds. As the number of monastic sites and networks grew around the Mediterranean and beyond, monks worried about the corrosive effects of this new kind of community even as they celebrated its potential for progress. That included its implications for distraction. Concentration could benefit from collective action, but it could also falter in the presence of other people.

Debates about the attention economy of social media today seem like a retread of this premodern paradox. In theory, a community of monks could help an individual monk by connecting her to others who shared her sense of purpose. Together monks could build new social norms in the service of their shared values. In the process they could inspire each other, empathize with each other, and teach each other by pooling their knowledge and abilities. John Climacus said in the seventh century that monks worked like rough stones knocking into each other: eventually their tumbling would make their sharp edges smooth. But he had in mind something more like erosion than a rock fight. As John and many other monks knew all too well, monks could uplift each other, but they could also break each other down. Communal life cut both ways.[2]

Abandoning the world, or trying to abandon the world, was the first step in becoming a monk and stretching the mind in concentration toward the divine. The next step was learning to work with others who shared the same cognitive and spiritual goals. But the promises and pitfalls of living with other people made it hard for monks to agree on what the best social arrangement might be. Should a monk live alone, or in a community? If in a community, what kind of regulated life was best to keep monks focused? What kind of leadership did they need? And how could they be there for each other without dismantling their attention to the divine order? Monks knew that most people can't live completely alone. But how, then, could they possibly escape distraction?

✳

EPHREM THE SYRIAN, who sang the praises of the solitary life, suggested in the fourth century that the monks who lived alone in the remote spots of Syria and Mesopotamia enjoyed a state of tranquility that was surpassed only by the silence of the tomb. By contrast, his younger contemporary Basil of Caesarea gave a long list of reasons in the 360s and 370s why communal monastic living was better than going it alone. Basil argued that solitude was selfish, and that living with other people was an opportunity to constantly practice the commandment to love your neighbor and to serve a common good. He pointed to the ways that a group of monks working together could do more than the sum of its parts—not only because nobody was totally self-sufficient (in a basic survival sense), but also because an organized community could combine its strengths to maximize the good it did. Even prayer was more potent when monks prayed together. And Basil added that there were disciplinary benefits, too: when you lived with other people, they could check on your behavior and let you know where there was room for improvement. And yet some monks remained so horrified by the idea of ever living in a community that they made a show of living with wild animals instead—or at least, there were plenty of stories circulating to that effect.[3]

Both sides of this argument were grounded in a shrewd understanding of human psychology. Proponents of the solitary life thought that advanced forms of prayer were possible only in isolation, because even fellow monks could be a distraction. Dolphins surface only in calm waters, they said. But the advocates of communal monasticism were suspicious of the self-delusions that could persist in isolation. John Climacus, who had lived as a hermit himself for decades around the turn of the seventh century, was concerned about how easy it was in isolation to convince yourself that you were making a lot of progress: "A solitary horse can often imagine itself to be at full gallop, but when it finds itself in a herd it then discovers how slow it actually is." In the eighth century Joseph Ḥazzaya warned that if a monk had not thoroughly trained himself before withdrawing into solitude, his own cell could turn on him, launching evil thoughts at him like stones from a slingshot. (Joseph himself had certainly not spent his whole life in a cell: he was born to Zoroastrian parents in Iran, captured and enslaved by Arab traders, and sold to a Christian in northern Iraq, before converting to Christianity, becoming a monk, serving as an abbot, then striking out as a solitary.) And although nobody would have mistaken Joseph and other standout solitaries for imposters, one of the most common critiques of solitary monasticism was that many hermits were flashy, inauthentic performers who were only pandering to the public appetite for sensational holy men. People who keep posting about their productivity on social media evoke similar grumblings today.[4]

And although they didn't have to contend with social media, monks still worried that solitude was actually very hard to come by. Already in the early fifth century some of them had a creeping feeling that the age of "true" eremitic life, the life they idealized in their stories of the desert elders who'd flourished only a generation or two earlier, was starting to fade. Striking a tone that was both nostalgic and judgmental, they said that the desert fathers and mothers had become tourist attractions. The solitary monks who lived in Egypt and the Levant grew frustrated that their work was continuously interrupted by men and women who had come to them for advice, healings, or spiritual souvenirs—or who moved next door to try the anchoritic life for themselves. Some monks came to the conclusion that the popularity of monastic solitude had diluted its potency. One of John Cassian's informants, Abba John of Diolkos, left the desert after it became, essentially, a scene. He had loved living alone. He thought it was harder than living in a community but also more exhilarating. He told Cassian that he used to become so focused in thought that he forgot he had a body and lost his sense perception entirely. To remind himself to eat every day, he'd had to put seven loaves of bread in a basket at the start of each week, like a rudimentary pill organizer. But the desert had gotten crowded, and he thought that hermits these days were nothing like the hard-core ascetics of old. They were even putting cheese on their lentils![5]

FIGURE 6   This building was part of the large monastic community known as Kellia—"the Cells." By the 700s this particular "cell" had more than sixty rooms. Kellia had been expanding
and densifying for centuries, and by the ninth century there
were over 1,500 buildings besides this one across an area of
about twenty-five square miles. Each walled complex in the
community was outfitted with everything a monk or monks
needed, including cooking and craft areas, one or more bedrooms, receiving areas, toilets, a garden, and a space to pray.

But although many monks drew a clear distinction between
solitary and communal monasticism, the two forms often blurred
together in practice—which is not all that surprising given the
sheer diversity of monastic arrangements in Late Antiquity and
the early Middle Ages. In Egypt the site of Kellia, which Evagrius
had called home for fifteen years, consisted of a constellation of
hermitages that were built only a few hundred feet away from each
other, and the neighborhood became even higher density over the
centuries (fig. 6). Many communities in the Levant were organized
in the form of lavras (or *laurai*), where monks lived in separate
cells but celebrated liturgies together and shared some common

facilities. Other arrangements involved hermits who were affiliated with monasteries but lived apart from them, as was the case
at the influential monastery of Izla, perched over the great city of
Nisibis: here monks would "graduate" from living in the community to living in individual cells, after a three-year trial period. The
monks at Lindisfarne, a monastery on a tidal island in northeast
England (and best known today as the site of the Vikings' first
raid in England), used its little neighboring islands as solitary get-
aways. And in the eighth and ninth centuries, the coasts of Anatolia were home to thriving "colonies" of mountain-dwelling monks
who were simultaneously alone and closely networked. These are
just a few of many examples.[6]

Even the advocates of more straightforwardly communal
monasticism devised many competing theories about how to create a spiritual collective. Monasteries didn't run on faith alone.
They needed to be carefully designed and regulated, according to
the monastic engineers who puzzled over their mechanisms. The
surviving evidence overflows with different approaches to making monastic communities functional, in the form of suggestions,
guides, rules, and narrative exemplars—not to mention countless adaptations and revisions to those suggestions, guides, rules,
and narratives.

While these sources aren't entirely reliable as guides to how
monasteries actually operated, they were written with the challenges of monastic discipline very much in mind, which makes
them a rich source for the struggles that monastic theorists identified and tried to alleviate. As more than one monk fretted, if an
outsider were to crack open a book of monastic rules, it could leave
an unflattering impression. But it is not just monks' shortcomings
that stand out in these sources. It is also their inventiveness, and
their determination to explore humans' capacity to change.[7]

Monks themselves understood that there were many possible
ways to configure and concentrate a group. Making comparisons
between different forms of monasticism, and criticizing the alter-

natives, was something of a pastime. The monks of Wearmouth-Jarrow in northeast England repeatedly pointed out that *their* system of monastic rules represented the best of what all other systems had to offer. They noted proudly that their founder, Benedict Biscop, had traveled extensively, and that he had visited a total of seventeen monasteries and selected the best elements of their rules to compile his own set of policies for his monastery back in England.

But the Venerable Bede, the most famous monk of Wearmouth-Jarrow, would also observe that some monks did not welcome such experiments. In his account of Cuthbert of Lindisfarne, he noted that intense and exhausting conflicts had erupted when the abbot tried to implement a new system of rules at that monastery. This story about the resentments born from monastic management-consulting is conspicuously absent from Bede's main source for Cuthbert's life, an anonymous text written by a monk at Lindisfarne around 700. It's possible that Bede wrote about Cuthbert's trials to highlight his own high regard for certain forms of monastic discipline. But it is also possible that the Lindisfarne monk-historian had deliberately omitted a painful institutional memory. Such debates about corporate culture could cut to the quick.

Think of a monastic rule as a yoke for the "necks of your minds," the bishop Ferreolus of Uzès told his monks in the mid-sixth century: it was a technology for harnessing psychological power. And there were many variations on its specs and applications.[8]

✳

DAILY ROUTINES WERE a case in point. Monks did agree that they were a practical strategy for fighting distraction. They believed that it was necessary to keep some kind of regular schedule in order to maintain their spiritual concentration. Their regimented workdays were famous enough to become punch lines: in Beirut in the fifth century, when one law student tried to convince his fellow law student that, with a perfectly calibrated schedule, they could make time for both religion *and* work, his friend joked, "You won't turn me into a monk!" Centuries later, daily regimens were still a standout feature of monasticism. Hildemar of Civate, who wrote an extensive and enthusiastic commentary on the *Rule of Benedict* around 845, suggested that simply following the *Rule*'s daily schedule alone would amount to embodying almost all of its larger principles.

Before the ninth century, however, the Benedictine *Rule* was not an obvious consensus choice, not even in the Latinate world. (It's also worth noting that the *Rule* was probably not even written by Benedict of Nursia: Anglo-Saxon monks began attributing it to the protagonist in Gregory's *Dialogues* a century or two after it was written.) Throughout Late Antiquity and the early Middle Ages, monastic schedules came in many permutations, each representing different psychological and sociological rationales. Augustine of Hippo said wistfully in his book *The Work of Monks* that he wished he knew how the apostle Paul had divided up his day. It would have offered monks clear and useful guidance.[9]

But Paul hadn't done that; monks were on their own. They avidly shared stories about successful monks' routines—like how writers today want to know how other writers work and maintain their focus. Monks heard about a hermit named Alexandra, who spent her days spinning flax from dawn to mid-afternoon, before she mentally reviewed the lives of various Christian heroes (patri-archs, prophets, apostles, martyrs), then finally had a snack and thought expectantly about her own death. They heard about an elder named Julian Saba who had his monks pray outside all day in pairs: one monk would stand and sing fifteen psalms while the other knelt in worship, then they'd switch, back and forth, from dawn to dusk. They read John Cassian's famous overgeneralization that all Egyptian monks sang psalms and worked simultaneously, all day long, while monks in the Levant set fixed times for their psalmody—and his account itself spawned a range of imitators.[10]

The premise of any schedule was that different activities helped condition a monk in different ways, and the process of variation itself was also supposed to be psychologically beneficial. Alexandra had told a visitor that her daily program kept her from getting bored. Antony was remembered to have said that switching between work and prayer and work and prayer was the solution to distracting thoughts. Even the Virgin Mary was said to have reaped cognitive benefits this way. A seventh-century tradition, probably written at a women's monastery in Gaul, suggested that Mary had stuck to a monastic schedule during the decade when she lived in Solomon's temple, and that her regular intervals of prayer, work, and study had made her unshakable (*constans, immobilis*). The routine transformed her thinking, which set the stage for nothing less than the Incarnation: "You have prepared a dwelling-place for God in your mind," an angel told her, and three days later, she was pregnant.[11]

Unlike solitaries such as Alexandra or special cases such as Mary, monks who lived in a community were usually synced to the same house schedule, because collective participation was supposed to help everyone concentrate. In almost every community, the schedule centered on the trifecta of manual labor, reading, and prayer. But the differences were in the details. In the early sixth century the bishop Caesarius of Arles expected the men and women in his monastic communities in Gaul to read until mid-morning and then do their assigned chores for the rest of the day, with periodic times throughout the day for prayers. But his contemporary Eugippius, who served as the abbot of Castellum Lucullanum in southern Italy, expected his monks to work until noon, read until mid-afternoon, then work again—a schedule also punctuated throughout the day by prayers. In yet another variation, about eighty years after Caesarius and Eugippius, Isidore of Seville told *his* monks to vary the order of reading and work depending on the season, and he also gave them a siesta in the summers.[12]

Such differences stemmed from contrasting assumptions about the mechanics of concentration. Even when the schedules were similar, the reasoning behind them diverged. Some theorists thought it was best to pray and work at the same time, because work was an anchor that kept the mind from slipping around, or because work and prayer quieted the body and mind at the same time, or because manual labor helped monks stay awake in their late-night prayers, or because prayer made work easier. Others countered that work was supposed to *empty* the mind of all thoughts. John Climacus, writing in Sinai in the seventh century, thought conversely that having to busy your hands while you prayed was an amateurish approach to concentration. It worked, but it was something of a shortcut.[13]

If there was not much of a consensus in the early Middle Ages about why manual labor was a good thing, there had been even less agreement centuries earlier.[14] In the fourth and fifth centuries, some Syrian monks had worked toward another ideal: they strove to praise God nonstop, rather than reliving the trauma of agriculture that God had inflicted on humans since the fall of Adam and Eve. This position was criticized from many sides. But the solitary monks who embraced it were also celebrated by lay Christians across the prosperous countryside of the Levant. They valued the monks' service as spiritual leaders to communities that remained locked into the agrarian cycle.

As it happened, communal monastic projects came to embody the opposing view, inspired by Egyptian monks in particular, that physical work helped monks foster financial and mental stability. But this model still depended on the support of outsiders—on the substantial donations of land, money, and food that allowed monks to dedicate many hours in their days to other forms of discipline. The less support a monastery had, the more its monks had to work to sustain themselves.

Every monastic schedule implicitly took a position on the ethics of labor. But there were also psychological and sociological tensions at play. When a single monk did not stick to the rules it threatened to destabilize the system for everyone. So how could a schedule manage monks both as individuals and as a group? Ferreolus of Uzès was thinking about this when he formulated policies for the monastic community he had founded in what's now southern France. He knew that his monks would complain about their work assignments. Farming and craft labor could be overwhelming for people who had never worked a day in their lives. They might protest, "I'm too old," "I don't feel good," or "It's too hard!" Ferreolus insisted that even if these excuses were true, every monk still had to work *somehow*. Catch fish! Weave nets! Make shoes! Even the monastery's dog had a job to do: the monks were allowed to have a guard dog to keep wild animals out of the crops. But Ferreolus predicted that his aristocratic recruits would miss their elite entertainments so much that they would try to take the dog hunting—and he warned them in advance that this would be unacceptable. The hypothetical guard dog needed to stick to its work assignment, just like the monks. They were all part of a system of labor that was designed to help monks concentrate on God against an array of enticing alternatives. Submitting to that shared routine was supposed to reorient the mind itself.[15]

While monks worked, they were not supposed to talk to each other—or at least, they were told to avoid chitchat. This was a point on which all monastic leaders agreed. Today we tend to think of vision as the sense perception that is likeliest to distract us. But in late antique and early medieval monasteries, speech was thought to be even more distracting than sight. The monks who moralized chatter said it loosened monks' minds from their bridles. They compared its effects to ravages of wildfires, late frosts, and demolitions. Their argument was that its effects were systemic. A talkative monk could hijack the thoughts of his companions at work, prayers, meals, or downtime. He could get them thinking about any random thing that didn't matter. He might even make them laugh, which deflated the seriousness of monastic training and made everyone seem juvenile.[16]

A few monasteries were celebrated for cutting out talking completely, such as the famous Pachomian monastery of Tabennesi in Upper Egypt. But some monks had mixed feelings about the virtue of silence. The abbess Sadalberga, for example, was praised by her hagiographer for her verbal restraint—but also for being a snappy conversationalist. It wasn't until the tenth century that total silence became more widespread in monastic practice. The monks of Cluny, in central France, decided that they would use their voices only to praise God, in their lengthy liturgies. And in order to communicate without speaking they developed an elaborate system of hand signs (though *this* language could be abused to the point of distraction, too). Some monasteries emulated the monks of Cluny; others criticized them for dispensing with tradition. But that "tradition" had always been mixed.[17]

Rules governing speech couldn't fix everything anyway. Monks might remain quiet at work, but the work itself could become too absorbing, so they were warned of the risks of concentrating too deeply on their chores. They were also supposed to resist the urge to work overtime for the sake of finishing a job: it caused the schedule to seriously malfunction. Work was *never* a reason to skip prayer, as Rabbula of Edessa pointed out in the fourth century. Many rules insisted that the instant monks heard the signal for services, they had to drop what they were doing—though some made exceptions depending on the nature of the work. (Pens and needles were easy to drop, less so sick patients in the infirmary.) Still, the mind could be slow to catch up to the switch. Isidore of Seville observed that even when work was supposed to be over, unfinished projects had a tendency to linger in the mind and become a distraction. Transitions were tough—an experience that monks shared with today's toddlers, college students, and most other people.[18]

The other key components of monks' schedules, reading and liturgies, involved a similar mixture of benefits and risks to monks' attention. John Climacus asserted confidently that "everyone can pray in a crowd." And monks loved to share stories about feats of liturgical concentration. Palladius, for instance, reported one about the Cappadocian monk Elpidius, who barely moved a muscle when he got stung by a scorpion during the night service. With lapidary control Elpidius simply crushed the creature with his foot. But stories like that were especially riveting because most monks found that praying together was not in fact as easy as John Climacus said it was.[19]

After all, communal prayers and liturgies (including the daily offices and the Mass) did not always mitigate distractions; sometimes they magnified them. Monks needed to be reminded that they should be doing this work "with total concentration," with that active mental stretching that was such a crucial part of their practice. But some of them still found themselves spacing out, or staring vacantly, or looking around the room—even when they were personally officiating the Mass. They stood outside the church and talked, or they raced to beat each other to the office, then wheezed and palpated their side cramps instead of singing. They chatted in pairs while everyone else sang. They made each other giggle. They yawned or coughed or sneezed or blew their noses and spoiled the moment. They prayed too loudly and ostentatiously, and when they made their ritual bows they invaded their neighbors' personal space. They tried to hurry through their material. They fidgeted or sat down or even left in the middle of service because they were tired of standing. And when the liturgy was actually over, they dawdled or made too much noise when they exited the church, which bothered the monks who had stayed behind to pray even longer.[20]

They also showed up late to church in the first place, especially to the prayers that they performed in the middle of the night, which of course occasioned debates about whether to let the tardy monks in. Then the monks who actually made it to the services sometimes dozed off once they were there. Monastic theorists had a number of responses to that problem, too. Sleepy monks might have to stand while everyone else sat, or leave the church for some fresh air while everyone stood—though the risk of the latter solution was that the monks might not come back. Could lateness and sleepiness instead be solved closer to the source? Cassian recommended following the Egyptian model of keeping prayers short, especially at night: there was no point in trying to hold marathon services, because monks would inevitably drift. (Cassian also knew very well, however, that monasteries were highly creative when it came to their services, and it was a fantasy to expect all of them to switch to an identical model.) Some monastic leaders focused on the sleeping schedule and wondered whether monks should go back to bed after praying in the middle of the night. Others tried to regulate the transition between sleeping and waking. The *Rule of the Monastery of Tarn* seems to have envisioned curfew checks to make sure that monks were in their beds at bedtime. The *Rule of the Master* even advised monks to sleep fully dressed, so that when it was time to get up for prayers, they wouldn't putz around hunting for their clothes in the dark.[21]

✳

EVEN THOUGH SCHEDULES ALONE could not solve the problem of distraction, they were a pervasive strategy for disciplining monks' minds through the power of consistency and collective energy. But they were only part of the formula for social support. As much as monks benefited from working and praying together, they also needed authority figures to guide them. John Cassian repeated what Abba Moses had told him: monks needed good teachers to counsel and encourage them when things got difficult. Others emphasized that obedience was the most important lesson to learn from a superior, because it was a crucial first step in learning self-discipline. Obedience got monks in the habit of "killing off" (*mortificare*, as Cassian put it) or "amputating" (*koptein*, as the *Apophthegmata* frequently put it) their impulses and personal preferences. In order to concentrate on the divine, especially as part of a group, monks needed to stop thinking so much about themselves.[22]

But the training was tough and frustrating, especially for people who had been accustomed in their former lives to the privileges of power. In the fifth or early sixth century a Latin preacher named Novatus tried to spin it to one monastic community by suggesting that obedience to an abbot should actually come as a relief. Rather than objecting to their food allotments or trying to switch their seating assignments at dinner, monks should be glad that their abbot was doing so much of their thinking for them. Other monks preferred to advocate obedience by sharing stories that winked at the counterintuitive virtue of following orders for the sake of following orders. There was one about the desert father Mark, whose teacher Silvanus spotted a wild boar and insisted that it was a buffalo. Mark simply agreed with him. Or a student of John of Lycopolis was said to have watered a dead tree branch that John had stuck into the ground, just because John told him to. Nothing miraculous came of this: the branch stayed dead. The remarkable thing was that the student kept watering the branch, for an entire year, until John told him to stop.[23]

But despite their agreement that authoritative leadership was an important element of monasticism, monastic engineers envisioned a wide variety of practical models for their communities. Some kept things simple. They said it was the abbot's or abbess's job to delegate work assignments to their monks (because monks would otherwise be inclined to pick jobs that were easy or prestigious or fun). And they told monks to follow the superior's orders without foot-dragging, grumbling, or talking back.[24]

Many also insisted that monastic leaders needed to monitor their monks' very thoughts. This had been a key element of Pachomius's work as an abbot: his monks would confide in him about their bad thoughts, and Pachomius would determine what each monk's thoughts reflected about his true ideas and feelings, in order to advise an appropriate course of action. Columbanus, who founded several monasteries in Gaul and northern Italy in the late sixth and early seventh centuries, was likewise a vocal advocate for what might be called cognitive transparency. He emphasized that thoughts were consequential, just like actions were, and he wrote a penitential that assigned penance to monks for "sinning by think-ing," whether they had thought about murder, sex, stealing, deser-tion, hitting someone, getting drunk, or just eating extra food in secret. He also expected his monks to confess such thoughts or "mental agitations" (*commotiones animi*) before they attended Mass. Other theorists asked monks to share their disturbing thoughts with the abbot as soon as they arose, or to check in three times a day, or to meet periodically but less frenetically. And at a monas-tery that John Climacus greatly respected, monks kept little books with them at all times, so they could fastidiously jot down their thoughts to show their superior later.[25]

Some theorists suggested that such protocols were rooted in a profound moral obligation. The abbot was more than a disciplinar-ian, they argued. He was the lifeline to heaven. His scrutiny and care made the monks' progress possible, and conversely, his negli-gence could imperil the entire community. His soul was burdened by theirs: God would hold an abbot accountable for every single monk who had been entrusted to him. Toward the end of the sev-enth century, the bishop Valerius of Bierzo suggested that more abbots should see things this way. He ranted about the monas-tic leaders in northwest Spain who weren't bothering to crack down on their subordinates' bad behavior, as if they assumed that God would not blame them personally. But Valerius was sure that God would!

In the sixth century, the abbot Eugippius argued that *this* was why an abbot should make so many decisions for his monks, down to the clothes they were assigned and the food they were served. To the monks, these restrictions might feel like martyrial torments. To the abbot, they were careful calculations in a massive ledger that he would eventually hand over for the ultimate audit. Like-wise the *Rule of Benedict* expected an abbot to root out problems in his monks as soon as he spotted them, rather than ignoring them or hoping they would solve themselves: all these problems were *his*. But even among communities with a less vertiginous sense of pastoral power, the disclosure of thoughts to a mentor was crucial, because it helped a monk identify and dismantle the hidden barriers that kept her mind distracted from God.[26]

It was a responsibility that required finesse. All monks were supposed to be treated as equals, which was a staggering expectation in a deeply hierarchical world. But at the same time, each monk had to be disciplined differently, because each psychological profile was distinct. There was no panacea for misbehavior, as Ferreolus of Uzès pointed out: an abbot had to determine what exactly a monk's mental "illness" was before prescribing the perfect antidote.

On top of that, abbots and abbesses had to balance the needs of the individual patient (or delinquent) with the community's own interests. The *Rule of the Monastery of Tarn* suggested that the superior should discipline a monk privately if most monks were unaware that he had done anything wrong, but the punishment should be public if the infraction was common knowledge. John Climacus was particularly impressed by how one abbot had handled a criminal who wanted to become a monk. He orchestrated a dramatic ritual of confession so that the initiate's sins would be forgiven. But he made sure that it was enacted in front of everybody, so that the horrific crimes they heard—and the pardon that the monk received anyway—would motivate everyone else to confess their sins, too.[27] Mental discipline was collective, but it was also customized. Monastic leaders had to be sociologists and psychologists at the same time.

＊

YET REGARDLESS OF THEIR skill or efforts, an abbot or abbess could not keep a community together on their own. The famous Benedict of Nursia, whom Gregory the Great celebrated in the second book of his *Dialogues*, quit his very first job as a monastic supervisor, because—according to Gregory—there weren't any good monks at that monastery to help him out. In fact his monks had tried to poison him.[28] The monks themselves needed to be good influences on each other; otherwise their minds would be ungovernable.

Of course, what counted as "good influence" was up for debate. Some monasteries emphasized the importance of cultivating emotionally supportive spaces. Jonas of Bobbio suggested in his *Rule for Virgins* that all the women in a monastic community should foster a culture of love—by praying for each other, forgiving each other, and governing their own actions out of consideration for everyone else. That was one strategy, at least. In this and in many other monasteries, monks also needed to keep an eye on each other. Some monasteries created official positions to accomplish that. The Pachomian monasteries divided their monks into subsidiary houses, each of which was led by a housemaster and a deputy housemaster. Similarly, the *Rule of the Master* assigned one or two supervisors to look over groups of ten monks each. But chains of command could be contested. The women of the White Monastery, one of the communities in Shenoute's federation, were more or less satisfied with the three ranking sisters who supervised them. But when Shenoute decided to subordinate everyone to a male deputy who outranked even their superiors, some of them were furious: they wanted the autonomy to determine their own protocols and forms of discipline. When Shenoute decided to appoint a deputy anyway, the women monks made their displeasure known, by talking back, standing their ground in other disputes, withholding information, and refusing to meet with Shenoute's representative.[29]

Mutual surveillance was another option. Some communities expected monks to tell their superior when they saw a fellow monk violating the rules. Others encouraged them to call each other out on their behavior rather than cover for them—to "be abbots to each other," as the preacher Novatus put it. And they were often forbidden from defending their brothers or sisters when they were being reprimanded.[30]

Unsurprisingly, a management strategy reliant on tattling had its problems. For one thing, monks could take it very personally. In the sixth century Dorotheus of Gaza—a monk at Tawatha who would later found his own monastery—sent several letters to his spiritual mentors anxiously asking what to do when he saw his fellow monks doing something wrong, and how to behave toward a monk who snitched on *him*. His correspondents, the solitary ascetics Barsanuphius and John, told him not to worry about what other monks thought. This advice was something of a refrain for them, but other monastic leaders were slightly more sympathetic. Augustine of Hippo had asked his monks to think about their responsibility to speak up in terms of public health: they were helping the members of their community get medical treatment when they were wounded.

Or maybe monks should follow scripts? Columbanus designed a dialogue that a monk was supposed to enact if he heard a brother say something wrong. The monk should take a moment to be sure that his companion had really spoken inaccurately. Then he should remark, "Sure, if you're recalling it correctly, brother!" This was supposed to prompt the other monk *not* to double down on what he'd said but instead to reply, "I do hope you remember it better! In my forgetfulness I've overstepped in my remarks, and I'm sorry that I misspoke."[31]

Columbanus's monks probably didn't take this suggestion literally. Or at the very least, we can't assume that they did, since monastic rules cannot tell us whether anyone actually followed them. (After Columbanus died, some of his monasteries became intensely polarized about how to operate in the spirit of their founding father. Their arguments did not proceed according to his idealized dialogue.) But it is at least clear that the stiffness of that little script was designed to defuse the charged situation of disciplining one's peers. There were monks who took offense at being corrected by their siblings, and there were monks who found too much enjoyment in doing the correcting. Although Columbanus's script was unusual, many of his fellow monastic leaders tried to

establish ground rules for mutual monitoring. A monk wasn't supposed to stare or make comments or joke about how much her
fellow monk was eating, for example. (Fasting could devolve into
a competitive sport, and more than one monastery was roiled by
individual monks who conspicuously outperformed all the others.) Likewise a monk was not allowed to take physical discipline
into her own hands: at the very least, she needed permission from
her superior to hit a fellow monk who deserved it. Some monastic
leaders didn't allow monks to correct each other at all and simply
told them to mind their own business.[32]

Provisions like these were supposed to minimize the friction
inherent in peer-to-peer discipline, but monks could start fights
that had nothing to do with pedagogy or protocol. Sometimes they
just misbehaved. They called each other names, like "devil" and
"stupid servant." They retained their classist prejudices and looked
down on the monks who did not have pedigrees to speak of. They
performed mean impressions of each other. They lied about each
other, and were overly suspicious of each other, and resented each
other for seeming to have it easy. And once they were mad, they
avoided each other rather than make up. They stewed in their
anger, reacted passive-aggressively, and made a performance of
refusing to eat because they were upset.[33]

A touch of conflict could be a good thing, or at least this is what
Basil of Caesarea tried to suggest in the fourth century. How could
a monk practice patience if he were not surrounded by other people
who constantly seemed "to thwart his wishes"? But as all monastic leaders recognized, even minor annoyances could escalate. And
when the collective spirit started to break down, as Abba Joseph
once told Cassian, monks' prayers wouldn't work anymore. Cassian's mentor Evagrius had said the same thing: you could not hold
on to your grievances and also hold on to God at the same time.
It was cognitively impossible. So monks were urged to cool down
quickly, and make amends. Many monastic guidelines liked to

quote Paul's letter to the Ephesians: "Let not the sun go down upon your anger."[34]

After all, the company of other monks was supposed to be beneficial. That was the point of the shared routines, the authority figures, the cultivation of mutual love or surveillance or both: cognition could be strengthened collectively. It was also one of the most important lessons of the stories that circulated about monks who lived in pairs: living in a committed monastic relationship helped monks triumph over their mistakes and failures. Even in larger communities, mutual support was understood to be so powerful that monastic leaders enforced social isolation for a monk who had committed a particularly serious offense. Monks were expected to value each other's company, even if they could see its benefits only by being deprived of it.[35]

※

YET MONASTIC LEADERS never forgot that the collective power of a community could also be destructive. They knew that the challenges of communal life—the challenges that monks were supposed to experience in a monastery for the sake of their own self-improvement—could shade into abuse or neglect and thereby shatter spiritual attentiveness. The welfare of individual men and women concerned them, as did their institutions' finances: founders and donors did not want to see their investments mismanaged. So monastic theorists asked monks to report mistreatments and threatened to get the ecclesiastical authorities involved. They advised abbots not to be so stingy with food and clothing that the monks would have legitimate grounds for complaint. Even the high-minded Shenoute had said in the fifth century that monks were entitled to complain about the cooking if it was truly unappetizing. Some hardships were essential to communal projects. Others could be debilitating distractions.[36]

Or worse: conflicts within a community could become intrac-

table, and those conflicts could erupt and become a public sensation and thereby threaten the delicate support system that monks
maintained with the world. Palladius's *Historia Lausiaca*, a generally warmhearted account of his monastic travels that he wrote
in the early fifth century, shared a few unflattering stories about
the Pachomian federation, including a disturbing account of how
a petty fight involving a false accusation led two women at the
esteemed monastery of Tabennesi to commit suicide. Palladius
approvingly noted that many of their sisters were punished in the
aftermath, because they hadn't done anything to resolve the conflict before it became serious. The story was supposed to underscore
the monastic principle that even small sins could become toxic if
left untreated—and also that monasteries depended on monks'
mutual discipline. Or as the abbot Dadisho' explained it to the
monks of the Mesopotamian monastery of Izla in 588: one brother's lapse, if left unchecked, could lead to the "confusion of the
community," which in turn could become "a cause of scandal and
damage for many."[37]

Dadisho' made this observation when he was new to the job.
He had just succeeded Izla's founding abbot, Abraham the Great,
when he recorded this and other rules. A regime change was always
a vulnerable time for a monastery, and Dadisho' knew it. Just a
year later, another prestigious monastery at the other end of the
Mediterranean experienced exactly the kind of scandal that had
worried the East Syrian abbot. The incident reveals how deeply
Dadisho''s contemporaries saw individual minds in the context
of communities, and how seriously they took the consequences of
social "confusion" and distraction.

The scandal started in 589 at Holy Cross in Poitiers, a monastery
that had been founded by the Merovingian queen Radegund only
a few decades earlier. Relying on her luminous reputation and also
her connections, Radegund had recruited women from all ranks
to Holy Cross, including two princesses who were her first cousins thrice removed and technically also her step-granddaughters.

Eventually she joined her own monastery, too. But there were probably tensions between the women of Holy Cross even while Radegund was alive. The obligation of monks to treat all monks equally, regardless of their former status, is a recurring theme in most monastic rules. It was certainly a subtext throughout the *Rule for Virgins* by Caesarius of Arles, which Radegund had adopted for her monastery. Caesarius's sister, the abbess Caesaria of Arles, also noted in a letter to Radegund that her well-born monks should be more concerned with their humility than their social rank. The point always needed stressing.[38]

Apparently, it didn't take. After Radegund died, and after the death of the monastery's first abbess, who had been a close friend of the queen, elitist grievances boiled over. The two princesses and some forty other monks walked out of the monastery in protest. Their leader, one of the two princesses—Princess Chrodield—put their primary concern in blunt terms. The new abbess, Leubovera, had subjected them to "great degradation": "We are being debased in this monastery as if we weren't the daughters of kings!" Throughout the year in which the rebellion took place, Chrodield never missed an opportunity to mention her royal connections.

The princesses registered their complaints with several bishops and two kings. But they were disappointed by the responses they received: Had the monastery's system of rules—Caesarius's *Rule for Virgins*—been broken? Or had any crimes that concerned the secular courts been committed? If not, the monks had no case. They might resent the principle of equality that made their social stature irrelevant, but that was a structural feature of monasticism, not a glitch.

The princesses' response was to enlist armed warriors to help them seize properties belonging to the monastery. They assaulted the tenants on those lands to coerce them into rendering their services to Chrodield instead. They broke into Holy Cross, kidnapped the abbess, and looted the monastery. It took a showdown with the police force of Poitiers to suppress the rebellion. The offending monks were hauled into court. Multiple people died in these confrontations; many more were injured.

At a trial convoked by the kings and bishops, Chrodield tried to ground her elitist complaints on a firmer legal footing, by representing the abbess as a nobody whose unwarranted taste for luxuries contravened the *Rule for Virgins*, in particular its emphasis on a strict separation between the monks and the outside world. None of her accusations won the court's sympathies, though the bishops acknowledged that Leubovera had veered into some gray areas— by playing board games, for example, and hosting an engagement party for her niece. They were not as upset by these things as Caesarius himself would have been: he had advocated an unusually strict policy of enclosure, in which women monks were never allowed to leave their monasteries, but many more Christians in Gaul supported monastic models that did not involve total lockdown. The bishops concluded that it was the princesses who had committed actual crimes. As punishment they were excommunicated and told to perform penance.

The princesses were so furious that they went on to accuse Leubovera of committing treason against the Merovingian king Childebert II—a claim that the king was willing to investigate. But he found it, too, to be unsubstantiated. One of the princesses asked for forgiveness and returned to Holy Cross. But Chrodield never went back.[39]

Gregory of Tours, the historian who narrated this entire saga and who had been personally involved in the conflict, also mentioned another casualty of the chaos: as the rebellion took its course, some of the monks who never left the monastery ended up pregnant anyway. This was a flagrant violation of Caesarius's *Rule for Virgins*, but Gregory and the other bishops concluded that these monks (*monachae*) were innocent. The revolt had so destabilized the community that the pregnancies didn't count as crimes. The bishops' reasoning underscores the optimism that many early medieval Christians felt about monasteries as institutions. They were certain that monks could be stronger when they were part of a regulated community. But they also recognized that schedules, hierarchies, and mutual support were still vulnerable to the misbehavior of individuals. Even a monastery was a potentially "unsafe space."[40]

After the Holy Cross revolt, a monk of that monastery named Baudonivia encouraged her sisters to remember their founding mother as a model of the *mens intenta*, of a mind constantly stretched out to God. Unlike Radegund's other hagiographers, Baudonivia thought that it was crucial to highlight Radegund's routine concentration, as if by representing her this way she could refocus the community as a whole.[41] But not even tightly organized social structures could solve all the problems of disaffection and distraction—no matter how well designed the schedule was, or how supportive the culture of leadership and mutual observation were. It was necessary to go deeper, into monks' very bodies, to reconfigure them.

CHAPTER 3

▦ BODY

MONKS LONGED TO LIVE LIKE ANGELS, AND THE angelic life meant something very specific to them. Humans, like angels, were rational beings. Humans, like angels, were capable of thinking abstractly and making principled judgments, and therefore capable of appreciating the complexity of creation and praising its creator. But as monks felt all too palpably, no human on earth could truly live like an angel—because humans had bodies, and angels did not. Angels did not feel deficient. They did not feel separated from the rest of the world by the stuff of matter. They certainly never felt grimy, or sleepy, or turned on, or hungry. Angels were pure consciousness. They spent all their time celebrating God and the universe he had created: their concentration was perfect and continuous. Humans were constrained by biology and physics, and the limitations of that existence inevitably led to distraction.

Some lucky monks got the chance to experience what it was like to be an angel just before they died—to hear, at last, the songs of praise that were normally inaudible to humans, performed perpetually by an ever-attentive choir.[1] Before that moment came, monks could only ever aspire to angelic concentration, and as part of that effort they opted to work with their own bodies for the sake of their minds, rather than to deny that their bodies existed.

Today we think of "wellness" as a product of both body and mind, and the spiritual well-being that monks sought was premised on this partnership, too. But the approaches they took to their physical training are not exactly intuitive now. They were suspicious of grooming and sleeping, for example, so for the sake of optimal cognition some of them avoided baths and built devices to interfere with a good night's sleep. Their behavior was more comprehensible a millennium and a half ago, but even then monks did not always agree on best practices, because their goal was an elusive synthesis of body and mind that could elevate them above the world's distractions.

This meant making adjustments to a working relationship that was already hard to fathom. Most Christians in Late Antiquity and the early Middle Ages saw themselves as a composite of material and immaterial parts, as bodies that had been joined with souls/minds/hearts/spirits—terms that were overlapping and sometimes functionally interchangeable. They pictured this anatomy in strikingly different ways, because, as the monk Anastasios of Sinai observed around 700 CE, there were no straightforward answers in the Bible, or for that matter in medicine, and "human beings are obstinate, inquisitive animals" who would never stop asking difficult questions about the soul and the body and their relationship to each other.[2]

Some imagined the mind as physically located in the chest cavity. Some divided the soul into different cognitive functions and assigned them to specific parts of the body accordingly: rational thoughts in the brain, emotions in the heart, and physical urges in the liver, all linked by breath and blood and nerves. Others thought the soul was present throughout every part of the body: it was "tied to the innards" (as Faustus of Riez put it in the mid-fifth century) and permeated a person's thoughts. Some figured that the soul-mind had a kind of astral body that could travel beyond the fleshy body and make itself visible to other people. Still others argued that the soul and its related mental faculties were completely shapeless and bodiless but were still somehow affected by the body until it died. These were just a few of the models on offer.[3]

But monastic writers only infrequently explained their views in any diagrammatic way. They were much more concerned about how to choreograph the material and immaterial parts of themselves; even their most basic discussions about monastic practice reflect a conviction that the two were always working together.

The partnership had its problems. Bodies nudged the mind to think about baths and naps and sex and food with frustrating regularity. And if a body got everything it wanted, its pleas would only become more persistent. It was not only "the world" and other people that could distract monks from their work. Monks' own bodies could betray them. Physical pleasure "clouds" the mind, as Gregory the Great put it at the end of the sixth century. Two decades earlier Abraham of Kashkar had put it even more bluntly to his monks at Izla: "If the body [is] not quiet, the mind cannot be quiet."[4]

Some monks thought this called for war. The desert father Dorotheos reportedly said about his body that "it is killing me, I am killing it." Sensational stories circulated about monks who seemed to share his fatalistic view. Whether in the spirit of self-crucifixion or penance or brutal self-discipline or enslavement to God, they branded themselves, or wound themselves with rope or chains that cut into their flesh, or locked themselves into tiny cages.[5]

But such monks were outliers. Most monks preferred collaboration to combat: rather than reject their bodies, they tried to discipline their minds *through* their bodies, and their bodies through their minds. They saw human beings as profoundly somatopsychic and psychosomatic creatures. The body conditioned an individual's experiences, perceptions, and ideas. In reverse, those nonphysical operations also shaped the body. So just as the body was a monk's partner in crime, it was also a necessary partner in her progress. "It is truly astounding how the incorporeal mind can be defined and darkened by the body," John Climacus exclaimed in the seventh century. "Equally astonishing is the fact that the immaterial spirit can be purified and refined by clay."[6]

The range of practices that monks developed to discipline their bodies goes today by the shorthand of "asceticism," a term of early modern vintage derived from the ancient Greek *askesis*, which could mean physical or mental training or both. But monks were not the first to develop body-and-mind regimens as part of a larger overhaul of the self. They were drawing on philosophical and medical traditions that stretched back centuries, and on Christian theologies that emphasized God's enfleshment in Jesus as the medium for redemption. Physicians, Platonists, Jews, Stoics, Cynics, Neoplatonists, and early Christians subscribed to substantially different theories about the nature of body, soul, and divinity. But they generally agreed that the soul was influenced by the body even though it ranked above the body, and that consequently the body needed to be scrutinized and refined through a combination of medical, athletic, and moral conditioning.[7]

Christian monks in Late Antiquity and the early Middle Ages saw grooming, sleeping, sex, and eating as primary targets of their physical training. But they energetically disagreed about technique. Sometimes their divergent recommendations were rooted in contrasting cosmologies and theologies. But usually the disagreements had to do with competing body-mind kinetics: How should they be trained together? The place to start is with grooming, which might seem like a minor subject, even a distraction in itself, but which in fact illuminates how monks saw bodies and minds as linked in the first place.

✳

A MONK'S APPEARANCE was more than skin-deep, but Christians delighted in stories about how surfaces could be misinterpreted. In Gregory the Great's *Dialogues*, shepherds who spotted Saint Benedict thought he was a wild animal because he was wearing animal pelts and lurking in the underbrush near his cave. A peasant came to visit a holy cleric in Ancona whom he had heard about, but when he entered the church and actually saw him, he was so unimpressed that even when others confirmed to him that *this* was actually the famed Constantius, he concluded that the man was not as great as he had been led to believe. When the Ostrogothic king Totila first saw the bishop Cassius of Narni, he thought his red face indicated a drinking problem—but God would go on to disprove Totila's snap judgment. The bishop just happened to have a ruddy complexion.[8]

It wasn't that appearances didn't matter. Gregory was only trying to teach his audience to interpret appearances more accurately, because in late antique and early medieval culture, exterior states were revealing of intangible realities. Stoics had seen the body as representing the condition of the soul, precisely because the two were linked. Late Neoplatonists argued that the body reflected deeper truths—or as Proclus put it in the fifth century, "We are in fact images of the intellectual realities." In this way of thinking, a beautiful body was a portrait of a mind attuned to the divine essence of beauty: the physical state expressed an intellectual one.

One did not have to be a Neoplatonist to notice that bodies also revealed the social conditioning that had trained them to move and speak in specific ways. Most late antique persons thought that even the skin, a seemingly superficial wrapping paper, expressed one's values and resources. Hence the appeal of a good Roman bath. The bath complexes that were ubiquitous in cities and on aristocratic estates provided more than a spa day. They also harnessed the elemental forces of fire and water to make bodies healthy and reconnect them with the energies of the universe. The clean and shiny bodies that emerged from the baths reflected this cosmic connection. Just as importantly, the baths *strengthened* this connection, because the body was not just a mirror but also an instrument of spiritual health. To clean was to clarify *and* to strengthen the self.

This would have been obvious to the elite bathers who could afford to spend so much time caring for their bodies.[9]

Monasticism was part of this culture of appearances—to an extent. Monks accepted that bodies could be symptomatic of the soul *and* cultivated to shape the self. But their view of this relationship resulted in grooming habits that were pointedly countercultural. That included a moratorium on baths. The desert mother Silvania reportedly said, "I am sixty years of age, and apart from the tips of my hands, neither my feet nor my face nor any one of my limbs ever touched water." Ephrem the Syrian suggested that "by the washing of the body the soul becomes polluted." Fulgentius of Ruspe gradually eased into monasticism by adopting ascetic practices in phases: the last thing he did before joining a monastery was to cut out his trips to the baths. And when the monk Severus became the patriarch of Antioch, he ostentatiously dismantled the bathing facilities in his official residence.[10]

High and dry: this was the goal. A "dried-up" body, deprived of its beloved baths, was both the means and the result of pulling away from the world and stretching the mind up to God. Men and women deprived their bodies of this short-term gratification to focus on the good things that would last an eternity. A grubby exterior emphasized and clarified the interior. And because it was so difficult for converts—especially elite converts—to give up their baths, dirtiness could become its own source of prestige. In the later fourth century, after spending a couple of years as a monk himself, John Chrysostom argued that an aristocrat was actually likelier to impress the public after converting to monasticism than he was in his former guise: "He would not amaze everyone as much as he does now by being dirty and unwashed, wearing a rough garment, bringing no followers and being barefoot."[11]

Not everyone saw things this way, which is precisely why John chose to write his treatise *Against the Opponents of the Monastic Life*. Even monks themselves were divided about the politics of bathing.

Some worried that giving up baths entirely was an oxymoronic performance of humility, that it fostered feelings of self-obsession rather than obliterating them. One possible solution to this problem was to tie bathing standards to a monk's level of experience. New or young monks should be dirty and poorly dressed, to transform their priorities by transforming their physical selves. (This took time and effort: one monastic founder had to remind his elite recruits that they were not supposed to wear cologne.) But once monks matured, they should degrease, because unkemptness could become its own distraction: a monk whose values had reoriented to an ascetic regime could start feeling vain about his griminess. Other monastic leaders, thinking medically, argued that monks' bodies should be healthy, that baths were at least necessary for sick ascetics, and that a medically advisable treatment was not the same thing as a splurge.[12]

Besides the disagreements among monastic moralists and policy makers, the monks who populated their communities also sometimes objected to the constraints on their personal hygiene. They thought their allotted clothes were too cheap or too worn and tried to donate them to the poor on the pretext of being charitable. They complained about the infrequency of laundering. In the sixth century, the abbot Eugippius of Castellum Lucullanum (near Naples) had had enough of these arguments: squabbling about your monastic habit, he told his monks, showed that the habits of your heart left something to be desired.[13] The monastic regimen certainly took some adjustment. But these tiffs also speak to monks' equivocations about the criteria for aligning the outer *habitus* with the inner one. Which came first—the bath or the distraction? Could a monk concentrate without giving up grooming?

Haircuts were a similar flash point. Unlike their counterparts in China, who always wore their hair in a topknot (if they were Daoist monks) or shaved it completely (if they were Buddhist monks), Christian monks could not come to a consensus about hairstyles. Some desert fathers had worn their hair long, in the mode of the biblical prophets. One monk was even praised for having *never* cut his hair, which was both a sign and a technique of his intense discipline. Some women ascetics, conversely, completely shaved their heads or cut their hair very short. But other Christians reacted with alarm to these choices. They were partly concerned about the same counterproductive showiness of monks who never took baths. They were also worried that men who wore their hair long and women who shaved their heads were rejecting the gendered traditions of grooming in the late Roman world, and some saw this as unacceptably radical. Augustine of Hippo, for example, insisted that long hair made monks seem even more effeminate than they were already perceived to be. Masculine identity was so defined by "the world"—by family, ownership, public service, and the military—that the men who gave it all up had to strenuously redefine masculinity in terms of their new rigorous training. Long hair made it harder for monasticism to look manly.[14]

But Augustine was writing at a time when men's fashions were rapidly evolving. In the late fourth and early fifth centuries, elite Roman men were taking a cue from the military. They were swapping out their togas for pants and belts. They were putting on cloaks and brooches. They were growing their hair down to their ears or longer. These choices might have originally been popularized by immigrants from east of the Rhine and north of the Danube who had been recruited to the Roman army. But whatever the origins of the soldierly style, it had become ubiquitous in the imperial military, and civilians were picking it up, too. So although long-haired monks were sometimes caricatured as emasculated barbarians, others would have found such a judgment to be retrograde. Roman, "barbarian," and soldierly identities were blurring, and as a result, men's stylistic syntax was shifting.[15]

As hairstyles continued to morph over the centuries, so did Christian monks' debates about the body-mind balance: monks should shave their heads completely, or tonsure them partially, or never shave their faces or legs or armpits, or cut their hair regularly,

FIGURE 7 Christ with a "Celtic" tonsure. His bald pate peeks just above his carefully styled curls.

or leave their beards untrimmed, or keep their facial hair neatly clipped, or tie their hair up but not too ostentatiously. These seemingly small details were taken seriously because they were part of the physical training by which men and women were supposed to make adjustments to their bodies in order to reorient their minds' priorities. In this environment some monks were not above lampooning each other's haircuts. The lavishly illuminated Book of Kells, produced in Britain or Ireland around the year 800, represents Christ sporting a Celtic tonsure—shaved at the crown and partially down the back of the head (fig. 7)—while a sinful monk is styled with a "crown" cut that, after about a century of pressure from Romanizing English reformers, had become the dominant method of tonsuring in the British Isles by the time this manuscript was made. Proponents of the crown tonsure liked to think of it as emulating Jesus's crown of thorns, but the Kells portrait was not so flattering: the artist depicted the crown tonsure as shaggy and disheveled (fig. 8).[16]

FIGURE 8
This uncouth
cleric, positioned
over the word
peccaverit ("he
sinned"), wears
his hair in a
mangled version
of the crown
tonsure.

But as energetically as some monks debated their grooming practices, others warned that it was possible to become overly focused on the superficial aspects of their training. When Poemen, the *Apophthegmata* favorite, was asked why he washed his feet when other monks did not, he was unapologetic: "We have not been taught to kill our bodies, but to kill our passions."[17]

✳

NOT THAT MONKS COULD rest easy with this advice. In fact, monks were not supposed to be well rested at all, because they figured that restricting sleep actually enhanced their concentration and acuity. As with grooming, monks approached sleep as an opportunity to discipline their bodies to reframe their states of mind. But critics also called attention to the limits of this method: a body could be overexhausted, and the mind would suffer the consequences.

Drawing on the judgments of Greek physicians and philosophers, many monks thought that the mind experienced a kind of paralysis or captivity during sleep, and that it was either totally inactive or more vulnerable to distractions. Reducing sleep, or sleeping poorly, had the beneficial effect of restricting the mind's susceptibility to distracting dreams and demons. Cutting back on sleep also carved out more time in the middle of the night for vigils or liturgies.[18]

The contrast between sleeping and prayer could not have been starker. Monastic prayer was a muscular activity. When monks were not mixing manual labor and prayer, they were still usually supposed to pray standing up, with their arms outstretched (fig. 9). The posture kept them from falling asleep again; it also straightened out the mind. The *Instructions of Horsiesios* advised the Pachomian communities that "when you pray, if you wish not to be negligent or distracted by many thoughts, then, when your hands are outstretched, do not hasten to drop them to your side, for through fatigue and pain these thoughts will come to an end." Beyond counteracting distraction, the physical act of standing was supposed to guide the mind upward. "Let us stand during psalmody so that our mind harmonizes with our voice," instructed the *Rule of Benedict*. The "stylites"—those monks who planted themselves on pillars—took this ascent to the extreme. Simeon, the most famous of the stylites, was celebrated for his marathon standing, "a thing whose very narration is beyond mortal man without God's help," according to his Syriac hagiographer. Theodoret of Cyrrhus reported that even when one of Simeon's feet became grossly infected, his concentration never crumpled. And Jacob of Sarug composed an exuberant metrical homily in which Simeon actually cuts off his own festering foot and continues to stand on one leg on his column, while praising God and consoling his amputated foot that he would rejoin it in the afterlife.[19]

Even without a pillar to stand on, a monk was supposed to be upright, literally, and the hagiography of the desert elders was full of imposing examples that were supposed to encourage him or her to stay that way. The abba Arsenius was quoted as saying that "one hour's sleep is enough for a monk if he is a good fighter." Every Saturday at dusk Arsenius would stand facing east, with his back

FIGURE 9
In this seventh- or
eighth-century wall
painting from the
Egyptian monastery
of Bawit, an ama
(monastic mother)
named Askla extends
her arms in prayer.

to the setting sun, and pray with his hands outstretched until the sun shone on his face on Sunday morning. His example made a deep impression on later generations of monks, whether they spoke Greek, Latin, Syriac, Arabic, Georgian, Armenian, or Geʿez. The Palestinian abba Euthymius, for one, devoured the stories he'd heard about Arsenius, and he decided to sleep sitting up rather than lying down—or sometimes even to sleep while standing and holding on to a rope that he had attached to the ceiling.[20]

Other monks devised their own personal sleeping contraptions. Members of the Pachomian federation famously slept in reclining seats. So did monks at the monastery of Amida, in northern Mesopotamia. They also stood on posts, strapped themselves to walls, and hung ropes from the ceiling to loop under their armpits. The monastery of Qartamin in what's now southeast Turkey preferred even lower-tech options: here the monks rolled back and forth while they were lying down so that their bodies were never motionless, or they squeezed into narrow closet-like cells, where it was impossible to sit or lie down at all. And the abba Sisoes of Calamon somehow suspended his body over a cliff, to scare himself into staying awake.[21]

But it was impossible for most monks to act like this. Sometimes it wasn't even advisable: an angel reportedly chastised Sisoes for his cliff stunt and told him never to teach it to other people. Macarius of Alexandria once stayed outside for twenty days to avoid falling asleep, but even he went inside eventually, because he worried that if he didn't sleep at some point, "my brain would have been so desiccated that eventually I would have been driven to distraction." Other monks agreed. It was possible to restrict sleep so excessively that both body and mind became weak and unfocused. So monastic leaders often offered more temperate advice. Sleep when you are exhausted. Wake up before you feel fully rested. And be careful what you think about right before you fall asleep, so that your dreams don't take a turn for the worse.[22]

Most monks did not need persuading about the virtues of moderation. They were involved in a more rudimentary struggle against the desire for comfortable bedding. It's not that monasteries were stingy about beds. They usually allowed monks some basic comforts. A ninth-century typikon or foundation document for the monastery of Saint John Stoudios in Constantinople, for example, allocated each monk a straw mat, a goat-hair mat, and two wool blankets. And excavations of monastic complexes in Egypt show that some monks slept on elevated platforms carved from rock or clay (though whatever textiles they put *on* the beds are long gone), and that they also slept outside in the summer, to make sleeping easier on hot nights (fig. 10). In cooler seasons, some monks may have heated stones and date seeds to warm themselves: this is one of the ways that archaeologists have interpreted the cubbies that were next to their beds.[23]

But many monks thought that such allotments were insufficient for their needs. Despite the hagiographies they had heard about monks forgoing beds entirely, some of the men and women who had converted to monasticism still wanted to make their beds with plush mattresses, pillows, comforters, sheepskins, and beautifully decorated coverlets. Their preferences betrayed their former privilege: elites were notorious in Late Antiquity and the early Middle

FIGURE 10 Three clay beds lining the walls of a monastic bedroom at Deir el-Bakhit in Western Thebes (cell 27), from the late sixth or early seventh century.

Ages not only for their love of baths but also for their love of a good bed. Shenoute even skewered the aristocracy for providing blankets to their puppies! The famously sleepless Arsenius had been a senator at Rome before he headed south to the Egyptian community of Scetis in the fourth century—but most elites' bodies could not stand the shock of conversion so easily. For this reason Augustine of Hippo suggested that rich people who had converted to monasticism should be allowed to have special bedding, because otherwise the new life would be too tough for them to handle. As he often pointed out, ascetic challenges were relative, because bodies were inescapably conditioned by class.[24]

Given that the solutions for sleeping were imperfect, it is not surprising that some monks wished they never felt tired in the first place. A monk wrote John of Gaza to ask how he could avoid feeling sleepy at the start of spring, when the days got longer and he was likelier to drift off into an unfocused malaise. John felt it, too. The struggle with sleep and distraction was frustratingly persistent—and John, for once, didn't know what to say.[25]

*

MONKS' TRIALS WITH grooming and sleeping are less well known today than their infamous commitment to giving up sex. Many of them would have been annoyed to hear this. In a rhetorical conversation between a Christian named Zacchaeus and a philosopher named Apollonius that was written between 408 and 410, Zacchaeus argued that monks who gave up sex alone were the lowest-ranking monks in the game. Not only were they still living in their homes and keeping company with the same people as before; they were also outperformed by monks who had changed their ways of dressing, sleeping, eating, and praying.[26]

Sexual renunciation was just one of many psychosomatic-somatopsychic practices that mattered to monks. And it was one of many practices whose parameters they debated, because although they generally agreed that it was necessary to stop having sex, they were not so sure what they should do to stop *thinking* about sex. That was a key problem. It was maybe the most obvious distillation of the challenges presented by the connections between mind and body. Monks wanted to train their bodies to help their minds. But they also wanted to train their minds to help their bodies—to help their minds in turn.

Historians have found that strategies for sexual restraint tended to be strikingly unisex in Late Antiquity and the early Middle Ages. Christians generally agreed that souls were not sexed, and although many monks believed that it was impossible to transcend gender while inhabiting a specific and socialized body, they did not think the differences between men and women mattered much when it came to mental and physical discipline. Men and women experienced the same struggle of sexual desire and took up the same training to surmount it. Male monastic communities were perfectly happy to adopt monastic rules that were originally written for women, and vice versa. But it was also the case that women monks were often praised in unabashedly masculine language, as if the male writers who celebrated them could think of nothing more laudatory than to say that they seemed manly. In this respect, the language and conception of virtue was impoverished.[27]

But most monks nevertheless seem to have assumed that women and men were training on equal footing, and that both female and male bodies had enormous potential to strengthen their spiritual practices. For just as with not-bathing and not-sleeping, monks saw not-having-sex as a beneficial regimen, rather than as a punishment or negation of the body. This theory was much older than monasticism itself. Centuries before monks incorporated celibacy into their training, pagan, Jewish, and early Christian communities had believed that sexual restraint had medical, philosophical, and spiritual benefits. Some Christian groups even suggested that everyone who was baptized should refrain from sex, but the majority opinion was that sexual restraint need only involve delimiting sex to marital sex. That was abstinence enough. And most Christians who advocated total celibacy assumed that it was something to practice later in life, by adults who had already had children.

Yet by the late third century, some Christians were choosing at a young age to be virgins for life, and as the leaders of Christian communities reflected on the potential benefits of lifelong virginity, some of them came to conclude that sexual renunciation resulted in tranquility. "Tranquility" was a state of calmness and balance that philosophers had celebrated for centuries. As the thinking went, the body-discipline of sexual restraint steadied the mind. Some suggested that by transcending the turbulence of the physical body, a virgin could experience the angelic peace of paradise even before he or she died.[28]

Some early ascetics and monks were so assured of the power of celibacy that they lived with members of the opposite sex without fear of sexual attraction: they were certain that virginity fortified their minds completely. But in the course of the fourth and fifth centuries, monks began to lose confidence that virginal tranquility was so unshakable. This was partly due to complex theological differences. The disagreements, however, also boiled down to technique: many monks had come to see the body and mind as too codependent for one to completely stabilize the other. Cassian, for example, thought that even when a monk was celibate, he could become distracted by sexual thoughts anyway. Erections and wet dreams were not so much failures of the body as diagnostic signals that the mind itself was perturbed. Sexual restraint *required* composure rather than generating it on its own. And so, Cassian concluded, true chastity—the asexuality of both body and mind—had to be cultivated over a lifetime.[29]

By the fifth century most monks would have agreed that abstinence was both a physical challenge and a mental one. Still, they developed varying training plans to reach a state of calm. Some monks, to take an especially contentious practice, went so far as to castrate themselves. They were inspired by a passage in Matthew (19:12) in which Jesus praises those who "have made themselves eunuchs for the kingdom of heaven." They were also informed by certain medical theories in the Galenic tradition, which ventured that a lack of sperm also drained the body of sexual desire; and by certain gnomic traditions popular in ascetic circles that seemed to imply that castration was an acceptable strategy to keep the body from sinning. If a body part "leads you to intemperance," one saying went, "better to live temperately without it than to perish whole." Castration helped a monk avoid distractions that might otherwise damn him.

A few monks countered that the logic of self-castration was flawed. They argued that eunuchs still experienced sexual desire and were still capable of having sex. A more common objection was that monks were supposed to castrate themselves only metaphorically. Self-castration wasn't a solution; it was a workaround. A monk who cut off his own testicles or had them surgically removed, no matter the resolve he had summoned in that moment, actually betrayed a *lack* of self-control. He had been unable to stand up to his own mind—the ultimate challenge.[30]

John Moschos, a monk who surveyed many ascetic options in the eastern Mediterranean in the seventh century, pushed this line of reasoning even further. Even if a monk's sexual desire were to be miraculously obliterated, he claimed, there would be nothing to celebrate, because it was actually the struggle against arousal that made a monk physically, mentally, and morally fit. He offered the example of a monk and priest named Conon who got aroused every time he had to baptize a woman. Instead of trying to surmount his weakness, he quit the ceremony in embarrassment. When a miracle made it so that Conon never experienced sexual desire again, he returned to baptizing—and yet John Moschos refused to give Conon any credit. His desexualization was a hollow victory because he hadn't trained his mind to achieve it. But not everyone shared John's judgment. Although self-castration had been forbidden by Roman jurists and high-profile ecclesiastical councils centuries earlier, their pronouncements were not always heeded or enforced. Even in John's day some monks continued to castrate themselves (particularly in Egypt and Palestine), some continued to object absolutely, and yet others came to accept their eunuch colleagues.[31]

Many monks were willing to simply cut off heterosocial encounters completely, even if others believed that this, too, showed a lack of resolve. Male hermits often prided themselves on turning away women visitors. And it was common for both male and female monasteries to deny access to members of another gender, though they usually made exceptions for certain spaces (such as the receiving room, or the church), certain people (such as relatives and high-ranking clergy), and certain jobs (such as construction work, medical care, or eucharistic services). There are records of at least a few monks over the centuries who were assigned a female sex at birth but presented themselves as men and joined male monasteries. Their trans identities—which as historians have argued is an accurate and appropriate characterization—were often discovered only after they died, and although their fellow monks were stunned by such revelations, the initial shock usually gave way to admiration rather than outrage.[32]

Or at least, this is how early medieval hagiographers idealized such scenarios. Their portraits of trans monks suggested that encounters between differently sexed bodies were not an inevitable threat to monks' mental composure. Monks could exercise greater control than that. Other monks made this point about more routine interactions. Some averted their eyes from differently gendered people whom they passed on the road, for example, to limit the mind's opportunities for arousal—but other monks objected that this was only a superficial form of asceticism. It was the mind that needed to be sculpted and shaped, not the body alone. In one widely shared story, a traveling male monk who encountered a group of female monks moved off the road to avoid them. The highest-ranking woman in the group disapproved. "If you were a perfect monk," she told him, "you would not have noticed that we are women." Physical restraint could only get you so far.[33]

The hagiographical literature, as a result, is just as full of stories about monks who *were* willing to interact with people of the opposite gender. The *Apophthegmata patrum*, Theodoret of Cyrrhus's *Religious History*, and Gregory the Great's *Dialogues*—to take just a few highly influential traditions—each celebrate monks of both inclinations. Even a close-knit community could harbor opposing attitudes. In a sixth-century account of the abbots known as the Jura fathers, Gregory of Tours noted that one of them refused to see women, while another was warmly receptive to them.[34]

Monks tended not to discuss same-gender desire with the same vitriol as many of their contemporaries did (the former monk John Chrysostom being a notable exception). And as with the body's other desires, they tackled it with variegated ascetic repertories. Many communities restricted adult monks' interactions with younger monks, because outside the confines of the monastery, it was not uncommon for men in particular—especially elites, and often married elites—to have sex with youths of either gender who were enslaved to them. To discourage sexual activity between adults, some monasteries specified that monks should not share beds. But others *required* them to share beds, because sharing was itself a disciplinary measure meant to erode a monk's attachment to possessions. As Shenoute unsparingly pointed out in the fifth century, there were plenty of other opportunities for monks to check each other out, whether they were bathing, urinating, undressing, or just working or climbing in such a way that they revealingly exposed a calf or forearm. But monks emphasized the positive force of companionship more often than the pitfalls. Monks who lived in same-gender pairs, for example, were wary of becoming attracted to each other, but they also thought that it was vital to confront desire rather than to dodge it, and that on balance a fellow monk was likelier to be a source of support than a hazard.[35]

That social potential might even be multiplied. As the historian Albrecht Diem has noticed, starting in the sixth century, especially in Gaul, some monastic theorists were so confident in the power of collaboration that they believed its effects could minimize the vulnerabilities of individual monks. If a monastery as a whole adhered to its carefully designed policies, the monks' corporate body would be chaste, and their prayers would be effective. An individual monk might still be subject to stray erotic thoughts, but the concentration of the collective would prevail. This confidence helps explain the enduring popularity of dual-gender communities into the early Middle Ages—especially, it seems, in Gaul. If the virginal body was not strong enough to lift the mind on its own, a regulated system of social support would buoy it.[36]

This is not to say that the challenges of focusing on God had been resolved, or even that these monastic leaders thought they had. They knew that communities could fracture, as we've seen, and as the pregnant monks of Holy Cross knew all too well.

Besides, as far as the body was concerned, sex was not even the primary contender for a monk's attention. That distinction went to the body's most basic but inescapable seduction.

※

ABOVE ALL IT WAS HUNGER, not sex, that monks combated most doggedly in their struggle for self-control. When Palladius, the author of the beloved *Lausiac History*, went snooping on Macarius of Alexandria, he overheard him yelling—at demons, it turned out, but also at himself. Macarius was almost one hundred years old by that point. And he was still ranting about his inability to stop thinking about food.[37]

John Cassian put the problem bluntly. A full stomach weighed down the mind. It also produced erotic dreams. This was a medical and monastic commonplace: overconsumption caused cascading problems. Shem'on d-Ṭaybutheh, a monk who probably trained as a physician in southwest Iran in the seventh century, soberly enumerated the severity of the side effects:

> When the channels of the stomach are filled up and the organs which lead the light from the brain to the heart are blocked, the heart will be overspread with darkness, all the house will be filled with smoke, the limbs will suffer numbness, dejectedness will reign, the mind will be perturbed, the soul will darken, the discernment will become blind, knowledge will be hampered, judgment will be perplexed, (evil) thoughts will be set free, the remembrance of good things will be deleted from the heart, and the passions—the children of darkness—will receive fuel for their fire, will dance with joy, and applaud.[38]

But although hunger was a monk's most relentless and catalytic distraction, eating was also an opportunity to develop a robust disciplinary regimen. Daily acts of fasting and ingredient restriction could steadily transform the body and strengthen the mind. This is why Cassian described eating as the first in a series of Olympic events in which monks would compete over a lifetime. It was the foundation for all their future successes. Or their failures: as the monks of the Pachomian communities ironically pictured it, a monk who did not restrain his eating "becomes like a well that has been filled in, or spring gone dry, a river run empty; he becomes like a crumbled palace, an orchard already picked whose fence has fallen down."[39]

The concerns that we have already encountered—about body affecting mind, about mind affecting body, and about socialization affecting both—were therefore particularly sensitive when it came to eating, and the stories that monks shared about their ascetic heroes often included meticulous attention to their dietary habits. Antony ate bread and salt once a day, and sometimes even skipped his meal entirely. Rusticula ate only every third day. Portianus purposefully made himself thirsty by chewing on salt in the summertime. George of Choziba ate exclusively the table scraps his brothers left behind, which he squished together to make dumplings. Another George, this one in Sinai, subsisted on raw wild capers—so bitter they could kill a camel! Joseph of Beth Qoqa never ate *anything* that had been cooked. One elder had a craving for a small cucumber, so he hung it up on the wall to stare at rather than eat, as a way to chasten himself "for having even had the desire at all." And Jerome's *Life of Hilarion* tracked its protagonist's meals over the course of sixty years, noting precisely when he switched out his ingredients and why.[40]

Monastic communities tended to distill such extreme hagiographical precedents into a set of more moderate principles. Eat once a day, without snacking or stashing leftovers or getting takeout on the road. Eat for functionality rather than taste. And don't eat so much that you feel full. These basic guidelines aimed to energize monks' bodies enough to sustain them, while training them to manage their hunger, so that the mind did not become "enslaved" by a grumbling belly or "suffocated" and "emptied" by a full one.[41]

That didn't mean menus were spartan. A survey of the plant remains at Egyptian monastic sites found evidence of the consumption of fava beans, lentils, onions, olives, melons, parsley, radishes, carrots, fenugreek, dates, grapes, figs, pomegranate, citrus, blackberries, peaches, almonds, and jujubes. In the abandoned kitchen of the monastery of San Vincenzo al Volturno (sitting on the spine of Italy's central Apennines), archaeologists found discarded seeds of grapes and elderberries; the shells of walnuts, eggs, and mollusks; the bones of pigs and poultry; and the scales of several varieties of marine and freshwater fish. Of course, the foods monks ate were closely tied to their local ecologies and farms. Further variation resulted from the fact that even seemingly straightforward rules gave rise to multiple interpretations. Many monastic theorists thought that monks shouldn't eat meat, for example, but they defined "meat" in different ways, and the monastic communities who read and adopted these rules interpreted them idiosyncratically. This is at least what their trash suggests; archaeologists have found animal bones and bivalve shells at many a monastic settlement besides San Vincenzo. In some cases, the monks may have been serving these meats exclusively to their guests, employees, and patients. But in other cases, perfectly healthy monks were probably eating them, too.[42]

The dietary strategies that monks developed reflected their characteristic mix of traditional and radical impulses. They drew on long-established medical and philosophical traditions that had emphasized the physical, mental, and moral benefits of eating in moderation. They were inspired by both Hesiodic and Judeo-Christian mythographies about what humans ate when the world was new and uncorrupted: a medieval paleo diet. And they flatly rejected the celebratory forms of dining that were a fixture of life in elite Roman households—meals that many of them had enjoyed for years before becoming monks themselves. In their new communities, the daily communal meal took on the counterintuitive feel of a pit stop. Monks came together not to enjoy themselves, but to refuel.[43]

But the fact that monks were eating together still counted for something vital: it reinforced the feeling that they were training together. Monastic leaders were especially anxious about how communal solidarity could crack when their monks did not eat the same things. Both Shenoute (in the fifth century in Upper Egypt) and the author of the *Rule of Paul and Stephen* (in the sixth century in Gaul or Italy) even made a point of saying that monks could not bring their own condiments to the table: everyone had to eat *exactly* the same stuff. The women of the White Monastery were especially annoyed to learn that Shenoute had the same opinion about portion size. When he cut back on their daily rations, on the logic that the women and men in his federation should be held to the same disciplinary standards, some of them countered that their gender should make a difference. They wanted more to eat.[44]

Shenoute refused to concede in that case, but he and other monastic leaders made exceptions when they felt that individual bodies needed more targeted treatments. Not many of them repeated Augustine's suggestion that elite converts could be permitted to eat tastier foods, to help ease them into asceticism. But some of them tried to accommodate young and old monks and monks who were worn out from the harvest or other seasonal labors. Most agreed that sick monks deserved special treatment, too—though when patients received better food and more rest, some of their healthy colleagues resented them for it, while some of the sick ones tried to tough things out instead of eating the foods they were prescribed. Naturally, monks suspected each other of pretending to be sick for the perks.[45]

Those sorts of suspicions and criticisms endangered the whole project of physical training. As important as a sense of community was to a monk's personal progress, social pressure could lead her to mismanage her own body. And nothing was more sensitive than the subject of eating. When Jerome, writing from his perches in Italy and the Levant, took unnamed persons to task for overeating, monks all the way over in Gaul assumed that he was criticizing *them* specifically. This was why monks were sometimes told not to watch each other eat, even when they were sitting at the same table together. In the tightly wound culture of dietary scrutiny, even a joking remark like "How much bread have you eaten?" was potentially explosive.[46]

Competition was one problem. Obsession was another. The ascetic mentors Barsanuphius and John of Gaza received so many letters from a monk preoccupied with the logistics of fasting that they eventually told him that food wasn't the only thing he should be moderating. Defection was a third risk in communities that were too fixated on fasting: Evagrius advised monks not to emulate ascetics like Antony because severe fasting set unrealistic expectations for the body, which set them up for failure. The abbot Lupicinus was perhaps less sensitive to the risk of turning off followers. When he visited one of his monasteries in the Alps and saw that his monks had prepared a good spread of beans, vegetables, and fish, he dumped everything into the same pot and served them the result. Twelve monks quit on the spot. (Lupicinus's co-abbot was furious with him. Once again, the Jura fathers were not on the same page.)[47]

Fasting could even become self-destructive. Lupicinus actually told another monk under his supervision to dial down his fasting because he'd nearly killed himself. Even when it wasn't life-threatening, extreme fasting could have negative consequences for a monk's concentration. John of Dalyatha, a solitary nestled in the mountains of what's now northern Iraq, received letters from monks who kept falling asleep unpredictably because they were fasting more than their bodies could handle. Cassian pointed out, too, that overfasting could make a monk too exhausted to pray, and that it could also provoke bouts of binge-eating, which caused the mind's steadiness to teeter. John Bar Qursos, writing for the monks of Mar Zakkai in Syria in the sixth century, had noticed monks exhibiting this very problem when they attended Mass: the ones who had fasted too much were gorging themselves on the eucharistic bread and wine. "They are like greedy dogs eating their Lord!"[48]

Monastic theorists were also canny enough to notice, however, that the logic of moderation could be taken too far. It might make sense in certain situations to eat a snack if it could help a monk discipline his thoughts and stay in his cell. But thinking about snacks could itself become distracting. Likewise it might make sense to give monks extra food at harvest time, to keep up their energy—but monks could also use the work as an excuse to eat too much. And it might make sense to heed the medical views that excessive fasting would break the body, but this perspective might then inspire monks to selfishly argue that they needed wine to keep their liver and spleen healthy, or that they needed to interrupt a fast in order to stave off disease.[49] With fasting as with so many other situations, some monks were great at gaming the system.

Ultimately there could not be any surefire method for dietary training because monastic discipline was not about rejecting the body or even about disciplining the body alone. Monks who focused exclusively on their physical training were warned about the side effects of premature confidence, debilitating losses of energy, unexamined mental weaknesses, and inversion of their priorities. Instead monks were supposed to work out a finely tuned collaboration between body and mind (and other bodies and minds), because they were striving for no less than a total transformation of both. Only then would they experience a state of concentration as a fifth-century Syriac poet described it:

Their bodies are temples of the Spirit,
their minds are churches;
their prayer is pure incense,
and their tears are fragrant smoke.[50]

Monks developed countless strategies for grooming, sleeping, sexual restraint, and eating—which stemmed from countless theories about how the body should be trained to change the mind, how the mind should be trained to transform the body, and how sociability should be leveraged for the sake of both. But all of these ventures were anchored in a fundamental consensus that body, mind, and culture were linked. The problem was that the closeness of this relationship made cause-and-effect impossible to disentangle to anyone's satisfaction. As important as the body was to concentration, it could not offer a solution by itself, and monks looked to their books for more guidance.

CHAPTER 4

▤ BOOKS

E VAGRIUS OF PONTUS WAS CONSTANTLY THINKING about thinking. But he had not always led a life of the mind. Earlier in his career he had worked as a deacon in Constantinople and nearly had an affair with a married aristocrat. To escape that situation (so the story went) he joined a monastery on the Mount of Olives, in Jerusalem, which was run by an influential duo known as Melania the Elder and Rufinus of Aquileia—she a very religious and very rich Roman expat, he a scholar and monk. The three of them became close, but Evagrius left Jerusalem for the monastic communities that were thriving west of the Nile Delta. That is where he did most of his writing. But he still had his bad days. Even books could cause problems:

> When he reads, the one afflicted with *acedia* yawns a lot and readily drifts off into sleep; he rubs his eyes and stretches his arms; turning his eyes away from the book, he stares at the wall and again goes back to read for a while; leafing through the pages, he looks curiously for the end of texts, he counts the folios and calculates the number of gatherings, finds fault with the writing and the ornamentation. Later, he closes the book and puts it under his head and falls asleep.[1]

The struggle feels awfully familiar. But even if we can empathize with Evagrius, the experience he described from his vantage point in the fourth century was shaped by the distinct technological culture of Late Antiquity. The book—or more precisely the codex, made up of folded pages bound between two covers—was a comparatively new device in the fourth century. Monks were excited by its potential to help them improve their cognitive habits, but they were also concerned that books could become yet another accomplice in distraction. This tension resulted in arguments about what, when, how, and how much to read; it also generated a flurry of experiments to make books more cognitively compatible.

When the codex first emerged in the Roman Mediterranean, at some point in the late Republic or early Empire, it was not particularly popular. Readers preferred the scroll—sheets of glued-together papyrus that they rolled along a horizontal axis, right to left, and stored in cubbies or cases. It was what they knew best: the scroll was simple and durable, and it was where serious writing was supposed to be found.

Today scholars tend to agree that a small segment of the population in the Roman Empire took to the codex more enthusiastically. In the second and third centuries CE, Christians were much likelier to use codices than other writers and copyists were, though they also continued to produce and read scrolls. The codex format was typically used for notes or drafts, rather than for polished works, and that struck the earliest Christians as appropriate for the traditions that they read and shared about Jesus.

Subsequent generations experimented in earnest with this technology, which was anything but standardized, even once the gospel material itself had crystallized into something more stable and literary. Christians began to exploit the potential of the codex to contain very long texts, and anthologies of texts, which in the scroll format would have been unwieldy. In Late Antiquity and the Middle Ages "the Bible" usually consisted of individual books in separate codices. But Christians also created luxe editions known as pandects: complete Bibles, calligraphed upon the highly processed skins of hundreds of sheep, enfolded within a single volume. Pandects were not widely owned or used, but they were ideologically and technologically significant. Their format embodied the Christian argument that the New Testament had superseded the Old—that the Christian Bible, not the Hebrew Bible, was the final word.[2]

In the fourth century, as monasticism was rapidly evolving, and when Evagrius was describing what distracted readers looked like, the book was in a robust phase of development. Monks took up the technology energetically. Some of them got their scrolls and codices by buying them from scribes who worked for bookdealers or wealthy readers. But the other traditional way to acquire a book was to borrow it from a friend, and monks began borrowing and copying so many books that their communities became major centers of book production in Europe, the Mediterranean, and the Middle East.[3]

Some communities built up book collections that rivaled the libraries of obsessive collectors in major metropolises and the treasuries of imperial palaces and mosques. The Georgian monastery of Zedazadeni had 110 volumes by the end of the ninth century. The monk known as Simeon of the Olives accumulated 180 books, which he gave to his monastery north of Mesopotamia when he died in 734. In the eighth century Bede had access to more than 200 books at Wearmouth-Jarrow, which made his monastery's library the largest in early medieval England. By the year 860, the monastery of Lorsch, one of the most privileged and politically active monasteries in the Carolingian Empire, possessed around 470 books; and it had sent many others into circulation, by lending books and copying others on commission for friends and patrons. And at the White Monastery in Upper Egypt, Shenoute's successors oversaw the expansion of a collection that surged to something like a thousand volumes at the start of the new millennium.[4]

These were unusually large holdings. Most monastic libraries in the early Middle Ages probably had a few dozen volumes. But still, every monastic community owned books and shared books,

and even stylites and other solitary monks were part of this circu-
latory system. Most monks read every single day, because although
books might distract a reader's thoughts, they could also "clarify"
them—as Shem'on d-Ṭaybutheh reminded would-be hermits in
the late seventh century. Understanding the minds of monks, and
their approaches to attentiveness, requires an understanding of
their relationship to their books.[5]

✳

IT WAS AN AMBIVALENT RELATIONSHIP, like so many other
monastic practices. Not many monks were technological optimists.
They knew that books were not equally accessible to readers, and
they thought that using books, even when available, posed risks.
They revived arguments that philosophers had made hundreds of
years prior about the shortcomings of written texts in any form.
Copies of texts were expensive. They were faulty substitutions for
memory. And unlike learning face-to-face, from a teacher, reading
from a book (whether it was a scroll or a codex) did not involve any
dialogue—the pedagogical gold standard of the ancient world.[6]

On top of these issues, monks pointed out that books could be
distracting. In Late Antiquity and the early Middle Ages people
usually read aloud from their books, even when reading alone,
which would have made it harder for them to skim or skip or flip
through pages. Yet reading could still slide into disengagement, as
Evagrius had described.[7]

He did not blame the technology itself for these behaviors,
exactly. Evagrius was a voracious reader. He had even worked as a
scribe after moving to Egypt, and he compared good calligraphy
to the universe that God had created: both pointed to their makers'
care and craft. The real catalyst of a monk's distraction while reading was a condition that Evagrius and other monks called *acedia*,
the same condition that Evagrius's student Cassian would diagnose
in monks who exhibited signs of nosiness—that toxic combination
of restlessness and dissatisfaction that could make it difficult to do

or think anything. Acedia was not *caused* by books; a monk could fall prey to it without a book in sight. But books could intensify the paralysis. To a mind that was already conflicted, the codex-as-technology—its countable pages, its aesthetic interface, its pillow-like volume—distracted a monk from the ideas within it.[8]

Monks also made criticisms of the opposite kind, that the contents of books could be *too* engrossing. Some books were unpersuasive and boring: they were not the problem. But a book that won its reader over? "It becomes iron," the desert elders were remembered to have said, "and is excised with difficulty." And because it mattered what stuck in a monk's mind, there were frank discussions about what texts were worth reading. Monastic educators were wary of "pagan" authors—the poets, orators, and philosophers who had become canonized in the Roman educational system. They mostly preserved that system's pedagogical methods, while swapping out the traditional texts for biblical ones. But they rarely got rid of non-Christian texts altogether. They just handled them carefully. It was possible to love and mistrust them at the same time.[9]

The men and women of Pbow and other Pachomian monastic houses in Upper Egypt, for example, were copying and reading experimental and apocryphal Christian texts alongside Homer, Menander, Thucydides, and Cicero. At the monastery of Qenneshre, which sat on the Euphrates west of Edessa, bilingual monks translated all of Aristotle's works on logic from Greek into Syriac, because they wanted to better evaluate the theological and liturgical arguments that were simmering across Mesopotamia and the eastern Mediterranean. The confessional competition (and confusion) that was characteristic of the fifth to ninth centuries was also a powerful engine of scholarship and, ironically, cooperation: scholars were not above sending couriers to rival monasteries to read, borrow, and copy their books. Across the Mediterranean, Latin readers came up with ways to flag suspect material without scrapping it—such as marking an *F* or *FAB* in the margins of their books when they came across a story (*fabula*) that was blatantly mythological. These notes are the work of readers who were carefully reading non-Christian material rather than suppressing it. Some annotations even helpfully pointed readers to reference books on ancient myths, to help them interpret these stories as Christian allegories. Monks may have been wary of ancient texts, but their sense of what counted as "relevant" reading was capacious.[10]

Still, they had to remind themselves that all this reading was a technology for stretching the self to God. Buried in a book, it was easy to lose sight of that. In the Turfan oasis (in what is now northwest China), among a community of Christians affiliated with the Church of the East, a compiler assembled an anthology of ascetic texts in the ninth or tenth century. It included advice from Isaac of Nineveh, who had been active in the late seventh century in the Persian Gulf and Mesopotamia. Isaac warned monks—originally in Syriac, and now in the Sogdian of a Central Asian translator—not to indulge in wide-ranging reading if they already had a tendency to get distracted. The texts would overwhelm them, make it impossible to have "dominion" over their own thoughts, and lead the monks to mistake themselves for savvy intellectuals. Far west of Turfan, monks fretted over similar notions deep into the Middle Ages. It was crucial, as a Cistercian monk at Pontigny (in central France) put it in the twelfth or thirteenth century, to read what was in one's heart, more than the contents of any manuscript—*in corde magis quam in omni codice*.[11]

Not that all monks loved to read. Papyrus letters that have survived from late antique Egypt suggest that many monks there were more interested in developing administrative skills than in reading literature. In the sixth century Ferreolus of Uzès complained that monks preferred to relax after a day of hard work rather than read. And a story in the Greek, Latin, and Syriac traditions of the *Apophthegmata patrum* griped that monks' books were collecting dust: "The Prophets compiled the Scriptures, and the Fathers copied them, and their successors learned to repeat them by heart.

Then this generation came and placed them in cupboards as useless things."[12]

＊

THIS LAMENT WAS REPEATED for centuries. It reflects the expectation that, despite the risks that books entailed, most women and men who became monks were supposed to be reading regularly—even if they didn't want to. The standard had been set by Pachomius's monasteries in the fourth century. Although the federation centered on Upper Egypt, its monks' writings were translated into several languages as they circulated into Lower Egypt and around the Mediterranean. Pachomius and his successors had insisted that every monk should be able to read. Anyone who was illiterate when they joined the federation would be taught.

The rationale was that reading, together with recitation and memorization, would help monks internalize their sacred texts. Pachomian monks were expected to know the Psalter and the New Testament, or at least significant pieces of them, by heart. They would speak the text aloud when reading to themselves, and they would listen to their fellow monks' readings and to the powerful speeches of their leaders that artfully knitted scriptural passages together. Continuously, throughout the day, whether they were working, participating in the liturgies, or even traveling, they were supposed to recite the scriptures. Naturally, they shared stories of fellow monks who had taken these expectations seriously. They commemorated a monk named Jonas, for example, who had worked as the gardener for the monastery of Thmoushons. Jonas never slept lying down but instead sat on a stool braiding rope in the dark while reciting scriptures. He died on the stool with the rope in his hand. And he had to be buried like that, because rigor mortis had set in by the time his brothers found him.[13]

Monks like Jonas read and recited scripture in perpetual motion so that the biblical world of history and prophecy would suffuse the present, and so that the divine word would suffuse each monk herself. The result was a cognitive shift that was both large and small. Monks came to speak the scriptures not as a script but as their own words. And their minds were moved to take action in the cosmic drama that they had come to know so well. In their textual culture, scripture was not supposed to direct monks' attention temporarily so much as transform it completely.[14]

At the same time, these practices acted as a repellent against the demons who continued to wage their wars of distraction. Monks disagreed about tactics to deploy in retaliation. The Pachomian monasteries instituted a steady schedule of reading and recitation to function as a systematic defense against cognitive interference. Other monastic communities developed very different schedules (such as psalm recitations three times a day, or seven times, or midnight prayers, or psalms in shifts). Evagrius, who was a contemporary of the early successors to Pachomius, thought that monks needed countermeasures that were even more targeted. Demons could launch thoughts into a monk at any time, without warning. He called their weapons of choice *logismoi*: passing thoughts that could embed themselves into a monk's self if left unguarded (including the tranquilizer dart of acedia). But the right counterthought could keep a *logismos* from sinking deeper into the heart and doing real damage once it was lodged there. Evagrius insisted that the key was to act quickly, which required having an arsenal of readings at the ready. For example, if a demon forced a monk to think about how beautiful his parents' house was, in contrast to his spare little cell, a monk could counterattack with a psalm. "I would rather be a castoff in the house of God than dwell in the tents of sinners."[15]

Evagrius compiled an entire manual of scriptural verses that were custom-fitted to the sorts of thoughts that demons were likely to weaponize. He called this manual *Antirrhetikos: Talking Back*. It owed something to the Stoic conviction that memorizing maxims and other aphoristic texts could prepare a person for some unexpected confrontation. But the book also reflects Evagrius's highly specific sense of demonic warfare, and some monks took to it more than others. The Greek original does not survive. It was translated into Latin in the fifth century, but that version was not widely enough copied to have survived, either. The book was also translated into Sogdian and Georgian, and into Armenian and Arabic in the late Middle Ages if not earlier. Evagrius's Syriac-speaking readers were the book's biggest fans: there are several copies of the *Antirrhetikos* in Syriac, three to five of which are datable to the 500s. (Evagrius died in 399.) Given the survival rate of late antique manuscripts, that's a lot.[16]

Some monks argued that confronting demonic thoughts head-on like this was cognitively counterproductive. The recluse Barsanuphius told one of his mentees, who was struggling with precisely this problem, that stopping his reading, recitation, or prayer to deal with a distraction was exactly what the Enemy wanted. Instead, he should call upon God and continue to struggle through his work. Barsanuphius and other monks were also concerned that trying to suppress thoughts would actually result in a fixation on them, a theory that the historian Inbar Graiver has noted for its striking resemblance to the modern psychological concept of Ironic Process Theory.[17]

But although not everyone seemed to need or want a manual to help them face down demonic *logismoi*, the Pachomian and Evagrian conviction that texts were essential to ascetic psychology became commonplace in Christian monasticism. In the fifth century, when John Cassian was translating Egyptian ascetic culture for elite readers in Gaul, he even amplified the importance of reading and presented it as analogous to the way that rhetoric transformed students into powerful public speakers. The mind was always going to be churning through thoughts, so one might as well improve the material it was processing by reading often and thinking deeply about scripture. Eventually that reading would "shape" (*formet*) the mind into a version of itself. For Cassian's

Gallic audiences, the message would have been clear: asceticism was not the grungy, selfish fad that its critics said it was. Instead it was a serious education in the art of ethical living. And for ascetics who aspired to positions of public authority (as bishops, imperial or civic officeholders, and other power brokers), at a time when authority in the western Roman Empire was straining and sometimes fracturing from the tension of political conflicts, Cassian was offering an updated model of legitimate leadership.[18] He and later generations also subscribed to the conviction shared by so many monks and educators before them: reading was personally transformative. If you filled your life with the right kind of books, your perspective and behavior would change. The words in the mouth became part of the heart, *in corde et in ore*. The book becomes iron.[19]

In the generations following Pachomius, Evagrius, and Cassian, monks took to their books. Most of them would not have gone to a designated library to do so: they tended to stash their books all over the place, not unlike modern bookworms. They kept books in the church for reading at the liturgy. Around their living spaces they kept books on shelves and in boxes, cabinets, or niches cut into the walls. Deluxe manuscripts might be stored in treasure chests. Occasionally there was a dedicated storage room if a monastery's holdings were especially extensive. And monks also kept books in their bedrooms. Most monastic rules assumed (or even stipulated) that monks would check out books from the community's collection. Sometimes this came with caveats: monks should be careful not to damage the codices they borrowed, and they shouldn't become so attached to them that they thought of the books as their very own.[20] (Possessiveness was, after all, a slippery slope to distraction.)

Even though monks in the early Middle Ages embraced the late antique endorsement of reading, monastic leaders continued to debate how best to integrate this technology into their daily lives. They often said the best time to read was in the morning, though sometimes the time slot was pushed back in the summer so that work could start earlier, in the cool of the morning. But they disagreed about how long a monk should read every day—one and a half hours? three hours? more?—before it became counterproductive. And should monks read during the nighttime liturgies if they were exhausted from working in the fields? Others argued for periodic bouts of reading throughout the day, in between shifts of praying and working. Reading could be a reward on Sundays. Alternatively it could be assigned as homework, to combat bad thoughts that needed specific textual antidotes. It could be a way to keep monks from chatting in church before the services started. Or it could serve as a substitute "job" when monks claimed to be too weak to do farmwork. Some monastic guidelines suggested assigning a monk to read to others while they worked. Most insisted that someone read aloud at mealtimes. The mind and mouth chewed together, they loved to say: variations on this theme abounded in monasteries from Persia to Spain.[21]

But nobody recommended reading nonstop. Isidore of Seville, who was himself famously well read, reminded monks that they needed to perform manual labor, too, like the hardworking apostles in their books. Physical work was an important part of monastic discipline, but monks also knew that it was virtually impossible to concentrate on your reading if that's all you ever did. Constant reading damaged the eyes and "distorted" the brain, as Joseph Ḥazzaya noted—and as a survivor of kidnapping and enslavement, Joseph was not one to exaggerate.[22]

✳

EVEN AT THE RIGHT TIME of day, books couldn't change monks and their minds by themselves. The sentiment of enthusiasts such as Epiphanius of Cyprus—"the mere sight of these books renders us less inclined to sin, and incites us to believe more firmly in righteousness"—was not widely shared. As Leander of Seville put it in the sixth century, monks needed to maintain a steady grip (*adsiduo retentaculo*) on their reading and praying to escape the devil, and even then, it was always an awfully close call.[23] Distraction began well before a book ended up as a makeshift pillow. Monks had to *work* with their books, and working required focus—even though, paradoxically, reading was also supposed to help them focus.

So monks were taught to read proactively. This meant adopting reading practices that were in some ways significantly different from modern habits. Rather than speed-reading or skimming, or aiming for breadth over depth, monks were supposed to read slowly and carefully, and to read the same things repeatedly. A set of monastic guidelines from northwest Spain called the *General Rule* (*Regula communis*) recommended that monks read texts about the holy fathers over and over, then populate their minds with those narratives, even when not actively reading them, picturing the saints as though they surrounded them on all sides. This imaginative overlay would help them avoid missteps as they moved through their own lives, like a virtual support group. The *General Rule* was making its recommendations in the mid-seventh century, to an unusual demographic. The monks it addressed were mostly peasants (men and women alike) who had converted to monasticism along with their families, households, and even entire villages. It seems that to resist the encroachment of local elites upon their lands, rural landowners in Gallaecia were forming monastic corporations as a way of protecting their property and preserving their communities. The abbots who composed the *General Rule* observed these developments uneasily and tried to establish some basic regulations. One of their priorities was to instill a sense of obedience and concentration on God. Their advice about books is unusual only for spelling out the reading process so clearly: they thought this audience needed it.[24]

Monks also engaged with their readings by writing notes in the empty spaces of their books. We might assume that they did this out of boredom or distraction, and sometimes that was true. Irish scribes in particular, some of whom were monks and many of whom were professionals, would scribble down comments that didn't have much to do with their material—about the weather, about the birds outside, or about how they felt cold or sick or hung-over (figs. 11a/11b).

But more often than not, early medieval writers and readers wrote in the margins to stay alert. They expressed approval of or disagreement with what a text was saying. They outlined the topics of a main text, to make the logical flow of the material clearer. They flagged certain passages that were worth remembering, reading again, or signaling for the next reader (fig. 12). And sometimes they offered an extensive and well-researched commentary around the main text, or cross-referenced other readings and lessons. For example: when an Irish intellectual in Gaul named Sedulius Scottus made a classroom anthology of texts in the middle of the ninth century, he laced it with notes such as "Read Pomponius's commentary on Horace, which I read at Lorsch." When someone familiar with Sedulius and his colleagues copied this anthology later on, he added even *more* annotations that identified who had written the previous annotations.[25]

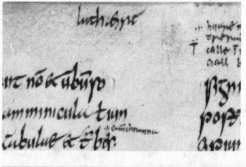
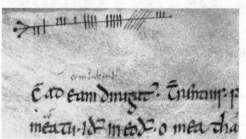

FIGURES 11A/11B Two marginal comments in Old Irish in a copy of Priscian's Latin grammar, one in the Latin alphabet (above) and the other in Ogham (below), note that the monk(s) had a "massive hangover" (*lathærit*).

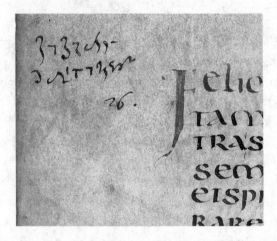

FIGURE 12 In a copy of Augustine's sermons made in the sixth or seventh century, the shorthand in the left margin of this page notes that "the place where he talks about humility and confession is short but sweet (*brevis et bona, ubi dicit de humilitate et confessione*)."

These marginalia reveal a world in which monks were working to concentrate and to help the readers who would take up the same books after them to concentrate, too. Their notes speak with surprising directness, even though we rarely know their names, let alone their biographies. So it is always notable when scribes introduce themselves directly. In the eighth century at the monastery of Speculos ("watchtower," in northeastern Syria), a chatty deacon named Saba was proud enough of his calligraphy to write, in the copy he made of the Book of Kings, that he "never made a blotted tau"—the last letter in the Syriac alphabet. A few thousand miles west of Speculos, just east of Paris, a group of ten monks at the monastery of Chelles produced a three-volume set of Augustine's *Interpretations of the Psalms* around the year 800. Each woman signed her name at the end of the section that she was assigned to copy. Nine of those names survive. One was Gislildis (fig. 13), whose name suggests that she might have been related to the abbess of her monastery, Gisela. If that was the case, she would have *also* been related to Charlemagne, Gisela's brother and (more famously) the ruler of the Carolingian Empire.

What is more certain about Gislildis is that she was a sharp reader, because she added notes to the margins of the material that she copied, in the form of single letters or shapes that highlighted themes in the text that were especially important to Augustine's theology and that were also pressing topics of discussion at the Carolingian court. For example, Gislildis consistently highlighted Augustine's use of the Psalms to express how one needed to know oneself, and to own up to one's faults, before being able to know God (fig. 14). The book was not hers: she and her sisters produced these volumes for the bishop of Cologne. But Gislildis seems to have taken notes for her own interest and benefit anyway, marking the material that mattered most to her, and probably archiving it in her memory in the process.[26]

Even if we can't identify most early medieval bookmakers, we can still appreciate that many of them were ingenious graphic designers. They experimented with the technology to enrich the

FIGURE 13   After copying Augustine's commentary on Psalms 31–38, Gislildis signed her work at the end of the quire: "Gislildis wrote this."

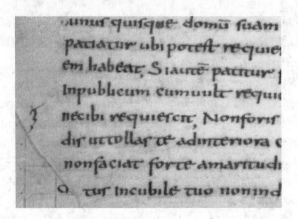

FIGURE 14 With a zeta in the left margin (shorthand for "Look it up!"), Gislildis singled out Augustine's comment on Psalm 35:5 (Ps. 36:4: "He deviseth mischief upon his bed") that peace can't be found in the outside world but rather "in the bed of the heart, so you should lift yourself into your innermost self-knowledge."

reading process—not necessarily to make it easier, but certainly to make it more revelatory and transfixing.

Some of their practices are still in use today. In Late Antiquity, texts were typically written incontinuouslinesofcharacters, without any spacing between words. A Latin grammarian named Pompeius, writing in North Africa around 500, commented that a text formatted like this could easily be misread at first glance. He gave an example from book 8 of the *Aeneid*: CONSPICITVRSVS could be read to say either "a bear took notice" (*conspicit ursus*) or "a sow was noticed" (*conspicitur sus*). This was partly a joke, since Pompeius was referring to a famous scene in a famous poem, but still, *scriptio continua* could be difficult to parse (fig. 15).

Although late antique scribes did not invent word separation (Romans had already tried then ditched it in the first century CE), they increasingly preferred it, and by the eighth and ninth centuries it was common practice. Meanwhile, scribes working in Syriac, whose writing system was strictly consonantal, began

FIGURE 15   An example of *scriptio continua*, from a copy of
Virgil's *Aeneid* made in Rome around 400 CE. CONSPICITVRSVS
appears at the end of the third line. Fortunately for readers of
this manuscript, the previous folio depicts Aeneas looking at a
big pig. No ambiguity there!

introducing dots to their writing system to differentiate between
words that looked identical on the page (such as *mlk* and *mlk*) but
that, when spoken, were two different things (*malka*/king, *melka*/
advice). By the seventh and eighth centuries these dots were functioning as straightforward vowel markers. Syriac texts still use dots
in these ways.

Punctuation was another literary shift we owe to Late Antiquity and the early Middle Ages. Originally these punctuation
marks were used only to cue the cadences of public speakers. But
they came to serve an ancillary function of providing readers with
syntactical and semantic information, such as indicating where
a thought started and stopped—an especially useful thing for
inflected languages, in which word order is very flexible.[27]

In the mid-sixth century Cassiodorus described punctuation as
providing an illuminated pathway to perception. The man definitely knew his way around a document: he had served as a high-
ranking administrator for the Ostrogothic kingdom in Italy and
in the course of his various jobs navigated an ocean of paperwork.
In his retirement he founded a monastery in southern Italy that he

called Vivarium and fostered a vigorous book culture there. So if Cassiodorus felt this way, we can guess how readers who were not as educated or who weren't reading in their native language felt about graphical aids such as word separation, dots, and punctuation. The most enthusiastic proponents of punctuation in Europe, in fact, were monks from the British Isles who had learned Latin only in school—unlike their colleagues on the Continent, for whom Latin was still a spoken language into the eighth century.[28]

Book designers went beyond these linguistic modifications. They experimented with page layouts and analytical graphics that could legitimately be considered forms of data visualization avant la lettre, because they aimed to illuminate certain ideas and patterns that their texts contained, to achieve the greater goal of gently shaping readers' attention.

Ideally, even before pen touched parchment, the "data"—the text itself—would be organized in an engaging way. The stories of the *Apophthegmata patrum* (those popular traditions about the desert fathers and mothers) were arranged and rearranged in different formats with this principle in mind. Some versions of the narratives grouped all the stories about the same person together, then sorted the cast of characters alphabetically; others organized the materials by topic, such as poverty, patience, and how to deal with thoughts about sex. The point, as the collection that was organized alphabetically explained, was that "a narrative which is the work of many hands is confused, and disorderly, and it distracts the attention of the readers, for their minds are drawn in different directions and cannot retain sayings that are scattered about in the book. Therefore we have tried to gather them together in chapters, so that they will be in order and clear and easy to look up, for those who want to benefit by reading them."[29]

Scribes likewise formatted their manuscripts to help readers track a text's progression. They indicated changes in topics or sections by writing headings in a different color of ink, and often in a different script, to demarcate it clearly from the main text. They used larger or ornamented initials to signal significant spots in the text: a new chapter, a shift in perspective, or a rhetorically distinct passage (fig. 16). They used the obelus (—, ÷, /) to flag passages that did not represent the opinion of the author: these marks were supposed to keep a careless reader from assuming that controversial material was authoritative (fig. 17). They used crosses to transport readers into sacred space via the portal of the page. They drew portraits of alert monks to jolt readers into the correct frame of mind (fig. 18).[30]

But the very richness of early medieval book culture was also a source of anxiety, because readers were daunted by the amount of material in circulation, even if that amount was only a very small fraction of what is available to us today. There were countless commentaries on the Bible, for example, and even the most erudite monks felt inundated when they sat down to make sense of their scriptures. Their favorite solution to this problem was, ironically, to make more books, compilations in particular: the anthology, the synthesis, and the mashup were beloved literary forms in Late

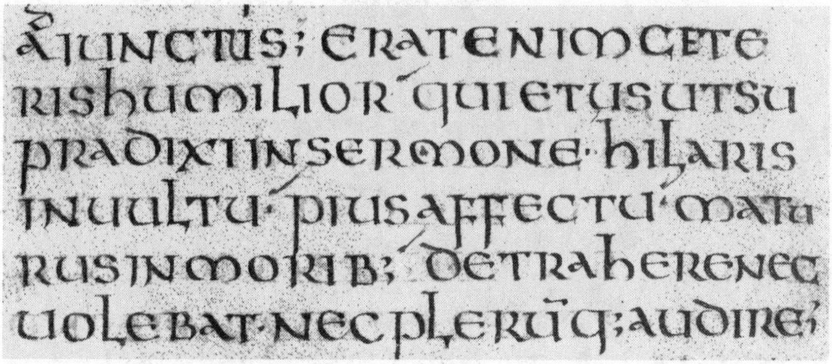

FIGURE 16 In this small book dedicated to the life and death of Wandregisel (the treasurer turned monk), a scribe has filled select letters of the uncial script with yellow pigment. The effect is to accentuate some of Wandregisel's qualities on the page: he was taciturn (*quietus in sermone*), cheerful (*hilaris in vultu*), pious (*pius affectu*), mature (*maturus in moribus*), and reluctant to disparage others (*detrahere nec volebat*).

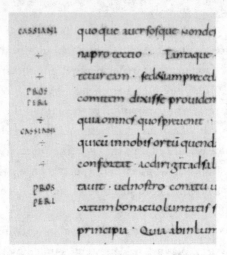

FIGURE 17 A ninth-century copy of Prosper of Aquitaine's *God's Grace and Free Will*, in which the arguments of Prosper's opponent—John Cassian—are marked with obeli (÷) in the margins. The scribe also took the additional precaution of writing Prosper's and Cassian's names every time the speakers switch.

FIGURE 18 A monk's head stands in for the letter O at the start of an antiphon. He models the alertness that monks should mirror as they sing this song, to combat (as the liturgical poem goes on to describe) the discouraging and distracting forces within themselves that feel like blindness, binding traps, and noxious smells.

Antiquity and the early Middle Ages. Compilers would curate a selection of texts and combine them into a single new codex, to sharpen their force or highlight certain themes by virtue of a strategic edit. They did this even with their scriptures. Individual books from the Bible could be paired with hagiographies, prophecies, or historical continuations. Or they could be formatted to allow commentaries to fit their pages: the scriptural text would sit squarely in the center, while abbreviated commentaries would surround it. This latter technique was popularized at the Italian monastery of Fulda in the early 800s, and after that, monks beyond Fulda continued to tinker with it. In the 840s, for example, a monk named Otfrid produced a copy-and-commentary of Acts and the Letters of James, Peter, John, and Judah that featured a three-column layout, plus reference symbols to help readers toggle between the main text and the exegesis that framed it (fig. 19).[31]

The seemingly humble column had also been crucial to the success of some of the most grandiose book and visualization projects of Late Antiquity. First among them was a massive biblical concordance known as the *Hexapla*: this was the passion project of Origen, a philosopher and Christian theologian who was active in the Mediterranean cities of Alexandria and Caesarea in the first half of the 200s. Origen dove into the *Hexapla* after moving to Caesarea in the 230s. One of his goals seems to have been to provide a more stable version of the scriptures for his fellow Christians, who were still a small minority in the third century. There were several Greek translations of the Hebrew Bible in circulation: if they could be compared to each other and consulted against the original Hebrew, Christian readers could be better informed, and ideally come to appreciate that one translation in particular (the Septuagint) was superior to the rest. Origen also seems to have hoped that these scriptural mechanics could help Christians more capably defend themselves in polemical arguments with Jews. In any case, Origen and his collaborators—a scribal staff, Christian and Jewish consultants, and one very rich patron—ended up pro-

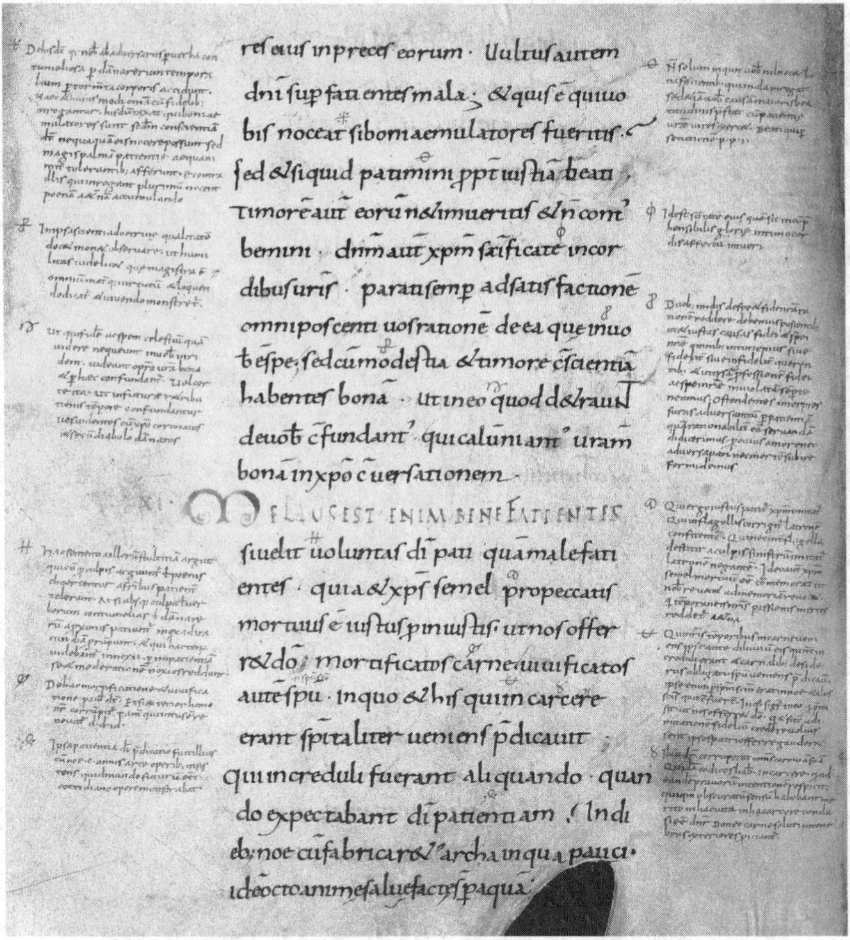

FIGURE 19   Otfrid's annotated copy of the Acts and Epistles, which he made at the monastery of Wissembourg in the 840s, deploys many textual technologies: word spacing, punctuation, a three-column layout that enfolds the biblical text within commentaries to it, symbols above the biblical text that point readers to the margins, and a rubricated line in *capitalis rustica* set against the brown Caroline minuscule of the main text (corresponding to 1 Peter 3:17).

ducing something unprecedented: a reference work on the order of forty codices, each arrayed with parallel columns of Hebrew, Hebrew transliterated into Greek, and multiple Greek translations. These thousands of pages of tabular concordances represented a technological breakthrough that pulled readers deeper into their sacred texts.[32]

Unfortunately the ur-*Hexapla* no longer survives. But an off-shoot of Origen's project attests to the enduring appeal of its biblio-technics. The Syriac *Hexapla* (fig. 20) came into being in 616–17 as a monastic venture at Enaton, in the suburbs of Alexandria, where many people living in the Levant and Mesopotamia had fled during a multidecade war between Rome and Persia. It consists of a Syriac translation of the Greek Septuagint as the latter had appeared in the original *Hexapla*, while making reference to other Greek versions of the Old Testament (and also Syriac *translations* of other Greek versions). The stark difference from Origen's *Hexapla* was that the Syriac tradition ditched the other five columns of the original. But the Syriac *Hexapla* does preserve his editorial marks, to indicate the spots where the Septuagint diverged from the Hebrew: asterisks point to gaps in the Septuagint that Origen supplemented with other Greek translations, and obeli identify material that is not present in the Hebrew original. Even though the Syro-Hexapla is "only" one primary block of text—apart from the textual variants noted in the margins—it was still an enormous undertaking. Timothy I, the patriarch of the Church of the East in the late eighth and early ninth centuries, had collaborated on several copies of the work, and he concluded that "no text is so difficult to copy out or to read as this. . . . I nearly lost my sight!"[33]

A little less than a century after Origen created the *Hexapla*, a bishop of Caesarea named Eusebius would take a cue from him in producing a different kind of concordance—this one not biblical but historical. Eusebius had read the *Hexapla*. He had also pored over many ancient chronicles, histories, and chronographs—chronological lists of rulers, officeholders, and other temporally

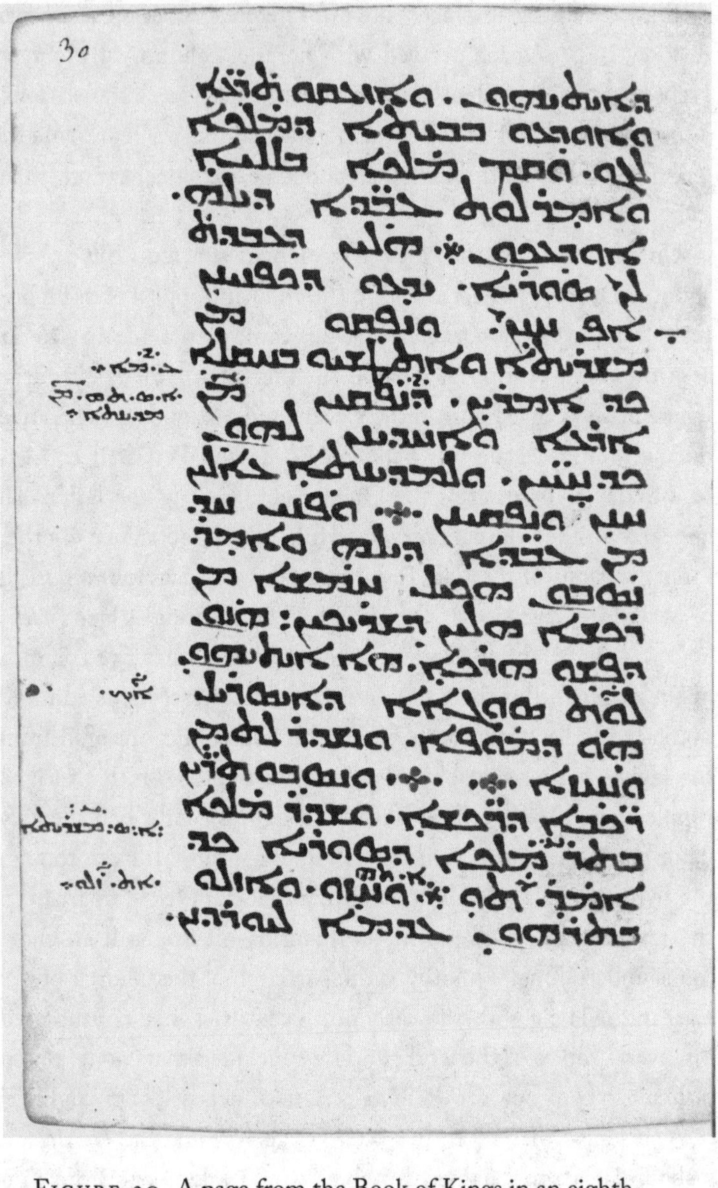

FIGURE 20 A page from the Book of Kings in an eighth-
century copy of the Syro-Hexapla.

significant sequences. In the course of his reading he was struck
by the plurality of systems for reckoning time. When considered
separately, each offered only a partial glimpse of the past. So he
undertook a massive universal history that he called the *Chronici
canones*, which did for the historical record what Origen's *Hexapla*
had done for biblical philology: it lined disparate chronologies up
across the page, to organize a massive comparative dataset (fig.
21). The chronicle's coordinated timeline allowed readers to cross-
reference an event across multiple dating systems while watching
parallel historical universes unfold. Even more clearly than Origen did with his *Hexapla*, Eusebius designed his technological
medium to accentuate his message. Through it he suggested, by
force of visual argument alone, that the Jewish patriarchs predated
the heroic figures of Greek history and mythology. And it was no
coincidence that Eusebius, who had lived to see the first Roman
emperor convert to Christianity, had the *Chronici canones* culmi-
nate in the single timeline of the Roman Empire: all historical
roads led to Rome (fig. 22).[34]

The book certainly caught the attention of numerous audiences. Early medieval readers noticed Eusebius's politics—the very
format of the *Chronici canones* made it hard to miss—and some
of them chose to dismantle it. The architects of a history that is
known today as the Fredegar Chronicle, which was compiled in
Gaul in the middle of the seventh century, drew on a Latin version
of Eusebius's history that had been penned by Jerome—the influential monk who had benefited from rich patrons in Rome and
who is best known for his Latin translation of the Bible known as
the Vulgate. Rather than winnowing all of world history down to
Rome, in the model of Eusebius-Jerome, the Fredegar chroniclers
expanded it again to follow the varied trajectories of diverse peo-
ples in the Mediterranean and Europe. Now, in lieu of an imperial
history, they emphasized the political and ethnic multiplicity that
characterized the early medieval landscape. Such a radical revi-
sion to Eusebius's work meant that the original visual layout had

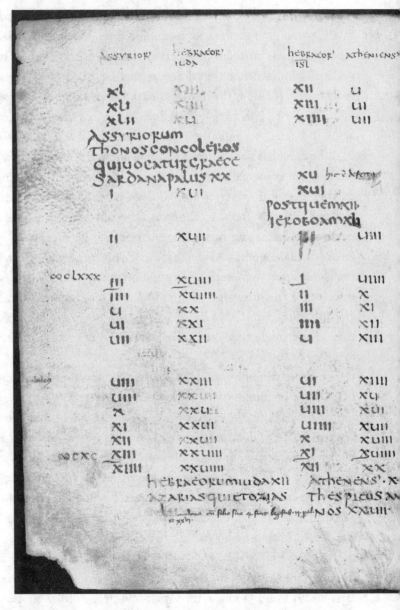

FIGURE 21 Eusebius's *Chronici canones* doesn't survive in Greek, except in later excerpts and abridgements. But Jerome translated the work in 381, and his version was a hit in the Latin-speaking world. This two-page spread in the earliest sur-

ATINOR'	LACEDEMONIOR'	CORINTHIOR'	AEGYPTIOR'
CU	XIIII		XXUI	XII
CUI	XIIIII		XXUIII	XIII
CUIII	XUIII		XXUIIII	XIIII
CUIII	XU		XXUIIII	XU
			postquicunta	
			celothis XIII	
CUIII	XUI		XXX	I
CX	XUIII	uti pocnices	XXXI	II
CXI	XUIIII	makeobianu	XXXII	III
CXII	XUIIIII	erunt	XXXIII	IIII
CXIII	XUIIII		XXXIIII	U
CXIIII	XXI		XXXU	UI
		CORINTHIORUM UIIII ACEMON XUII		
CXU	XXII		I	UIII
CXUI	XXIII		II	UIIII
CXUIII'	XXIIII	Sardanapallus	III	UIIIII
CXUIIII	XXU	eodem tempore	IIII	X
CXUIIIII	XXUI	Tarsumatq. anchialem	U	XI
CXX	XXUII	condidit inprotio uictusa	UI	XII
CXXI	XXUIII	barboco medose metince dioconcke maui	UII	XIII
			AEGYPTI XXIIII DYNASTIA UI PETU BASTIS XUI	

<small>Sardanapal. lustrapuin anchialos. didit</small>

viving copy of Eusebius-Jerome (made in Italy in the mid-fifth century) shows the parallel histories of the Assyrians, Hebrews of Judah, Hebrews of Israel, Athenians, Latins, Spartans, Corinthians, and Egyptians.

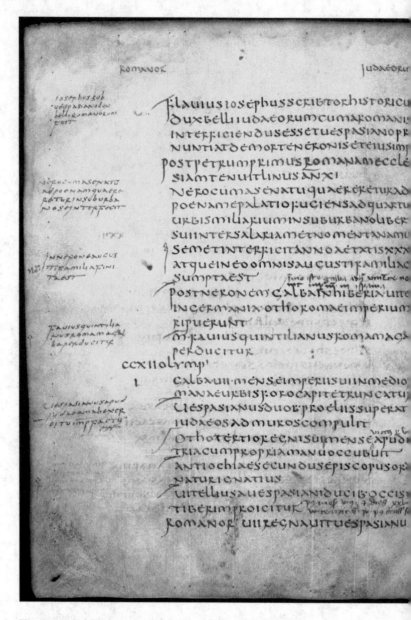

FIGURE 22 Deeper into the same copy of Eusebius-Jerome, the many separate threads of history have collapsed into a single timeline defined only by the Romans and the Jews, and on

ROMANORUM

JUDAEORUMREGNUMFINITUMEST

ANN LIIII MENS XI DIET XXII

UESPASIANUSAPUDIUDAEAMIMPERA XXV
TORABEXERCITUAPPELLATUSETBELLUM
TITOFILIOCOMMENDANSROMAMPERALE
XANDRIAMPROFICISCITUR
CAPITOLIUMROMAEINCENSUM

TERTIUSIUDAECAPTAETHIEROSOLYMIS XXVI
SUBUERSAS SESCENTAMILIAVIRORUMINTER
FICIT IOSEPHUSUEROSCRIBITUNDECIES
CENTENAMILIAFAMEETGLADIOPERISSE
ETALIACENTUMMILIACAPTIUORUMPUBLI
UENUNDATA UTAUTEMTANTAMULTITU
DOHIEROSOLYMISREPPERIRETURCAUSA
ATVMORUMFEREFT FUISSEOBQUAE EXO
MNICENTEIUDEAADTEMPLUM CONFLU
ENTESURBEQUASICARCERESUNTRECLUSI
OPORTUITENIMINHISDEMDIEBESPASCHAE
EOSINTERFICIINQUIBSALUATOREMCRUCIFIXERANT

Collicitur OMNETEMPUSINSECUNDUMANNUM
UESPASIANIETNOUISSIMAMEUERSIONEM
HIEROSOLYMARUMAXU ANNOTIBERIICAE
SARISETABEXORDIOEUANGELICAEPRAE
DICATIONIS ANN · XLII

Acaptiuitate LUTEMQUAMABANTIOCHO
PERPESSISUNT ANN CCXXXVII
PORROADARIISECUNDOANNOSUBQUORUM
TEMPLUMAEDIFICATUMEST AN DXC
Aprimaautem AEDIFICATIONETEMPLISUBSO
LOMONEUSQ ADNOUISSIMAMEIUS
RUINAMQUAESUBUESPASIANOFACTAESTAN DCCII

the right page, the narrative becomes exclusively Roman with a caption at the top that reads, "The kingdom of the Jews has come to an end."

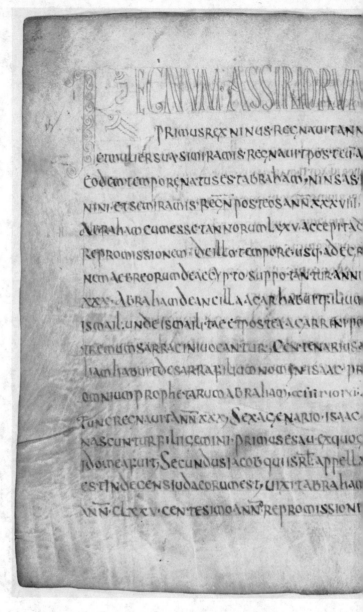

FIGURE 23 This is the oldest manuscript of the Fredegar Chronicle. It was copied in Gaul around 700, just a few decades after the text was composed in the 660s. The compilers' new version of Eusebius-Jerome begins on the left page and has

CURABRAHAM·CENTESIMOLXANNE·CUMESSET
TUNCIACOBDISCENDITINMESOPOTAMIA·ETSER
ABAN·ANNUSXIIII·PRODUASFILIASQUASACCEPIT
·LIA·ETRACHIL·ANN·CCMO·POSTREPROMISSIONE
IUSISAAC·ANNORU LXXX·FILIUSEIUSIACOB·CUI
NNORCX·ADHUCUIUENTE·ISAAC·IOSEPHFILIUS
ANNORXVII·UINDETUSESTINAECYPTO·CMOXXXMO
NESSITIACOBIAMSECUNDOANNFAMIS·INGRESSUS
ISINAECYPTO·IACOBCMOXL·MOVIIMOANN·OBIIT
TANSDEXPO·CMOXMOANN·CUMIMPLISSETIOSEPH
R·FIUNTAUTEMOMNESANNIQUOSACERETINAE
FECERUNTCCXVOBHOCABEOTEMPORECONPO
RQUODIACOBCUMFILIISSUISDISCENDITINAECYPTO
MOANNREPROMISSIONISNATUSESTMOYSISCUM
NNORLXXVI·EROPHRIGNAUITINAITUCAAQUOUSQ
ECAPTIUITATEFIUNTANNICCCLVCCCMOXLMO
MISSIONISANNOMOYSISAECYPTODERELINQUENS
MOPHILOSOPATUR·AEBREORU·LXXMOANNACUM
ENERISEXAECYPTOAEBREORCONFESEFFICITUR·

conspicuously blended the distinct timelines of ancient history into a single composite narrative about the political diversity and interactivity that characterized the world in both past and present.

to go, too. The columns and parallel chronologies came down. In their place, the Fredegar Chronicle presented a single spool of history, in which the historical threads of many nations were wound together in a single text (fig. 23). Once again, the format intensified the message.[35]

Another Eusebian experiment proved to be even more popular in the history of book design: a grid for the gospels, known today as a canon table (though this is technically redundant because *kanon* was the Greek term for table). The gospel had not always been imagined as a fixed form of four narrative texts. But by the fourth century, the accounts ascribed to Matthew, Mark, Luke, and John were viewed as canonical, and Eusebius developed a cross-referencing system that allowed Christians to read these four texts with and against each other, by indicating where they narrated the same events or ideas in their own distinct ways (figs. 24, 25). The section numbers in the table were keyed to numbers in the main text, so that readers could toggle between the concordance and the gospels (fig. 26). The tables also functioned as a mnemonic device. Advanced readers could internalize the data that was compressed into a single page (in the form of architectural columns and rows of numbers) and use it to navigate speedily through their own memories of the four narratives.

Eusebius was clearly onto something, and readers of the gospels from Ethiopia to Ireland took advantage of his device. Along the way, they customized. Some added a column to the tables that summed up the biblical episode (in case readers didn't have the passage numbers memorized). Others added mini-tables to the foot of every page, so that readers would not have to flip to the front of the book to look up the concordances. They added portraits or pictorial symbols of the evangelists. They added more numerical subdivisions in order to multiply the possible parallels. But whether they decided to make modifications or not, early medieval readers were using Eusebius's system to pay attention to larger patterns and rela-

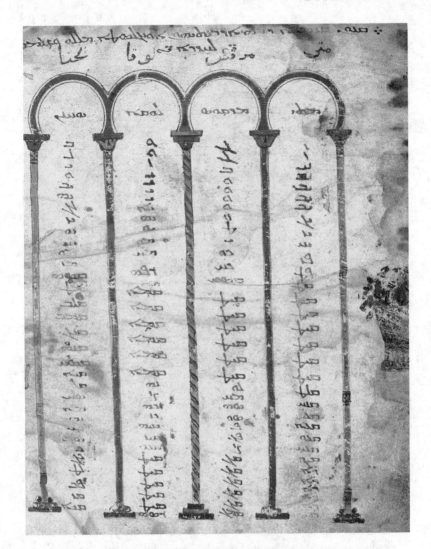

FIGURE 24 A modified version of Eusebius's first canon table in a Peshitta (Syriac) bible from the sixth century. The columns for the gospels of Matthew, Mark, Luke, and John are ordered from right to left to accommodate the direction of Syriac script.

FIGURE 25 A version of Eusebius's third and fourth canon tables in the Abba Garima Gospels I, made in Ethiopia in the sixth or seventh century. The references here are treated as lists, rather than as a grid that can also be read horizontally. Ethiopian Christians were less interested in the tables as a reference system than as a visual testimony to what were believed to be miraculous correspondences between different narratives about Jesus. The lush headpiece, topped with a flock of pigeons and ducks, amplifies this sense of divine dispensation.

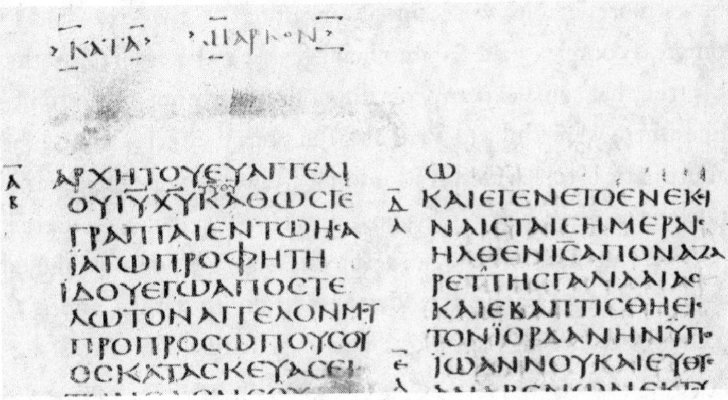

FIGURE 26 The Codex Sinaiticus is a Greek bible that was copied in the mid 300s, and it is the earliest surviving manuscript that uses the Eusebian reference system. The red marginal number-letters come in pairs: the upper figure indicates the section number, and the lower figure tells the reader which canon table to consult for the concordance. Here, at the beginning of the gospel of Mark at the top of the left column, the letter alpha marks the first section and the beta below it points the reader to the second canon table (which aligns the shared material that is specific to Matthew, Mark, and Luke).

tionships among the gospel texts. The tables drew them deeper into their books.[36]

Christians were not the only ones experimenting with book technology in the early Middle Ages. Early copyists of the Qur'an devised all sorts of ornamented shapes to mark the ends of verses, even when the rest of the text itself was written in unspaced Arabic; and they also seem to have been inspired by Syriac scribes to introduce dots or strokes to their own previously ambiguous abjad (or consonantal alphabet).[37] So monks were participating in a larger culture of early medieval graphic design that spanned the Middle East, the Mediterranean, and Europe. The spectacular contributions they made to that culture were born of the desire to enhance the working relationship between readers and their books: to make things more legible, to accentuate meanings in the texts, and to compress complex material into manageable and memorable units. It is true that some experiments didn't find many fans. And sometimes there were kinks to work out. But both the successes and the failures attest to a widespread interest in helping readers concentrate on their books through adjustments to the technology itself.[38]

When modern critics of distractedness suggest that we should be reading more books, they owe something to monks' efforts to make this technology a more effective partner in their own struggles to concentrate. At the same time, the monks' work went beyond technical adjustments to page layouts and text. They also developed practices of reading—slow reading, communal reading, repeated reading—so that their technology would not overtake them. The researchers today who suggest that even video games and TV shows can help us concentrate, at least when *certain* games and shows are used in *specific* ways, reflect views of tech that are fairly analogous to the monks' own attitudes.[39]

If developments in book design and reading practices made books more user-friendly, however, they were not supposed to simplify the concepts contained in their pages. In monastic culture especially, a smartly visualized text was intended to help readers plunge into the complicated stuff and stay there.[40] And in order to concentrate on that complexity, monks developed practices of reading and thinking that went well beyond engagement with any single codex. These practices took them deep into their memories.

CHAPTER 5

MEMORY

JOHN CASSIAN WAS FRUSTRATED THAT EVEN WHEN HE was singing or praying or reading, the contents of his memory still managed to distract him. The poetry that he'd read when he was younger kept edging out his meditations. He said that it had "dyed" his mind: no matter how hard he tried to kick out the "silly stories and military histories" that his mind had soaked up from so many poems, the war heroes of his memories were still part of its fabric. The unsparing observation of distraction-in-action was one of the many things that Cassian had learned from Evagrius. And as he admitted to the desert father Nesteros, what he observed in his own practice made him feel hopeless.

We often blame our memories for blanking, but monks were likelier to accuse theirs of being hyperactive—and this was an additional threat to their attention. Yet Nesteros didn't blame Cassian for remembering this stuff. He only thought that Cassian had been tackling the problem from the wrong angle. It was impossible to empty your mind completely, no matter how much you disliked its contents. But you *could* restock it and reorganize it, filling it with things you actually cared about and making them easier to access. He offered Cassian some design suggestions based on a biblical template: his mind should become a room that was furnished well, but sparely. He pictured this room as an ark containing two stone tablets, a golden jar, the rod of Aaron cut from the tree of Jesse, and two angels on guard. These furnishings, he explained, represented the durability of the law, a bottomless memory, eternal life, and literal and spiritual knowledge, respectively. This was how a refurbished mind could look. Cleared of cognitive clutter, it became a house of God.[1]

For Nesteros and Cassian and their contemporaries, the work of renovation was just as important as the finished product—precisely because they saw the memory as more than a collection of *memories*, more than a storage unit of things to recall. Yes, its contents were important. A monk's memories were always with her, supplied her with material to think about, gave her templates for guiding her perceptions and experiences, and served as her reference point for acting ethically. But the memory was also the very instrument that she used to design and build new mental structures from the materials she had at hand.[2] In Late Antiquity and the early Middle Ages, the memory was where monks did some of their most complex concentrating.

To do that, monks learned how the memory worked—rather than treat it like a black box, as we often do today. Then they took advantage of its mechanisms. They used this construction site and its machinery to reorganize their past thoughts, draw themselves deeper into present thoughts, and establish new cognitive patterns for the future. They were after modes of thinking that felt proactive rather than passive, to engage in a kind of work that was itself a form of deep attention.

Monks employed mnemonic strategies that enhanced recollection, and they learned to repurpose the memories they already had—all the while keeping their minds in motion. These practices were complex, creative, and difficult. And like every other facet of monastic culture, they catalyzed debates about their benefits and risks. But the hope was that the memory's work would make monks architects of their own cognition. By displacing distractions, it had the potential to deactivate them.

*

THE FIRST STEP IN USING the memory more adroitly was to notice what made things memorable, and to design memories accordingly. Monks knew that memories were tightly associated with places. The ark-sanctuary that Nesteros described is one example of this: he conjured for Cassian a clearly defined space so that it would be easy to revisit. Likewise monks often read and wrote about things that mattered to them in the form of geographic narratives—voyages, pilgrimages, cosmographies, mapped catalogs—as a way of anchoring knowledge spatially. Moving through those places in the imagination helped set information in order and allowed monks to recall it later. The monastery itself could be used in this way. For an individual monk, a familiar cell or monastic complex accumulated layers of experiences and associations over time and in the process became a kind of warehouse of memories. Monks were trained to think in these ways. Their techniques were similar to what we know today as the "memory palace," which involves stocking an architectural space with imagistic items to recall, like a more elaborate and ornamental version of Nesteros's ark. Monks in Late Antiquity and the Middle Ages didn't use that exact mnemonic; they and their contemporaries thought it was "cumbersome and gimmicky." But like the memory palace, many of their devices were spatialized: they involved attaching ideas to meaningful places.[3]

Monks also knew that engaging multiple senses at a time would help something stick. Cassian and Nesteros had used sensory terms to describe the experience of remembering: ideas that stayed in the memory were visible, tangible, fragrant, sweet, and animated. These were not so much metaphors as they were descriptions of how things entered the memory and what it felt like to revisit them. And in the multisensory media culture of late antique and early medieval monasteries, there was plenty to perceive. This was especially true of their churches: many communities thought that sacred spaces should flood the senses with vitality and beauty.

Take the sense of sight. Church interiors, in this aesthetic, emphasized an interplay of colors, light, surfaces, and materials that was designed to delight human vision, but also to destabilize it. Densely decorated surfaces kept the eyes moving. Textiles were embroidered with metals and gems. Marbles and mosaics looked like paintings. Paintings of textiles seemed to soften the stone surfaces they covered. Indoors seemed to become outdoors by conjuring nature and hinting at the heavens. These spaces were capable of "strik[ing] men's eyes with irresistible force," as one sixth-century commentator put it. The mind was supposed to be energized but also stunned.

At the Red Monastery in Upper Egypt, every inch of the monks' church was brilliantly painted in the course of the late fifth and sixth centuries, and the results attest to the late antique aesthetic of abundance. The monks of this community were part of Shenoute's federation; they built this particular monastic complex in the same monumental style as Shenoute's White Monastery, about a century after the abbot had died. The Red Monastery is the best surviving example of painted architecture from the late Roman world: many other buildings—including the White Monastery—were scraped of their surfaces when modern tastes skewed plain and white. The Red Monastery's paintings avoided this fate because they were hidden for centuries beneath layers of structural mud and brick. Now in their restored state, wide-eyed portraits of monastic leaders, saints, and biblical figures look out from the semidomes and niches of the basilica, and they are surrounded by trompe l'oeil architectural features, mixed with actual architectural features, that create dancing multicolored surfaces of marble, textiles, vegetation, animals, and geometries (fig. 27). The church attests to the

late antique taste for mixing color and pattern to "increase expo-
nentially the variety of visual stimuli," as the art historian Elizabeth Bolman has characterized it.[4] Rather than distracting, these
stimuli and this style were supposed to immerse viewers, engage
them, and enhance their ability to remember the experience.

The Red Monastery is a special case in some ways. Most monastic churches were not nearly as large as the ones that Shenoute and
his successors built. Some communities could not afford to deco-
rate their churches at this scale, and others were opposed to it on
principle. Pachomius had worried that such beauty could make the
mind "stumble" if monks paid too much attention to it; and the
Cistercians of the twelfth century would famously insist that surfaces should be spare, so that it was easier to meditate with *mental*
images. It's hard to track the aesthetics of monastic churches comprehensively, because so few of them survive in anything like their
original state and because so many monasteries are hard to identify
archaeologically in the first place. Early medieval churches were
often expanded or renovated in later centuries, and many others
were damaged or destroyed by fires, earthquakes, warfare, demolition, or pollution, or were simply abandoned.

Still, archaeologists find glimpses. The monastic church at Khirbet ed-Deir, which was built into a rock cave a few miles southwest
of Bethlehem, features "carpets" of mosaics that cover every section of its floor, and the brightly patterned frescoes from the nearby
monastery of Khirbet el-Quneitira peek out from fragments that
were left behind by robbers. At the churches of the double monastery of Wearmouth-Jarrow, Bede's home in northern England,
surviving fragments of sculpture, plaster, and colored glass suggest
that these spaces were also densely decorated, with a taste for variety and dynamism that would have made sense to the monks of
the Red Monastery almost two centuries earlier. When a monastic
community built a church in Toledo (Santa María de Melque) after
the Umayyad conquest of Iberia, they took cues from the Levan-
tine architectural styles that the new ruling class had brought with

them. But they were traditional in other ways, and the fragments that survive of the church's decorative program had led archaeologists to believe until recently that the monks had built the church much earlier, because it so closely mirrors the style that had been established centuries prior.[5]

Sight was a crucial part of monks' cognitive practices, but so were the other senses. The rituals that took place in these same churches involved powerful stimuli of song and scent and motion and even taste. These sense experiences were not ornamental; they were essential to the body-mind partnership. The overlapping of sensory perspectives helped a participant come to grips with the complexity of God and the universe he had created. It also made things memorable.[6]

Texts were likewise designed to evoke intersensory experiences, even if they mostly only hinted at the senses rather than physically triggering them. Although Cassian and other monks complained about the stories they wanted to forget, they did not think that captivating stories were inherently bad. They respected the ancient principle of anagogy, which held that the practice of imagining abstract concepts in sensible forms helped people process and remember complex ideas. And Christians became especially interested in how texts could use sensory suggestiveness to transform a mind's perspective.[7]

That notion—described by one historian as the "visceral seeing" and the "corporeal imagination" of Late Antiquity—is on full view in hagiography. Whether they were writing about societies in the Middle East, the Mediterranean, or northwest Europe, all hagiographers shared the stylistic strategy of compressing arguments about theology, politics, and ethics into human-centered stories that would resonate with readers and listeners. And many hagiographical narratives unfold like a live show: there is vivid action, minimal but memorable scenery and props, powerful speeches, comedy, conflict, gore. The hagiographers themselves recede into the background, as if the memories they were making in their readers were not mediated at all.[8]

One example of this mnemonically astute style, originally written in Greek in the seventh century, introduces its saint through the eyes of a monk named Zosimas, who has ventured into the Palestinian desert:

> While he was chanting psalms and looking up to heaven with an alert eye, [Zosimas] saw the shadowy illusion of a human body appear to the right of where he was standing and performing the prayers of the sixth hour. At first he was alarmed, suspecting that he was seeing a demonic phantom, and he shivered with fear. But after he had made the sign of the cross and shaken off his fear (for his prayer had ended), he looked again and saw that in fact someone was walking in a southward direction. What he saw was a naked figure whose body was black, as if tanned by the scorching of the sun. It had on its head hair white as wool, and even this was sparse as it did not reach below the neck of its body. When Zosimas saw this, he was inspired with pleasure and, filled with joy at that incredible sight, began to run in the direction that this creature he saw was heading. . . .
>
> But as soon as [that creature] saw Zosimas coming from afar, it began to flee and run toward the innermost part of the desert. . . . Zosimas' pace was quicker, and little by little he drew nearer to the fleeing [figure]. When he had approached close enough that his voice could be heard, Zosimas started calling out these words tearfully, "Why are you running away from this old and sinful man? O servant of the true God, wait up for me whoever you are, in the name of God, for Whose sake you dwell in this desert. . . ."
>
> . . . [T]he fleeing creature descended [into a dry streambed] and climbed up again on the other bank, while Zosimas, who was exhausted and unable to run [any further], stood on the

opposite bank of the apparent streambed, and shed tears upon tears and [uttered] lamentation upon lamentation, so that his wailing could be heard by anyone in his vicinity. Then that fleeing creature cried out, "Father Zosimas, forgive me in the name of the Lord; I cannot turn toward you and be seen by you face to face, for as you see I am a woman and I am naked, and I am ashamed to have my body uncovered. But if you are really willing to grant one favor to a sinful woman, throw me the garment that you are wearing, so that with it I may cover my feminine weakness and turn toward you and receive your blessing." Shivering fear and astonishment overwhelmed Zosimas, as he told [us], when he heard her calling him "Zosimas" by name; for as the man was sharp in mind and most wise in divine matters, he decided that she could not have called by name a man whom she had never seen or heard about, unless she was clearly blessed with the gift of foresight.[9]

Although this episode is told as a story within a story—the hagiographer is reporting the experience of Zosimas—it still unspools as an action sequence. A chase mounts across a scenic landscape. The midday sun burns hot. There is direct dialogue conveyed with desire, weeping, shame, chills, and shock. There are images that keep mutating, so that a shadowy peripheral vision becomes a black-and-white creature becomes a naked woman yelling across a wadi. This structure produces two surprise twists: the "shadow" and "creature" is actually a woman, and this woman recognizes Zosimas even though she has never met him. And these twists foreshadow the text's larger argument that identities can change. We eventually learn that this woman, Mary, is a former sex enthusiast who came to see herself as a slut, then moved to the desert for almost half a century to fight her desires. By the time Zosimas encounters her, the desert and her self-discipline had darkened her skin, made her more masculine, and turned her into a saint.[10] All of this is distilled into a memorably constructed scene. Its artistry is striking but not unique: early medieval literature is full of narratives that were designed to condense complex arguments into lively tableaux that helped audiences understand and remember them.

※

HAGIOGRAPHY AND OTHER narrative texts were only occasionally illustrated in the early Middle Ages, in part because they were already so energetically visual in their storytelling. Deluxe codices that were produced with accompanying paintings tended to be books of the Bible, most often copies of the four gospels or the book of Genesis. But their images were not purely decorative nor even designed solely to aid the memory. They also communicated arguments visually and invited viewers to participate in the artist's analysis on the page. Such images helped viewers intensify their concentration by prompting them to think more deeply about things they already knew and remembered.[11]

Consider a single page from the Book of Kells, a set of gospels made in Britain or Ireland around 800 (fig. 28). It displays two texts from the Gospel of Mark—*erat autem hora tertia* (15:25) and *et crucifigentes eum diviserunt vestimenta eius* (15:24)—that narrate how the soldiers who crucified Jesus divided up his clothes in the late morning. The art historian Benjamin Tilghman has found that this page was designed to help a viewer interpret the two passages more complexly and to retain that understanding through the intertwining of textual and visual forms.

As Tilghman points out in his decoding of this illumination, Christians sometimes associated Jesus's garments with another textile in another part of the Bible—the curtains or veil of the Tabernacle, which Exodus 26:1 describes as blue and purple and scarlet twice dyed. They made this connection both because the veil itself was occasionally interpreted to represent the flesh of Christ, and because the veil and the garments of Christ were ripped apart during his torture and execution (according to the gospel narratives). So the colors of the veil of the Tabernacle are the colors that

FIGURE 28 A complex visual interpretation of two passages
from the Gospel of Mark (verses 15:24–25), in the luxe gospel codex known as the Book of Kells, produced in Britain or
Ireland, ca. 800.

dominate the page, including the purple that floods the scarlet text about dividing Jesus's clothes.

The association is reinforced by the two lozenges, or diamond-shaped panels, in the middle of the symmetrical golden frames. These lozenges are filled with a purple-and-scarlet pattern that other early medieval artists sometimes used when depicting the veil, while the shape of the lozenge itself was a familiar symbol for Christ's nimbus (or halo) and also for the cosmos itself, as if to suggest that Jesus would transcend this earthly fissure.

The four perfectly symmetrical rectangular panels embody another strain of commentary that associated the division of Jesus's garments with his own body and, more symbolically, the Christian Church, which would spread to the four corners of the earth. Jesus himself is split by these panels: his head emerges at the top right and his feet at the bottom left, clothed in the purple of the Tabernacle, divided but not dead.[12]

It was a lot to pack into a single page. But images were not supposed to be a shortcut. Rather, they encouraged the reader to pore over their difficult but beguiling puzzles, and in the process to form a rich set of ideas and memories that could be revisited even when the manuscript was out of sight.

Graphics also helped monks *organize* their memories in order to learn new things from them. If images could be used to connect different ideas, as the creators of the Book of Kells understood, they could also be used to sort them into groups. Ancient and medieval analysts of the memory knew that it is much easier to retrieve memories when they are divided (or "chunked") into a handful of units. Monks therefore used actual images, or described images for others to picture, not only to bring ideas together but also to differentiate them.

They loved to picture ladders, for example, whose rungs represented ethical choices that scaled higher and harder. Several monastic rules discussed the process of self-abasement this way, by assigning twelve acts of humility to twelve rungs on a ladder. Even more famously, in the 600s an abbot in Sinai wrote *The Ladder of Divine Ascent*, which became so popular in the eastern Mediterranean that its author was nicknamed *Klimakos*: "John of the Ladder." John's work is full of aphorisms, hagiographic vignettes, and witty metaphors. But it's also memorable because the entire ascetic guide is structured as a series of thirty steps or monastic practices that could help monks keep an entire system for ascetic discipline in the mind's eye, while progressing through the details that appeared at each rung.[13]

From the twelfth century onward, scholars and teachers became especially enthusiastic about trees, angels, and other mnemonic imagery that could serve similar ends. Trees and angels were already associated with the memory by the time that Nesteros had outfitted his mental ark with them some seven hundred years earlier. But historians have suggested that they became more appealing in the high Middle Ages because a boom in higher education had resulted in a renewed feeling of information overload. The figures helped university students and scholars break down the voluminous material available to them, and analyze and retain it through strategic storage.

The standard angelic device, to take one example from this category of images, was derived from a passage in Isaiah (6:1–2) in which the prophet has a vision of six-winged seraphim. This "perfect example of sensorial activation" (as one scholar has described the vision) made it a powerful presence in monks' memories. The angel was also an organizational avatar: it took the form of a figure with six wings, each with the same fixed number of feathers (typically five to seven, for optimal recall), with the option of further subdivisions for each feather (fig. 29). One of the texts that popularized this device—*The Six Wings*, probably written in England in the 1100s by the monk Clement of Llanthony—designated each wing as a separate practice of spiritual purification (confession, penitence, purification of the flesh, purity of mind, love of one's neighbor, and love of God), while assigning a subcategory to each feather (so on the wing of the purification of the flesh, for example, the feathers stand for restraint of the five senses).

Other people tinkered with this template to represent other forms of knowledge and interpretation. As a mnemonic device, the angel was not so much a subject as a scaffold. And once it was set up within the mind, a thinker used it to plunge deeper into an analysis of the topics and subtopics that she had fastened to it. Preachers found it especially useful for organizing their sermons. It helped them with the order of their talking points, and—as a bonus—if they forgot a feather in the course of their preaching, they could skip to the next one without stalling out. They sometimes even described their angels in their sermons, so that listeners could use the same packaging to transplant the ideas into their own memories.[14]

Angels and other such devices were only occasionally drawn out or painted in books. Their symmetrical and gridlike structures were supposed to be easy to picture and easy to recover with the mind alone—especially if a person had first *constructed* the image in her mind, rather than relying on a prefabricated model. This was true of all the mnemonic figures in use in the high Middle Ages, and it had been true centuries earlier, when monks had emphasized how important it was to take an active role in the formation of their own memories.[15]

ANCIENT AND MEDIEVAL techniques for memorization might seem like a lost art, but they have been revived today for competitive and practical uses. The journalist Joshua Foer, for example, has written about the modern breed of "memory athlete," one of whom—Ed Cooke—went on to cofound Memrise, a language-learning platform that blends ancient and modern mnemonic technologies.[16] But these modern applications tend to focus on rote memorization, which is not at all what ancient and medieval prac-

FIGURE 29 This is one of the earliest surviving illustrations of the six-winged angel as a topical-mnemonic figure. It accompanies a copy of Clement of Llanthony's *Six Wings*, and it matches Clement's conceptual organization exactly. The fact that some of the wings are braided together suggests that a viewer would have needed to animate the figure in her head, stretching the wings to sort out the order of topics and subtopics. The braiding would have also invited making connections across categories.

titioners were after. Monks were much more interested in what to do with their memories once they were already in storage. Systems for simple memorization, in themselves, didn't hold the same allure for them as they do for us; monks already knew how effective they were. What they found much more riveting was the work of using those memories to meditate.

They called this practice *meditatio* or *melétê*. It was not a state of stillness or letting go. *Meditatio* was all about movement, in keeping with the metaphors of concentration that monks used. Minds that meditated were supposed to warm up, jump, stretch, hold tight. They made cognitive connections that felt like gathering flowers, concocting a medicine, or building something from salvage. Monks could meditate while they read, or go off-book. The most basic meaning of *meditatio* was memorization. But more advanced *meditatio* involved linking memories together and in the process "remembering" something new.[17]

Scholars who have compared the meditative practices of different spiritual traditions have suggested that any form of meditation might be described as a technique of attention aimed at inner transformation—but they also note that meditation comes in many forms. Buddhist practitioners in early medieval China meditated in the hopes of obtaining spectacular visions that functioned as a diagnostic about their spiritual achievements. By contrast, their Christian counterparts to the west were more interested in meditation as a structured mode of analysis. For Christian monks, meditation involved a distinctive mix of what scholars today would call directive techniques and thematic structures: their meditations were purposeful and concentrative and worked like their memories did, by association.[18] To meditate on a concept, to think about what something was or meant, a monk searched her memory for something related to it. Then she'd build on that association, and the next, and the next. The goal was a gradual agglomeration of memories that evolved into something much more revealing than any single-sided view could be. It was an exploratory, probing way of thinking. It was a form of prayer but also an act of discovery and creation. It was a means to stretch closer to God, because to think more deeply about the world was to decode the communications that he was constantly sending. It was also a tactic to set the mind in motion without letting it wander aimlessly.

Christian monastic literature is full of examples of what meditation was supposed to look like, because the texts that monks wrote often preserve the meditational structure that had guided the formulation of their ideas in the first place. This was the case with the prologue of the *Rule of the Master*, for example, which was composed in the sixth or seventh century. The anonymous author explains in this prologue why he has called the text a *regula*—a measuring stick, ruler, or rule. The term forms the starting point of his meditation, and it prompts him to recall a passage from one of Paul's letters. Paul had explained to the citizens of Corinth that he is not a self-congratulatory leader. Confidence in one's power should be limited "to the measure of the rule [*regula*], which God hath measured to us." Already, in this first meditative link between two different uses of the same word, the titular "Master" is starting to define his *Rule*. Through the association he is suggesting that, like Paul, he has been deputized by God to speak with authority, as a teacher, for the purpose of saving souls. The nod to "the Apostle" (as he was usually called) also suggests that the *Rule*'s guidance is based in Paul's precedent.[19]

The meditation continues as the author thinks about how a rule is enforced. He concludes that it is through a combination of fear and love, by capping off the prologue with a cluster of biblical passages woven together through linked keywords and etymologies:

As the prophet says, "Thou shalt rule [*reges*, which shares a root with *regula*] them with a rod," meaning with the force of fear. As the apostle likewise said, "What will you? Shall I come to you with a rod; or in charity?" As the prophet said, "The scepter of thy kingdom [*virga regni tui*: *regnum* also shares a root with *regula*] is a rod [*virga*] of uprightness, in which thou hast loved justice and hated iniquity." And again as the Lord said, "I will visit their iniquities with a rod."[20]

A reader today of the *Rule of the Master* might be tempted to skip over strings of biblical quotations like this one, which are so characteristic of monastic literature, because they seem derivative rather than historically distinctive. But every meditation, every assortment of scriptural quotations, still involved curatorial choices and motives. This particular cluster is an ingenious recollection of passages that shared multiple elements in common (rods, rules, and justice), assembled without the help of an index or word search. Some biblical commentators had already tied some of these verses together, but this combination accomplishes something new. It braids together biblical motifs—and, implicitly, interpretive traditions about them—to present the *Rule* itself as authoritative, apostolic, educational, disciplinary, equitable, and divine.[21]

This argument-by-assortment would have been more transparent to its original audience, who inhabited an intense subculture, than to readers who are more distant from its context and its canon. But even monks needed to slow down to appreciate such a complex interplay of ideas, whether in the short meditational burst of this section of the *Rule of the Master* or in other passages and other books. In 721 or so, Bede reported that a pair of monks had sped through the Gospel of John together at the rate of one quire a day, or around sixteen pages—but only because one of the monks was dying, and they were trying to finish the whole book in a week! On a deadline like that, Bede said, reading was bound to be straightforward rather than searching.

But meditation had its own pitfalls. Monks who *did* take their time found that the practice could cross over from engaging to distracting, because Christian scriptures were a deep corpus with endless possibilities for cross-referencing and combining. Meditations ranged widely to explore the hidden layers of the world, but they also risked overwhelming a monk with possibilities. As Shemʿon d-Ṭaybutheh put it in the late seventh century, "If the eyes of the mind are opened, every word contains a volume." The practice could become so consuming that it distracted monks from work that mattered even more. To some critics, monks were supposed to be scrutinizing themselves rather than roving conceptually through space and time.[22]

After all, that meditational roving was not restricted to analyses about monasticism. Any topic could be the focus of this form of reading and thinking. The entire universe was in play. This was the premise of the collection of *Riddles* (*Aenigmata*) written by the abbot Aldhelm of Malmesbury in the seventh or early eighth century. Aldhelm structured his verses as a series of puzzles in which different components of the cosmos—bubbles, ostriches, pillows, constellations—describe themselves by diving past their superficial attributes into more complex ways of seeing. As the literary scholar Erica Weaver has pointed out, this "hermeneutic style" helped cultivate readers' attention. The *Riddles* "wander" through arcane vocabulary, wordplay, and shifts in perspective, to engage readers in difficult and surprising meditations.[23]

A similar principle underlay one of the most compendious works of the early Middle Ages: Hrabanus Maurus's *Natures of Things*. The book is some 250,000 words long. It is an encyclopedia of biblical figures, the earth's physical features and life forms, astronomy, and anthropology (including timekeeping, sports, crafts, urban design, domestic space, and more). But *Natures of Things* was also a guide to the inner meanings of all these phenomena. Through Hrabanus's own meditations, the text guided its readers to meditate and concentrate on the divine logic that stitched the universe together.

Hrabanus relied on lots of other books for this project. We know that medieval writers sometimes took notes on scraps of parchment as they read, but they also often compiled things from their memories. And when Hrabanus began *Natures of Things* he had decades of memories from his readings and meditations to draw on. He took on the project when he was in his sixties, after having spent nearly his whole life to that point as a monk at Fulda, in what's now central Germany, whose library was among the best in Europe by the time Hrabanus left in 842. But *Natures of Things* is not just an example of Hrabanus's own meditational practices. It also served as a cognitive springboard for his readers.[24]

This is not exactly obvious to us now. It can be hard for modern readers to stay focused on the text's twisting passages. But for monks who were part of the same media culture as Hrabanus, monks who knew the same texts and stories and ways of reading and remembering, the meditational mode was more immersive. They would have experienced *Natures of Things* not as a chaotic collage but as a kaleidoscopic rotation of familiar texts and themes—though as with any meditation, there was always a risk that exploration would turn into distraction. Hrabanus's text and other meditations might seem to meander, but they were attempting to cut sensible paths through an immense world of information, paths that could readily be followed by those with the right training.

If we look closely at what Hrabanus had to say about domesticated pigs, for example, we can see him making connections through linguistic and conceptual parallels. By layering texts and memories and collating their meanings, Hrabanus could lead his readers to concentrate on the divine communications that pulsed through everything:

The sow (*sus*) is called that because she roots up (*subigat*) pasture: that is, she searches for food by rooting the earth up. The boar (*verres*) is called that because he has great strength (*vires*). The pig (*porcus*) is named as if it were dirty (*spurcus*), for it gorges itself on muck, immerses itself in mud, and smears itself with slime. Horace says: "And the sow is a friend to mud." Our terms for filth (*spurcitiam*) and illegitimate children (*spurios*) also derive from this word. . . .[25]

Sows (*sues*) signify sinners, and the unclean and the heretical, and the Law established that because they hath the hoof divided, and cheweth not the cud (*ruminant*), the faithful are not supposed to touch their meat (*carnes*). They are the people who may accept both the Law and the Gospel, but because they don't ruminate (*ruminant*) on spiritual food, they are unclean. Likewise they are people who don't care about being penitent, and they signify people who revert to things that they had once lamented, just as Peter says in his letter: "The dog is returned to his vomit, and the sow that was washed, to her wallowing in the mud."[26]

When a dog vomits, he throws up food that was weighing down his stomach; but when he returns to his vomit, he loads up again on what he had just jettisoned. It's like people who lament their wrongdoings: by confessing them they throw up the mental wickedness that they had gorged on and which was weighing them down on the inside; but after confession, they seek that evil out and eat it up again. When the sow is washed clean while wallowing in the mud, she ends up even filthier (*sordidior*). And the person who laments his wrongdoing but doesn't stop doing it anyway subjects himself to more serious guilt, when he rejects the very pardon he could have obtained by weeping. So it's as if he's rolling around in muddy water, because as long as he is sapping the cleanness of life from his tears, he is making those very tears filthy (*sordidas*) in the eyes of God.[27]

"Pigs" (*porci*) also means unclean and decadent humans. In the Gospel: "If thou cast us out, send us into the pigs." And in this spot: "Cast not yet your pearls before swine (*porcos*)." Likewise "pig" means the spirit of an unclean person. In the Gospel: "And he sent him into his farm to feed pigs." Likewise "pig" signifies the sinners and the unclean, and it was written in the psalm about them: "Their belly is filled from thy hidden stores. They are full of pork (*porcina*), and they have left (*relinquentur*) to their little ones the rest of their substance." He is saying here that the Jews are full of unclean things, which are the "hidden stores"—in other words, things that are known to be forbidden by the Lord. "Pork" refers to what's polluted, because among other rules in the Old Testament, pork is designated as unclean. But the sinners also passed on other remnants (*reliquias*) to their children, when they cried out: "His blood be upon us and our children." Likewise "sow" (*sus*) in Solomon is a knowing sinner living indulgently: "A golden ring in a sow's snout, a woman fair and foolish." Likewise "sow" means the filthy thoughts (*sordidae*) of fleshy things (*carnalium*). Perverse actions result from those thoughts, as if they'd been roasted to perfection. Isaiah: "The people that eat swine's flesh (*carnem suillam*), and profane broth is in their vessels."[28]

This meditation is both original and not. Hrabanus based it on a clutch of commentaries that originated from North Africa, Italy, Spain, Gaul, and England in the fourth to eighth centuries. Technically his debts ran even deeper, because his sources also had their own sources. That is how early medieval exegesis worked: it was crucial to refer to authorities, who themselves relied on authorities, in trying to make sense of sacred texts. As more than one monastic author pointed out, you couldn't just bend the Bible to your own perspective.[29] But it was still possible to put a personal spin on the interpretive tradition, and this is what Hrabanus and most exegetes did.

For instance, he knitted a strain of anti-Jewish polemic into the meditation that his own sources had not really stressed, by suggesting (via Cassiodorus) that the pork eaters of Psalm 16 and Pontius Pilate's interlocutors in Matthew 27 indicated that Jews had bequeathed a sinful inheritance to their children. By the early Middle Ages it was a typical move for Christian exegetes to scrutinize the Old Testament for signs that Jews had not served God sufficiently, in order to argue that Christianity was the true path to salvation. But at the time he was writing *Natures of Things* in the 840s, Hrabanus was a conspicuously moderate voice among his contemporaries. The Carolingian emperors—patrons of Fulda and rulers of a large swath of western and central Europe—had styled their kingdom as a chosen people analogous to the people of Israel, and they had supported their Jewish subjects in highly visible ways, including patronizing Jewish courtiers and hiring what seems to have been an officer of Jewish-Christian relations. They did so in opposition to fierce objections that Jews and Christians should conduct their lives in strict separation from each other. Hrabanus himself had faced criticism for reading and quoting the Jewish historian Josephus, and for his interest in Jewish exegesis more generally.[30]

The passage also reflects Hrabanus's overarching objective to show that even seemingly simple pieces of the universe could be interpreted in many ways. The things that filled his books and his environment, even pigs, were not straightforward symbols. They were shape-shifters. And that called for a correspondingly supple way of investigating them. Sure, his meditation mixes metaphors. Its etymologies, by today's standards, are bogus. It samples from biology, history, and theology but does not treat any of them comprehensively. But Hrabanus's massive text was only a starting point, or rather, a vast array of starting points. There was always more to explore about a given subject. Hrabanus hadn't even exhausted the possibilities for meditating on pigs: when the Gazan solitaries Barsanuphius and Euthymius had exchanged letters three centuries earlier, they had combined some of the same biblical passages about pigs with entirely different excerpts, to direct their meditations toward the problem of unwanted thoughts.[31]

The universe was too vast for any single text or meditation to encapsulate it, and whatever logical order a person imposed on the world was never absolute. Late antique and early medieval thinkers knew this. The analytical style of *meditatio* was unapologetically subjective. The insights an analyst reached were shaped by the cognitive paths she chose.[32]

But meditation was also a collective endeavor. That was true in a diffuse cultural sense: the resources we have to piece together and the questions we ask will always be affected by what's available in the world around us. But it was particularly true in monasteries, where thinking happened in groups. Geretrude, who founded the monastery of Nivelles with her mother Itta and served as its abbess, memorized almost all of the Bible as well as some difficult exegetical material. The point of doing this, her hagiographer points out, was to convey everything she'd learned to her monks. And even when abbots did not turn individual questions about scripture into teaching moments for the whole group, many monks would have shared their questions and ideas with each other anyway.

The extended conversations that monks had at sessions like these often resulted in the texts that survive today. The consultations of Cassian and Germanus with their Egyptian mentors are one obvious example. And Cassian's friend Eucherius of Lyon wrote two enormously influential books of biblical interpretation that reflect years of discussions he'd had as a monk and bishop. Gregory the Great's important commentary on the book of Job had a similar origin story. Even the monastic rules that Basil of Caesarea developed in the fourth century were themselves the result of questions that his communities had posed to him over more than a decade. We attribute these texts to individual authors, but they were shaped by the ideas and memories of interlocutors, too. Meditational pathways were guided by groups. As personal as the work of concentration could feel, it fostered ways of perceiving and evaluating the world that were also profoundly social.[33]

✳

ULTIMATELY THE PRACTICE of meditation was supposed to produce a perpetual state of attentiveness. "The holy meditation in your heart should never stop," as Caesarius of Arles put it in 534: while the body worked or rested, the mind should be doing its intelligent exercises, moving through its memories—especially its memories of canonical texts—to better understand God. Two centuries later, a monk named Theophilos even transformed his cell in Nubia (at what's now the Egyptian-Sudanese border) to remind himself to do this: he covered his walls with writings designed to look like a series of codex pages, covered in Coptic texts divided into rectangular frames and accompanied by miniatures. His selections included opening lines from the Gospels, the Nicene creed, lists of saints' names, stories from the *Apophthegmata patrum*, and magical texts. Mural was memory. Ornamentation was concentration.[34]

Theophilos finished his project in 738. But the memory was a never-ending construction zone where a monk could build something monumental, constantly renovating and enlarging it, without being anchored to a book or blueprint. This line of thinking culminated in a guide that is technically not monastic or early medieval: Hugh of Saint Victor's *Little Book about Constructing Noah's Ark*, written between 1125 and 1130. Hugh was an Augustinian canon, meaning that he was one of many priests in the Parisian church of Saint Victor who lived according to guidelines they attributed to Augustine of Hippo. In some ways the Victorines (as Hugh and his colleagues have been dubbed) were the vanguard of a new medieval world: they helped usher in a culture of urban schools, civic engagement, and scholastic theology. But they were also the heirs of early medieval monasticism, and they took its cognitive lessons seriously. Hugh's *Little Book* is a brilliant example of how monks had learned to manage the mind as it meditated.[35]

In the book, Hugh (or a student taking notes on Hugh's lectures) teaches his audience what the interpretation of scripture should look like by building his own customized version of Noah's ark. Hugh might have painted his complex creation as a fresco in the Abbey of Saint Victor, but his *Little Book* explains that it circulated beyond the abbey's walls, and in the many copies that survive, the text was never illustrated. That's partly because the ark would have been better served by the large format of a wall compared to the small format of a codex. In any case it would have worked best within the memory itself, and medieval readers were prepared to internalize this exercise without painting it at all.

Hugh had chosen an ark because monks loved to point out that Noah's name in Hebrew, נוּחַ, means "rest" or "repose." They interpreted his ark from the story in Genesis as a kind of monastery: both were refuges for spiritual calm and stability. The ark was a model but also a metaphor for the work of monastic concentration.[36]

But in the *Little Book*, it is the model that matters most. Hugh starts at its heart, describing his artistic process to help later readers work up the image themselves. He begins with a small square, he says, set inside a slightly larger square, so that it looks like a square surrounded by a thin-banded perimeter. He sets a cross inside the smaller square, and has its arms extend to the band. He fills the cross with gold. He also colors the spaces that have formed between the corners of the smaller square and the crooks of the cross: the two top squares become a fiery red and the bottom two a cloudy blue. Now, within the band surrounding the square, he writes one letter on each side: an alpha at the top, to signal the beginning; an omega at the bottom, to signal the end. In the right side of the band he writes a chi and in the left a sigma: these are the first and last letters of "Christ" (Χριστός), and they also closely resemble the Roman numerals X and C, ten signifying the Ten Commandments and one hundred signifying the perfection that was possible among the gentile nations when they finally received the faith. He fills the band with two lines of color: a line of green in the inner lane and a line of purple in the outer lane. And at the center of everything, he sets a lamb, standing directly on the cross. This is Christ himself, the beginning and end, the Old Law and the New, a sacrificial lamb on the cross. The purple represents his blood; the green, eternal life. And the red and the blue represent

God's columns of fire and cloud that led the people of Israel in their exodus from Egypt.

Hugh continues to build. He surrounds the bounded square (and lamb and cross) with a much larger rectangle. This is the footprint of the ark. Then he "pulls" the central square up, as if out of the page or plane, so that it now sits atop a tall pillar. He proceeds to build a roof for the ark, with a timber from each corner extending to the purple-and-green perimeter of the central square. "Viewed" from the side, the structure now looks like a rectangular pyramid with its pointy top lopped off and a lamb standing at the summit. He divides this pyramid into three stories: the basic frame of the ark is complete.[37]

But Hugh was just getting started. His ark has infinite room for further engineering. He decides, for example, that the plane that runs from the ark's bow up to the pillar, and from the pillar down to the stern, should represent the course of sacred history: he populates this roofline with a parade of icons of biblical figures and popes—and leaves a blank space for the history to come. To do this, Hugh has to make choices about whom to include, and how to divide up those genealogies so that they correspond in some meaningful way to the geometries of the structure. Every phase of construction works in this manner. Hugh adds more rafters and explains what they mean. He paints the sides of the ark in alternating horizontal bands of color and gives reasons for those choices. He puts a ladder in every corner of every floor, twelve ladders in all: he stacks some of them up with all the books of the Bible, and others he fills with particular verses that he breaks up into parts and colors. He personifies states of being and imagines them doing various things on or near the ladders: Ignorance breaks a jar, Meditation picks up the pieces, Contemplation glues them back together. He writes words on many surfaces. He considers how the three floors relate to each other, and builds little pods along the outer wall of each floor, and pictures each pod as a different geographic location, and paints the inside of the ark's walls to represent still *other* pods that are actually other geographies, transforming the ark into the world. He surrounds the ark with an orb representing the globe and imagines around the contours of this orb the four seasons and winds and the zodiac and heaven and hell, while God sits enthroned above and embraces all of it.

The *Little Book about Constructing Noah's Ark* is a virtuosic performance of mnemonic and meditational techniques. Hugh deploys the familiar strategies of spatial organization, subdivision, and sense-activating details—but he does it to make *new* memories out of a meditation that is utterly absorbing. After his ark is built in his mind (and not only as a fresco on a wall), he can return to it whenever he wants, viewing it from angles that a painting cannot allow, zooming in or out, outfitting it with new attributes or asking new questions about the features he finds there. As Hugh wrote in another of his works, *meditatio* "loves to run through open space."[38] One of the best ways to discipline the mind was to give it a taste of what it wanted.

Monks' complex meditational practices, and the capacious inner worlds they constructed through them, may seem especially bizarre to us now. Most of us don't try to concentrate by roving through keywords and images and DIY panoramas. But that shouldn't make *meditatio* any less appealing. I teach a class for freshmen in which we try out different medieval cognitive practices to help students tackle their first year of college. Their favorite exercise, by far, is meditation in the mode of Hugh's *Little Book*. They pick a concept from one of their classes that they think is worth exploring—a little piece of organic chemistry, say, or coding or poetry—and they set up an imaginary construction site for it. To start building, they have to start associating, asking themselves how that one piece relates to *other* pieces, whether the connection is strong or weak, whether there's more to analyze and build. All that work basically amounts to high-level studying, but rather than being boring or intimidating, it's adventurous and immersive. It's also highly memorable—as students appreciate on exam days.

But as with so many other monastic techniques and technologies, the cognitive movements involved in this meditational practice could be risky. Cassian had already diagnosed the hazard back in the early fifth century: wide-ranging meditation could go off course. One of his teachers, Abba Isaac, had suggested a straightforward solution. To rein in your thoughts, Isaac argued, you should grip the lifeline of a single verse from the Psalms: "Oh God, come to my assistance; Oh Lord, make haste to help me." Isaac told Cassian and Germanus that they should think of it whenever they were struggling with distraction. Or even better, they should repeat the phrase nonstop in their minds—even and especially while they were working and traveling and eating and sleeping and going to the bathroom.[39]

This formula was supposed to remind a monk that God was always there to help, and that in fact she needed God's help to persevere. Repeating it endlessly was also supposed to push out all potential distractions. But Germanus and Cassian knew their minds well enough to know that this method still couldn't totally dislodge the ur-problem. They asked: "How can we hold on tightly to *that* verse?" Isaac seemed frustrated by the question, but he also admitted that the answer was circular. To keep your mind fixed on his formula, you still had to perform vigils, pray, and meditate!

The late antique and early medieval psychology of meditation is yet another example of how monasticism was not strictly a practice of self-deprivation. It is true that monks were asked to avoid saying things that would pointlessly stick around in their colleagues' memories. When Pachomius heard a monk mention that it was grape season, he launched into a tirade: "Some ignorant men, now hearing you name that fruit, will be tormented by the wish to have some of it!"[40] But the work of concentration was also about abundance. As Nesteros would point out about half a century after Pachomius's outburst, it was easier to flood the mind with new memories than try to excise the things that were already there. And the absorptive engineering projects that monks developed with those memories make clear how active their idea of meditation really was. There was so much complexity to attend to in the cosmos and in the moral landscape that infused it. They needed to get moving.

CHAPTER 6

▦ MIND

WHEN MONKS MOVED EVEN DEEPER INTO THEIR thoughts, they encountered the mind's most bizarre feature: its ability to work through information while observing itself on the job. And although today we might think of this reflexivity as a chattering interference, the monks saw it as a gift. To their minds, thinking *about thinking* was not a distraction at all. It was the ultimate way to steady the self. So they devised all sorts of ways to get inside their own heads.

The monastic strategies we have already seen—the practices that monks devised to maneuver through the world and through their communities, bodies, books, and memories—were like a set of concentric circles centered on the target of the mind. But even when monks conditioned their minds, they remained susceptible to distraction. Worse: to a well-trained monk, distractions became increasingly difficult to recognize as distractions! When a high-functioning mind experienced an interruption, it was as likely to be a flash of insight as a misdirect. Gregory the Great and Isaac of Nineveh (writing at the end of the sixth and seventh centuries, respectively) each pointed out that distraction and revelation could be strikingly similar. Both distraction and revelation felt like a loss of control. Both felt like the sensation of being drunk. And in order to tell between a cognitive "slip" (as Gregory put it) or "stammering" (as Isaac put it) on the one hand, and a sudden special encounter with something conceptually overwhelming on the other, the mind had to scrutinize itself for the answer.[1]

As a result, metacognition was a vital monastic practice for women and men in Late Antiquity and the early Middle Ages. Techniques ranged from the elementary to the advanced because a monk's "hidden person," as Abraham of Nathpar put it around 600, "starts out like a baby."[2] The mind needed to develop its baby-like babbling into an inner dialogue that adeptly monitored its movements and immobilized its distractions. This meant learning, through progressively harder exercises, to observe one's thoughts, evaluate them, animate them, enlarge them, and ultimately—briefly—make them motionless.

*

FIRST AND MOST FUNDAMENTALLY, monks had to acquire the habit of observing their own thoughts as they occurred. Basil of Caesarea expected the adults who supervised young monks to ask them what they were thinking about—and to do it often. In the process, the youths would learn to tell the difference between good and bad thoughts, to try to concentrate on the good ones, and to start watching their own thoughts automatically. More than half a millennium later, in the ninth and tenth centuries, monastic educators in England still taught these objectives, though their methods had changed: they encouraged child monks to participate in various theatrical exercises—performing dialogues between teachers and distracted students, for example—that helped them practice vigilance over themselves.[3]

Some took this cognitive habit more seriously than others. Monks around the Red Sea and the Persian Gulf liked to tell a story about a desert father who had used two baskets to keep track of his thoughts every day. Whenever he had a good thought he put a stone in a basket to his right, and whenever he had a bad thought he put a stone in a basket to his left. If his bad-thought rock collection outnumbered the good by dinnertime, he would punish himself by not eating.[4]

His behavior was riveting because it was so weirdly diligent. Most monks, even as adults, were not so organized. They still needed to be reminded to monitor their thinking and to be told why it mattered. Shenoute had stressed to his monks that God "walks daily (and) often, (but) always secretly, through all the inhabited world," as a means to motivate them to straighten up their minds in anticipation of God's visits. After Shenoute died in 465, some of his monks suggested in their hagiographies that Shenoute himself could peer into his monks' thoughts: the fresh memory of the formidable abbot was supposed to be further incentive for practicing self-surveillance.[5]

Other monastic mentors preferred that monks take the initiative, and they designed techniques to help them keep track of their own distractions. In the sixth century Dorotheus of Gaza recommended that his monks go over a mental checklist with themselves every day, like a kind of journaling exercise: Was I paying attention in psalmody? Was I held captive by turbulent thoughts (*logismon empathon*)? Did I listen to the divine readings? Did I stop psalmody or leave church early? In the late seventh century, Shem'on d-Ṭaybutheh took a different tack. He suggested allowing your thoughts to wander on purpose. Let them go as if they were livestock grazing in a field—"and then suddenly thrust yourself upon them vehemently and unawares, and hear, examine, and scrutinize with discernment what they are thinking and meditating." If this ambush revealed that your mind was actually thinking about business or travel or other people, you would know that you needed to ramp up your training—to make your mind likelier to choose better thoughts the next time it was let loose.[6]

"Discernment" was the operative word here, not only for Shem'on but for many monks, from Iran to Ireland. Observing one's thoughts was only the start of monastic metacognition. A monk was also supposed to investigate distracting thoughts and identify their origins, and "discernment" (*diakrisis, discretio, purshana*) was the technical term for this detective work. It was steeped in the psychology of Evagrius of Pontus, who in the fourth century had popularized the theory that thoughts entered the mind from different places. Some thoughts originated in the self. But God could also send thoughts into a monk's mind. So could demons. This meant that one's seemingly random thoughts were not all equally problematic. Some were good and some were bad. It was the job of the monk to tell the difference.

Evagrius had written his handbook of back talk, the *Antirrhetikos*, to rebut the thoughts that monks discerned as demonic. And monks shared stories of heroic elders who had fought with their bad thoughts so loudly that passersby could hear them. But these battles could begin only if a monk had detected that a thought was hostile. And that preemptive screening process was the work of discernment. The *New York Times* tech journalist Kevin Roose has argued that "attention-guarding" and "digital discernment"—that is, learning to evaluate the information we're bombarded with on our screens—are essential tactics that humans will need to thrive in the age of artificial intelligence and automation. But attention-guarding and discernment were singled out as survival skills more than a millennium and a half ago, long before anyone was worried about humanity's enthrallment to algorithms and robots.[7]

Even in Late Antiquity discernment was difficult, because it called for nonstop critical thinking. Monks had to gauge the contents and character of every thought that crossed their minds, and to hunt for contextual clues that would help them know whether to accept a thought or reject it.

Take a seemingly virtuous thought, like the impulse to fast. Fasting was often beneficial, but it wasn't *always* good, and if a monk got the idea to fast during Easter, instead of eating with his brothers on the holiday, his discernment should flag that thought as inappropriate. And because thoughts could be so misleading, monks were advised to do their detecting nonstop. When Dorotheus of Gaza had been practicing medicine at the monastery of Tawatha, he knew a monk there who was so unreflective about his suspicious thoughts that they warped his sense perception: he thought he witnessed his brothers commit crimes that never actually happened. Cassian shared a similar cautionary tale he'd heard from Abba Moses about a monk who tried to kill his son. The monk had assumed that God had given him the idea, just as God had commanded Abraham to kill Isaac. Unexamined thoughts, in short, were treacherous. Even the superficially beneficial or innocuous ones had to be analyzed carefully.[8]

Dorotheus said that discernment was a gift from God, who had put a divine seed or spark in humans when he created them "to clarify the spirit and allow it to discern good from evil." But Dorotheus didn't mean that monks were supposed to act as lone detectives. Monks were encouraged to turn to God for help, as Dorotheus's younger contemporary Columbanus advised *his* monks to do when they were trying to discern their thoughts. They were also supposed to ask their mentors for advice. One of the primary reasons that monasteries expected monks to share their thoughts regularly with their abbot or abbess was that monks needed assistance with the analytical process that discernment entailed.

Monastic leaders still tried to offer rules of thumb to help monks discern their thoughts on the spot, the moment that they came into their minds. But their advice was laced with ambivalence because they knew that generalizations weren't really enough to go on. A layperson who was gradually converting to monasticism in the sixth century exchanged many letters with the Gazan elder Barsanuphius about this problem. Barsanuphius had passed along a technique to detect the credibility of a thought: if you have a thought that something is good, followed by another thought that it *isn't*, you should pray. Then if you still think the thing is good, it probably is. But his correspondent wasn't satisfied: what if you thought something was good but failed to have a subsequent thought that second-guessed it? Was a thought that seemed like an

unalloyed good actually bad? Barsanuphius refused to give him a
straight answer. You couldn't always tell. Once again, consultation
with God (or someone else) was crucial.[9]

Barsanuphius's correspondent might strike readers today as
unreasonably paranoid. Such suspicions were not unlike the modern simulation hypothesis: questions about whether a demon is
misleading us, and whether we're living inside a digital simulation, are both rooted in the desire to find out if the things we
think we know are being manipulated by something else without
our knowing it.[10] And just as techno-philosophers have argued
that the possibility of simulated realities is a nontrivial issue, early
Christian monks treated thought-detection with utter seriousness,
because distraction was even more devastating when it was epis-
temologically suspect. It was worse to be distracted by something
that wasn't what it seemed—to fall for the trap of paying attention
to something deceptively good that was actually bad.

Monks therefore believed that the effort to find certainty should
be perpetual, an endless triangulation of one's conscience with
God and one's mentors. Unlike other forms of discipline, such as
fasting or reading or socialization, monks never suggested that it
was possible to overthink or overperform discernment. If a monk
exhibited symptoms that seemed obsessive, such as fixating on a
single intrusive thought or feeling entrapped by thoughts for an
extended period, the diagnosis was not excessive discernment but
rather a failure to discern things adequately. Monks were not concerned about "paralysis by analysis."[11]

Discernment itself could not be the problem, as far as monks
saw it, because discernment *arrested* problems. Or as the neuroscientist Adam Gazzaley put it, it worked liked a bouncer. Technically, Gazzaley was speaking about executive functioning in the
prefrontal cortex of the brain, rather than about discernment, but
premodern monks would have enjoyed the metaphor. It was especially important to arrest or bounce unwelcome thoughts as soon as
they appeared because monks believed that thoughts could repro-

duce on their own. They "nested" or "germinated" in the heart. They were also allelopathic: bad thoughts could work like a pesticide (or "compound of artificial ingredients," as Ferreolus of Uzès put it) that killed off the seeds of good thoughts. And the longer a thought was allowed to stay in one's mind or heart, the harder it was to eradicate. The benefit of accurate discernment was that it prevented a distracting thought from settling, metastasizing, and eventually doing real damage.[12]

But discernment had to happen quickly to keep a thought from evolving into a pernicious psychological problem. In his ninth-century commentary on the *Rule of Benedict*, Hildemar of Civate said that even a small little demonic thought needed to be smashed to bits as soon as a monk detected it, because otherwise the thought would get bigger and stronger and require a massive amount of effort to dislodge it. Dorotheus likewise pointed out that seemingly minor thoughts, if ignored, could lead to severe moral negligence. He also argued that it would become increasingly difficult to exercise discernment if a monk didn't do it regularly. In the athletics of metacognition, it was possible to fall out of shape.[13]

Evagrius had argued that the very act of identifying a demonic thought had the effect of disarming it. Say that a picture of gold suddenly pops into a monk's mind. The monk should not only take note of this distraction but also ask himself what was so agitating about it: was it the gold itself that was distracting, or rather an impulse to accumulate wealth? If he pinpointed avarice as the animating idea, he could track the thought back to a demonic force, because he knew that avarice was inimical to humanity and to God. The moment he made these connections, the thought could no longer bother him: "As you engage in this careful examination, the thought will be destroyed and dissipate in its own consideration, and the demon will flee from you when your intellect has been raised to the heights by this knowledge." To best the demons and keep their thoughts from sinking in, a monk had only to expose them.[14]

The fact that monks were expected to be in a constant state of self-surveillance and wariness may have been exhausting, but many also found it strangely consoling. Discernment enabled monks to distance themselves from their thoughts once they had detected them, so they did not have to judge themselves harshly when their passing thoughts were evil ones. Monks in the Greek-speaking world even got in the habit of talking about their thoughts as active subjects and themselves as direct and indirect objects. Comments like "The thought tells me" or "distresses me" or "devours me" or "suggests to me" helped reinforce the point that a monk did not have to identify with every thought that entered his mind.

John of Apamea offered similar consolation to the monk Hesychius in the fifth century. Bad thoughts that "float over the surface of the mind" could be easily brushed away. God would judge you only for what you allowed to sink in. Even recurring thoughts were inconsequential if handled properly. The desert father Poemen, who had come up with so many metaphors for dealing with distraction, was said to have spoken more plainly to one distraught monk: "Every time this thought comes to you say, 'It is no affair of mine, may your blasphemy remain upon you, Satan, for my soul does not want it.' Now everything that the soul does not desire, does not long remain."[15]

✳

THE WORK OF THINKING about thinking was supposed to continue in prayer. Or more precisely: monks were supposed to rely on metacognitive tactics when prayer was not going so well.

Monks were often told to pray as much as possible. "If it is only when a monk stands up for prayer that he prays," said one anonymous monk in the *Apophthegmata* tradition, "such a one is not praying at all." Prayer was, most basically, the ideal state of attentiveness. Monks might classify their various prayers as praise, thanks, requests, or conversations with God—but they were always acts of communication and outreach, a mind stretching itself to the divine. Monks therefore tried to pray constantly, on the logic that constant prayer would crowd out every other thought and fix their attention. But when monks watched themselves pray, they noticed that they still struggled to focus. This was not merely irritating; it was enervating. As John Climacus pointed out, "It is by means of distractions that devils try to make our prayers useless."[16]

It was the very experience of faltering during prayers that had led monks to moralize distraction so emphatically. The philosopher and theologian Origen offers a telling point of comparison. Although Origen's work became controversial in subsequent generations (he had been active in the third century), it still made a powerful imprint on monasticism, and on Christianity more generally. But Origen had not been all that concerned about distraction. He knew that Christians had trouble concentrating when they prayed. He advised against praying in the bedroom, for example, in order to avoid thinking about sex, and he disapprovingly noted that some Christians prayed while facing a good view outside because they thought it was "more inviting than looking at a wall." And he assumed that anyone who prayed was familiar with the experience of having random thoughts warp their attention away from God. But he was more invested in convincing his fellow Christians that it was worth carving out the time to pray in the first place, and he was fairly certain that if they treated prayer as an active exercise that required their sincere effort, they would be able to concentrate successfully.

In this respect Origen's views were fairly conventional for his time, even beyond the bounds of Christianity. Neoplatonists in Alexandria and elsewhere, for instance, seemed as unperturbed as Origen was about the risk of distraction. These philosophers, who usually just called themselves Platonists, saw all beings as having a single divine origin, and they strove to ascend to and behold that divine singularity, in part through the practice of prayer. Although they disagreed with each other about what a successful prayer required—some emphasized rituals and others emphasized the communication hub of the soul itself—they were similarly confident that their equipment would enable them to conduct their encounter with the divine unity successfully.[17]

But a century after Origen offered his recommendations, monks were finding, to their utter frustration, that distracting thoughts still hounded them even though they had made concentration and prayer their life's work. They thought it was best to pray purely out of a love for what was good—that is, to concentrate on God simply because they loved him.[18] But they also acknowledged that in practice, most monks needed additional assistance. Out of consideration for human limitations, then, monastic theorists developed a variety of imaginative exercises and metaphors to help the mind pray less distractedly. Here, too, monks made the counterintuitive move of thinking about thinking for the sake of singlemindedness.

One of the simplest of the metacognitive gestures they devised to improve the integrity of prayer was to imagine the mind corralling its thoughts back together—"gathering in the thoughts of our minds from all over the place," as the Syriac writer Sahdona put it in the seventh century—to serve as a preparatory mode of concentration. If thoughts could be let out to pasture, as Shem'on had pictured it, they could also be shepherded back together. John Climacus shared the same strategy with his readers after visiting a monastery near Alexandria, where he noticed that one monk was especially engaged in prayer. When John pressed him to explain how he could concentrate so deeply, the monk admitted that "it is my custom at the very start to gather my thoughts, my mind and my soul. I call to them and cry out, 'Come! Let us worship and fall down before Christ, our King and God.'"[19]

Deliberate goal-setting was another kind of warm-up. Basil of Caesarea pointed out in the fourth century that craftspeople set goals for themselves to get their work done, and monks could stand to benefit from the same sense of direction. A blacksmith imagined his client and commission as he forged an axe or scythe, and in the same way, a goal gave a monk's mind something to think about as it worked in prayer or in anything else. Antony was likewise quoted as saying that "whoever hammers a lump of iron, first decides what he is going to make of it, a scythe, a sword, or an axe. Even so we ought to make up our minds what kind of virtue we want to forge or we labor in vain."

There were many variations on this theme. Cassian's *Collationes*, an account of the consultations that he and his best friend Germanus had held with their mentors, begins with Abba Moses's advice that every monk needed to see his short- and long-term goals clearly. The desert father Dioscorus was famous for making New Year's resolutions, such as not speaking or avoiding cooked food. And another elder was quoted as telling a discouraged monk that he needed to picture "the finishing-post"—yet another monastic metaphor pulled from the world of Roman sports.[20]

Other strategies zoomed out even farther. Some monks visualized not only their thoughts but also *themselves thinking those thoughts*, as a way to reframe their prayers and keep them from meandering. (The technique bears a rough resemblance to the modern psychological exercise known as "distancing.") One popular variant in Late Antiquity and the early Middle Ages was to compare the abstract act of prayer to concrete, everyday interactions. Imagine that you were having a conversation with someone. How would you feel if they weren't paying attention to what you were saying? And what if you were speaking to a powerful person: Would you disrespect them by not paying attention? Or imagine that you were in a courtroom, pleading your case to the judge. Would you get distracted? These hypothetical scenarios were retold endlessly to suggest that distraction amounted to a failure of imagination. A monk who couldn't concentrate had not really registered that God was right in front of her.[21]

It was also a failure of feeling—a failure to feel that the divinity was worthy of the same attention in prayer that came so easily in more mundane situations. Consequently one of the most valuable diagnostics in evaluating whether a monk was truly focused on God was to check on his weeping. The assumption was that a monk who truly appreciated God's creations, sacrifices, and capacity to forgive could not help but weep in guilt and gratitude. The technical term for this state was "compunction" (*katanyxis, compunctio*). A monk who felt it was focused. She was locked into the moral orientation of the cosmos and her place within it. Or to use a more medieval metaphor, she was *unlocked*: as Shem'on d-Ṭaybutheh put it, "The master-key that opens the door to all virtues is a contrite heart, broken by repentance." And without a broken heart, he suggested, a monk "will not be freed from wandering." Tears made the mind attentive.

Compunction was so crucial for concentrating on God that monks who *didn't* feel it tried to manufacture a feeling that was supposed to occur authentically. One desert father suggested that monks could kickstart their weeping by thinking of anything that made them cry (like a sort of Method acting), or by physically hurting themselves, so they could graft their tears onto more important thoughts and prayers. But others saw this as a problematic shortcut. Abba Isaac told Cassian and Germanus that forced tears weren't the same as natural ones and suggested that worrying about feeling compunction was self-defeating. Or as Barsanuphius saw it, self-centeredness was precisely what prevented a monk from feeling compunction.[22] Learning to concentrate was a paradoxical process of self-reflection and self-effacement. It required frames of mind that helped pull a monk's perspective outside herself, so that concentration became intuitive.

Yet another set of strategies that were ubiquitous in early medieval monasticism centered on death, specifically thinking about one's own death and its consequences. Like other exercises aiming to improve a monk's attentiveness in prayer, death-centered thinking was a metacognitive method of redirecting a monk's thoughts and feelings. It was rooted in a robust ancient tradition of *memento mori* / *melétê thanatou*, which the Stoics in particular had advocated as a means to be attentive to the self. It was also an extension of the classroom exercises that were familiar to every student in the Roman Empire, in which they imagined themselves in the position of tragic heroes in perilous moments by writing speeches for them. Their homework answered questions like "What words would Odysseus say watching the Cyclops eat his friends?"

But death meditations were more than a legacy of other traditions. Christian intellectuals in Late Antiquity gave these exercises an eschatological flavor. They linked thoughts of death to questions about eternal consequences. A person should think about her own death to reorient her life, but she should also think about the *afterlife*, to include the divine system of recompense as part of her long-term calculations.[23]

Although many Christians had begun to think this way, monks took a characteristically cognitive approach to the matter. When they considered the prospects of death and divine judgment, they determined that even passing thoughts in the present could affect the soul's future. And they reminded and urged each other to think of *thinking* as a life-or-death situation. Cassian, for example, told his readers (quoting the abba Theonas) to imagine that they were walking a sky-high tightrope, where distraction could be fatal. A certain Babai advised a monk named Cyriacus to see himself perched over a canyon on the edge of a sword. In the late seventh century Dadisho' Qaṭraya suggested that a monk picture an angel at his right and a demon at his left, and to turn his head to look in different directions as he prayed, toggling between himself, the angel, the demon, and finally a mental image of a crucified God.[24]

These exercises also helped remind monks that once they did die, they would be better prepared for what came next. John Climacus—an abbot who saw "the whole of the monk's environment in terms of death" (as one historian has observed)—argued that God had made death unpredictable precisely so that humans would be better behaved: if they knew their exact death dates, they wouldn't get around to fixing themselves until the last minute. So to avoid an abrupt termination to the arc of their lives, monks tried to keep morally and mentally alert at all times. As Evagrius had learned from his own teacher, "The monk must ever hold himself ready as though he were to die tomorrow."[25]

Thinking of the soul's future beyond death was an extension of this strategy. Monks pictured themselves in heaven to feel energized and clear-sighted about their objectives. One monk noted that "when I become discouraged, I ascend to heaven and contemplate the wondrous beauty of the angels." This tip was featured in a popular story about twelve hermits who meet up to offer each other insights and instruction, based on their personal experiences in solitude. Other monks traveled even more widely: in Pachomius's many glimpses of heaven, he saw beautiful cities full of saints, trees forever in fruit, perfect weather, and perpetual daytime. And in the *Rule of the Master*, nestled among its many detailed proposals for a regulated monastic life was a sweeping vista of a place where it was always spring, where the food was always exactly what you wanted to eat, and where there was no indigestion—or even digestion at all![26]

And then there were days when monks imagined the worst. One monk working in the bakery of his monastery constantly looked into the fires of his oven and thought of "the everlasting fire to come." A monk named Simeon at a hermitage in Cappadocia scrawled death meditations on the walls of his living spaces, including a reminder that "the fire of death chases us, the death that sends us naked into the next world." Simeon also wrote his own epitaph on his tomb, which sat waiting for him in his chapel. In the absence of ready-made tombs, monks could improvise. John Climacus, always quick to offer a necrotic thought, advised his readers to picture their beds as their graves: "Then you will not sleep so much."[27]

Some monastic leaders encouraged their communities to visualize the horrors of eternal condemnation to make them more resilient. But monks were perfectly capable of imagining harrowing scenes without the assistance of an abbot. One monk, transported to the Last Judgment in his sleep, was terrified to see his own mother there. She yelled at him for not having done enough to save himself, after having made so much of an effort to abandon her for monasticism.[28]

Monks were welcome to picture heaven or hell, or simply to dwell on the fact of their own physical mortality, but the one thing that they were not supposed to feel in the course of these exercises was confidence. Isaac of Nineveh offered the example of a venerable monk whose own thoughts told him that he was happy and praiseworthy. Thanks to his discernment, the monk knew to resist these ideas. Happiness was premature. And monks were never supposed to feel pride. They were told to recognize it as a "fish hook" that caught them up in themselves. So this monk told his thoughts: "Why do you call me happy, while I am still alive? I do not know what will happen to me till my death."

One of the risks of being sure of salvation, as John of Apamea pointed out, was that "such an idea will give rise to you relaxing your concentration." A monk named Thomas explained to John of Ephesus in the sixth century that this was why he resented interruptions to his work: a whole human life was like a series of books that God would carefully review, and the thought of God's judgment rattled him so profoundly that he "effectively controlled his thoughts and collected his mind, directing it toward God . . . and thus shunned and dreaded and feared the waste of one hour only."[29]

The *Guardian* columnist and author Oliver Burkeman has returned to the tradition of *memento mori* / *melétê thanatou* in suggesting that the finitude of a human life—an average of four thousand weeks—should prompt us to focus on the things that matter to us.[30] Such guidance lacks the eschatological urgency that made cognition so serious for the monks who monitored it a millennium and a half ago, but it shows a similar didacticism: John wrote about his conversation with Thomas precisely because he was so impressed by the mental discipline that the monk had summoned from thinking about his own death. That metacognitive bent made

Thomas a model. The prospect of death and divine judgment helped monks steer their minds to God, in prayer and in all things.

∗

THOUGHTS OF DEATH and visions of the afterlife were obviously motivational. They provided perspective that helped monks pay attention in the present, particularly when they were speaking to God. But they were also adventurous exercises that catapulted monks past their minds' usual horizons, by offering glimpses of the divine logic that structured all of creation. Metacognition did not have to mean closing the mind up to itself. It could actually widen monks' perspective beyond themselves, beyond their minds and memories and books and bodies and communities and world, to encompass the entirety of the universe.

One of the most famous of these cosmic experiences was a vision of Benedict of Nursia, publicized by Gregory the Great in his *Dialogues*. Benedict had gone to his bedroom window in the dead of night to pray, and as he looked out from his tower he could see the entire world illuminated by light, as well as his colleague Germanus of Capua being escorted by angels to heaven. (Benedict later learned that Germanus had died at that very moment.) When Gregory recounted this story to his deacon, Peter, the deacon wanted to know how a glimpse of the globe was even possible. Gregory's answer was that vision was relative. To a soul that can see its creator, all of creation seems miniature by comparison. When someone experiences a vision like Benedict did, Gregory explained, "the coil of the mind gets straightened out" (*mentis laxatur sinus*) and stretches across the whole universe. The world did not get smaller; Benedict's mind got bigger.[31]

A good monastic field of vision was both microscopic and macroscopic. It helped a monk see how even the most seemingly minor of behaviors could reverberate beyond the physical world itself and reconfigure her fate. When a monk named Gibitrude was transported to heaven during a fever in the seventh century, God told her that she needed to give up the grudges she had been holding against three fellow monks. And when a monk named Barontus received a temporary trip to heaven in the 670s, it was not his three marriages or multiple affairs that concerned the celestial residents. He had made good on those shortcomings after abandoning his elite lifestyle and becoming a monk. Instead he was chastised by one of his dead brothers for not keeping the lights burning all night in the monastery's church, and Saint Peter himself told Barontus that his ultimate misstep was having kept twelve gold coins to himself after joining the monastery: he had to get rid of them.

Visions weren't always perfectly clear. When the abbess Sadalberga had a vision of paradise, she didn't recognize people she had known on earth, and they had to reintroduce themselves to her! As Gregory the Great pointed out, monks needed to exercise discernment on their dreams. Sometimes "visions" were just the result of overeating, or the product of preoccupations or demons. Sometimes they *were* genuine divine revelations, but the mind had to be careful, because misinterpreting the origins of a vision could lead to a misapplication of its message.[32]

Gregory offered this advice knowing that his readers were already treating visions as a precious navigational system. Monks told and retold stories of their visions eagerly. That is why we know about them, too. When a monk at the monastery of Wenlock (in what's now the West Midlands of England) had a such a vision, probably in the early eighth century, his experience was relayed to the abbess of another monastery, who told a monk working as a missionary across the Channel, who in turn wrote to *another* abbess in England about it. Everyone in this chain of transmission (and undoubtedly many other monks they knew, too) were enthralled by the monk's experiences—by the feeling of being drawn out from the body, peeling away the "impenetrable covering" (*densissimo tegmine*) of normal sense perception, and seeing the entire world and the parallel zone of the afterlife with superhuman clarity. They also shared these stories because, as their Buddhist contemporaries in China also observed, visions required interpretive assistance. As thrilling as they were to behold, it wasn't always obvious what they meant, even to monks with powerful discernment.[33]

In Christian monastic culture, such death-centric visions were increasingly frequent in the later sixth century onward, when Christians around the Mediterranean started strenuously debating the options that were available to help the soul's trajectory after the body died. Visions like the ones Barontus or the monk at Wenlock had, in which the soul travels to the residences of the dead, helped readers parse the choices and the forces that influenced their fates. Even though each vision offered a different view on what was possible or advisable, in aggregate they presented a panoramic perspective of human life that stressed the links between the small and the monumental, and between the past and the future. Such a metacognitive perspective not only mapped out the mind's way forward; it also motivated a monk to stick to that path alertly.[34]

Cosmic fields of vision became so appealing in the early Middle Ages that they were not restricted to death or to the near-death experience of a disembodied soul. Some monks embedded them in a state of mind that they called "pure prayer," the most advanced state of prayer that anyone could handle.

Pure prayer—or "undistracted prayer," as it was also called—was the brainchild of Evagrius, the keen-eyed theorist of the fourth century who made a deep impression on monastic cognitive culture. But the concept morphed in the hands of his successors, who brought new questions, traditions, and expertise to bear on it. In the Syriac-speaking world, most conspicuously in the Persian Gulf and Mesopotamia in the seventh and eighth centuries, monks explored and mapped the mental processes that pure prayer entailed with unparalleled enthusiasm.[35]

We don't know much about these monks apart from their work. They tended to be more interested in the mind than in their exterior lives, so although their writings are intimate and animated we know virtually nothing about them otherwise. What little we do know about them beyond their writings derives from brief entries in biographical compendia, most of which were drawn up centuries after they lived. But even this frustratingly patchy evidence still makes clear that these East Syrian monks were extremely well educated and plugged into overlapping social networks that stretched far beyond their cells.

These monks were therefore aware of the debates about the soul's trajectory after death that had engaged Gregory the Great and so many others in Europe, the Mediterranean, and the Middle East. In these debates, East Syrian Christians tended to take the position that the soul was dependent on its body for its perceptive faculties, and that after a person died, her soul would lie in a state of sleep until the Day of Judgment for all souls. In its "anesthetized" state (as one historian has described it), the soul was incapable of cognitive revelations. But although monks in the Church of the East were not particularly interested in visions of the postmortem soul, they explored the mind's cosmic horizons through the process of prayer.[36]

They were not writing for beginners. Pure prayer was a practice for experts.[37] These theorists tended to see it as the exclusive preserve of monks who retreated from communal living to spend weeks or even years in solitude. Only the solitaries who had already learned to monitor and discipline themselves in the more rudimentary domains of monastic practice were suited for this most advanced exercise. But the monks who achieved it would gain more than an elevated view of the universe. They would move *beyond* the universe to a state of total concentration.

The monks who formulated the concept of pure prayer saw it as the ultimate stage in a cognitive and spiritual sequence of prayer more generally. To make progress through that sequence, monks had to be prepared. Prayer was the act—the thought—of speaking to God "off-book." But that speech was not supposed to be whatever came into a monk's head. Prayer improved the more a monk worked at her other forms of physical, social, codicological, and mental training. Most monks believed as much. When Gregory told the story of Benedict's vision, he implied that going off-book was possible only if you'd begun with books in the first place. Reading scripture, paired with the exegetical habit of interpreting it through multiple layers, helped a reader to see into the depths of the universe. Once again, Isaac of Nineveh would have agreed with him. Isaac—born in Qatar, active in southwest Iran and northern Mesopotamia, and enormously influential among Syriac-speaking Christians—suggested that monks could gradually pull away from their books and meditations the more they internalized the material. In contrast, undertaking prayer without having read or meditated deeply meant that the mind's path to heaven would be much too murky.[38]

But with sufficient preparation, monks could progress to more advanced stages of prayer, where they spoke to God about the conceptual and moral systems that interlaced creation, and in the process caught glimpses of the universe as a whole. In the early fifth century a certain Asterius exclaimed to a monk named Renatus that "even setting aside the reward it brings of a future life, how great it is to have your feet fixed on the ground while the mind strolls with the stars through the vault of heaven!" Monks had many exhilarating examples like this to choose from. In the tradition of the *Apophthegmata*, "They used to say of a great elder that he was living at Porphyrites and that, when he lifted his eyes up to heaven, he used to observe everything that was in heaven and if he looked down and turned his attention to earth, he would be seeing the chasms and everything in them." The East Syrians wrote even more enthusiastically about these advanced stages, which they saw as experiences on the path to pure prayer. John of Dalyatha said in the eighth century that it was possible for a monk to range higher than the sky and deeper than the seas and abysses—sometimes for as long as an hour or even an entire day. Joseph Ḥazzaya (who was a generation younger than John) noted that a monk who successfully fended off demonic attacks during prayer would win "the sight of the two worlds"—that is, the current world and "the New World," a Syriac elocution for heaven. These views were also chronologically capacious. Shemʻon d-Ṭaybutheh said that an elevated mind could see all the events that had happened in the past, as well as everything that was currently taking place. Joseph Ḥazzaya went a step further and suggested that a monk in an advanced state of prayer could even see the future.[39]

Part of the thrill of these metacognitive moments, when the mind saw itself within the cosmos, was the unexpected clarity that came from gazing upon the whole world at once. Everything was in view, and yet the mind was stable rather than shifty. The East Syrian monks in particular liked to accentuate this surprising contrast between singularity and multiplicity. A monk accessed these expansive visions of creation, John of Dalyatha observed, through his own quiet heart: the enormity of the universe sat within the self. From his solitary cell in the mountains at Qardu (in what's now Iraqi Kurdistan), Mar Shamli wrote to one of his students to describe the feeling of having his mind grow so calm and his heart expand so much that it felt as if heaven and earth were contained within him.

In this scalar view of the mind's attention, examining even the smallest parts of the world could open up access to the totality. Any bit of the physical world could serve as a cognitive key to a vast system that God had designed meticulously. This was a sensibility that East Syrian monks shared with Christians farther west. The Irish abbot Columbanus even suggested in a sermon he delivered in Milan in the early seventh century that it was irresponsible to see things otherwise: "What kind of person explores celestial phenomena while knowing nothing of terrestrial ones?" Rather than get lost as they ventured down various rabbit holes, however, monks were supposed to synthesize these "individual realities" or "details," as Isaac of Nineveh put it, into a "single vision" that considered them "collectively." Behishoʻ Kamulaya, one of Isaac's many avid readers in the eighth century, described how a monk could start making those cognitive connections: "When he tries to gaze at the construction of the nature of creation, his understanding [or mind, *mad'a*] at once stretches out over God's creation, returning quickly like a lightning flash."[40]

Behisho' figured that all humans had been able to see things this way before Adam's fall. Gregory the Great (among others) had thought the same thing. Monks were only trying to repair the damage. The universe, because it had fractured in their minds, should be made whole again. Paradoxically, the more monks narrowed their focus, the wider their vistas became.[41]

But these dizzying exercises were only the penultimate part of the journey. The conceptual leaps between large and small, and the gradual integration of the cosmos's pieces, were supposed to lead to an even more enthralling experience of motionlessness. At last: *that* was the state of pure prayer. It was not supposed to involve "seeing" anything at all. Evagrius had insisted that the mind would not reach a state of pure prayer "unless it has transcended all the mental representations associated with objects"—though not without first thinking about "the diversity of bodies and worlds." Or as Joseph Ḥazzaya put it, the spirit's sight became so elevated that it even rose above "the contemplation of bodied things." The result was that all of creation became indistinguishable.[42]

As the very concept of bodiedness dissolved in this state, so did a monk's own bounded sense of self. The normal limitations on human beings disappeared. Barsanuphius of Gaza characterized monks who reached this peak state as "becoming all intellect, all eye, all living, all light, all perfect, all gods." Monks who experienced it said they forgot themselves. And this forgetting allowed them to become, as Philoxenus of Mabbug described it in the early sixth century, "entirely engulfed in [God], entirely commingled in all of him." Joseph Ḥazzaya saw the self as being so completely obliterated in this final stage of prayer that the mind became indistinguishable from divine light or truth. John of Dalyatha said that the soul and God were so illuminated in such moments that the soul saw its resemblance to God and became united with the divine light entirely. No single account was exactly like another because, as Isaac of Nineveh pointed out, the experience couldn't possibly be captured with any satisfying accuracy: "Precise terms can be established only for earthly matters."[43]

This was also a point at which concentration seemed to *resemble* distraction—when one form of mental drunkenness could be mistaken for the other—not only because the monks who experienced it might feel overwhelmed, but also because their stupefaction waylaid them from their work and liturgies. The advice they received at this stage sometimes contradicted what they had learned when they had trained in communities: rather than prioritize regular recitations and fixed schedules, they were told to skip them. Even the routine work of monasticism counted as a distraction the closer a monk got to pure prayer. This is at least what John of Dalyatha and Joseph Ḥazzaya suggested, but not everyone agreed with them. Once again, it was not clear what was best.[44]

But the question of discerning or deciding would become irrelevant anyway. The monks who thought this deeply about thinking remarked that when monks reached the highest state of prayer, they were no longer actually *praying*. Verbs did not make sense in pure prayer. Isaac of Nineveh thought that even the noun was misleading at this point: "Where thoughts do not exist, how can one speak any longer of prayer—or of anything else?" The mind became so motionless that thinking itself came to a stop. It moved beyond what today we would call "flow," because although flow involves unselfconscious mental absorption, a mind in flow still moves. Pure prayer, by contrast, was a state of crystalline stillness.

Metacognition was impossible at this point, too. The acts of self-monitoring that were so crucial to monastic mental discipline halted, because as the self dissolved, so did its ability to think reflexively. Behisho' had described the body and mind defeating their challengers, after which the mind finally squeezed through a little door into the innermost room of the heart, where the monk faced an image of himself and his soul. But that was an intermediate stage. In the ultimate state of pure prayer, second-order observation—reflecting on reflections—was impossible. As Joseph Ḥazzaya put it in the eighth century: "The intellect in this state is melded with that action which works in him and they become one. Indeed the light of the intellect is not separated from that sea in which it swims." Mind merged completely with the object of its thoughts.[45]

Unfortunately, pure prayer was only temporary. As the abba Paul had told Cassian and Germanus centuries earlier, nobody could hold God in their sight continuously. Monks' minds would invariably go backward—tottering, falling, slipping, collapsing, and being led away. This was part of the handicap of being human. Monks also took it as a sign that they needed a divine boost, a gesture they called grace, to experience those ecstatic moments at all. Isaac of Nineveh put it to God directly: "Without the power of your grace I am quite unable to enter within myself, become aware of my stains, and so, at the sight of them, be able to be still from great distraction."[46]

The writers who advised other monks on the process of pure prayer were generous with their encouragement and candid about their own frustrations, because the distraction that followed a sublime moment of prayer could devastate the highly educated and experienced monks who felt it. Joseph Ḥazzaya warned that the mind was especially vulnerable to the "demon of distraction" after it had experienced a state of stillness—a gentle reminder that this frustrating mental flip was something that even the most advanced monks experienced. The solitary monk Mar Shamli (who may have been Joseph's student) once wrote to one of *his* students to describe the vision of God that he had experienced in a moment of pure prayer. But rather than end on that high note, he went on to describe the shattering feeling of returning to normalcy. When visitors started coming to his cell again, Mar Shamli said he felt like "a widow who has buried her beloved." Shemʿon d-Ṭaybutheh had sympathetically compared a monk's mood shifts to changes in the weather: sometimes it felt like the sun was shining on the heart, and sometimes sadness shadowed the soul like a huge cloud. Such feelings were completely normal, and transient—but that didn't make them any less overwhelming, so Shemʿon recommended that monks read what their monastic heroes had shared about their own experiences. It would console them. And in fact Shemʿon had himself leaned on the experience of the elders: he noted that he'd borrowed the atmospheric imagery from the abba Macarius, one of Antony's most celebrated students.[47]

As seemingly transcendent as these experiences were, however, the East Syrian monks who delved into the subject of pure prayer were also rooted in a time and place in which that subject was particularly compelling and contested. Some of them were accused of suggesting that the personal experience of pure prayer short-circuited other forms of authority and contemplation. The monks themselves would not have agreed with such a characterization, but they were aware that other Christians did not think it was possible to perceive or experience God in this way while still on earth. And they recognized that to describe the experience in human language was to put limits on what was inherently unlimited. "How frail is the power of ink and lettering in a book," Isaac of Nineveh sighed, "to specify the exactness of the thing!" This is probably one reason he wrote so prolifically.

Christian communities read the East Syrians' work with interest but vacillated in their verdicts on them. One of Shemʿon's readers, for example, tried to tone down his more experimental concepts about divinity by writing down qualifications in his (or her) copy of the text. More notoriously, the writings of John of Dalyatha and Joseph Ḥazzaya were condemned by the patriarch of the Church of the East in 786 or 787. (This was Timothy I, the same patriarch who had complained about the ocular strain of working with the Syriac version of Origen's *Hexapla*.) But one of Timothy's successors lifted the condemnations half a century later, and even before that reversal, John's writings became so popular among West Syrian Christians that they nicknamed him "Saba," the Holy Elder—even though East and West Syrians were technically supposed to treat each other as heretics.[48]

The reception history of John's and Joseph's work is a reminder that Christian culture in Late Antiquity and the early Middle Ages was heterogeneous and argumentative—and also that ostensible sectarian boundaries were constantly crossed with alliances and sympathies. And although the studious examinations of states of prayer flourished especially in the Syriac-speaking world and were intended only for the most proficient monks, they were part of a wider monastic culture that saw the mind as the ultimate site of discipline and reward.

They were also part of a culture in which quick leaps between macro- and microvisions of the universe were just as thrilling to lay Christians as they were to monks. Augustine of Hippo had delivered sermons that "simulated" death for his North African congregations and encouraged them to see themselves in different moments in space and time, from different points of view, in rapid succession. Basil of Caesarea had preached about the wonders of the physical world and urged his own congregation to recognize God's master plan in the smallest details of creation—and when he accidentally skipped the subject of birds, listeners in the crowd made hand signals to remind him not to omit this beloved subject. Or to scale even smaller: among the Stadler collection of late antique Egyptian art, acquired by the family of an Alexandrian candy empire, is a finely carved hairpin topped with a tiny shrine upon a globe. This was an iconographic shorthand: the Christian cosmos in miniature, balanced on a woman's slender ivory pin to slip into the strands of her hair.[49]

What was distinctive about monks' own cosmic contemplations was that they were the centerpiece of a cognitive program aimed at total concentration on the divine. And as they moved through monasticism's many layers of discipline, even the most seasoned of them needed encouragement, because the work of attention was elusively paradoxical. That was not just because, as the essayist and novelist Joshua Cohen has put it, "To become conscious of attention is to create attention. To become conscious of attention is to destroy attention." The monastic paradox of attention was even more specifically the result of being *a part of* the cosmos and *apart from* the cosmos. The efforts to focus on God both sharpened the self and effaced it. The finely calibrated work to know and master themselves would allow them to escape themselves, to reconnect with a divinity that was inherently undivided.[50] But those hard-earned and God-granted moments of singlemindedness were only temporary. The mind, as a created thing among other created things, was bound to split again.

CONCLUSION

WOULD THE FLIES, BANDITS, AND STORMS OF DIS-
traction ever disappear? Monks were not optimistic. Even
after death, distraction stuck around. Or so a Syriac poet imagined it:

> *The soul having left the body,*
> *Is in great suffering,*
> *And feels much grief;*
> *And she is distracted*
> *Hither and thither,*
> *As to her destination;*
> *For the evil spirits desire*
> *That she should go with them*
> *Into the midst of Gehennah;*
> *And the angels also,*
> *That she should journey with them,*
> *To the region of light.*[1]

The soul is torn not only between the directives of demons and
angels. The metrical hymn goes on to suggest that the soul's distraction stems from her own conflicting feelings. She is sad about
her separation from the body that loves her. And she still loves the
people who outlived her. But she also rejects the world, and she

fears punishment for her sins. This is why "she is distracted . . . as to her destination." She cannot decide which way to go.

In the cognitive culture of early Christian monasticism, only a return to God would end the problem of distraction for good. As long as a soul remained a separate self in a universe that was characterized by variation and motion—by choices and differences and change—her attention was a volatile thing.

So although we might assume that our own difficulties with distraction are symptomatic of the pressures and seductions of twenty-first-century life, Christian monks in Late Antiquity and the early Middle Ages would have said that distraction is inherent in the experience of being human, even when the substance of those distractions is culturally specific. They probably would not have been surprised to learn that their Daoist and Buddhist counterparts were struggling with similar challenges in the same centuries: Chinese and Central Asian monks, too, were getting distracted in their prayers and liturgies, occasionally succumbing to alcohol or sex, and worrying about the unintended side effects of their physical and mental practices. (And as plenty of Chinese rules, commentaries, and meditational literature attest, these late antique monastic cultures were also invested in experimenting with tradition to solve their own socially specific problems.)[2]

Obviously, premodern monks' lives were very different from ours. And they chalked up their own distractedness to different causes than we usually do. Whereas researchers today blame distraction on sleep deprivation, boredom, poorly designed workplace cultures, and technological triggers, among other things, Christian monks ultimately faulted demons and deficiencies, the will, and the original split of humanity from union with the divine. But we share a fixation on the problem of distraction—thanks in no small part to the monks who cast it as a moral crisis in the first place—and a suspicion that our predecessors were better at dealing with it. In the seventh century, the leader of one of the most prestigious monasteries in Judea was quoted as saying that "in our fathers' time it was very important to avoid distractions. Now our cooking pot and our handwork rule us."[3] This narrative of decline is at least as old as Christian monasticism. It was enshrined in stories that celebrated Pachomius ignoring his demons, Simeon standing forever on his infected foot, Sarah never looking at her river, Elpidius squashing a scorpion without stopping his recitations. Compared to models like these, it wasn't only the mediocre monks who fell short as they raced each other to church, fell asleep while they were reading, or did mean impressions of each other. Even expert monks confided to their friends that they were underperforming—as John of Dalyatha bemoaned his own negligence, and as Mar Shamli mourned the limits of pure prayer.

But even though the past set a daunting example, the monks decided to make use of it. They figured that carefully studying the achievements of prior generations would help them improve themselves, including their concentration. That is one important reason why monks were avid readers, and why it is possible to find common threads of experience in a world as diverse and argumentative as theirs. Monks were bound together, if only loosely, by their shared storyworlds. The desert elders who populated the *Apophthegmata patrum* and other early narrative traditions became familiar and beloved mentors to monks across the Mediterranean, Middle East, and Europe, despite the centuries that separated them. Many of the monastic guides that recur in this book were also widely read, as later quotations and allusions and even the fragmentary manuscript footprints attest—whether it was the letters of Antony in the Caucasus, a treatise of Evagrius in a Christian outpost of Spain, or the quips of the East Syrian mystics translated into Sogdian at the oasis of Turfan.[4]

After all, the monastic work of concentration was never supposed to be exclusionary. Monks saw distraction in many dimensions—psychological, physical, social, cultural, cosmic—and their goals for concentration were likewise varied and expansive. They were certain that a focused mind could better connect the self to the divine while charting an ethical path through the universe. Besides the personal benefits of doing this, monks' battles also benefited the communities who supported and trusted in them, whether their fights to focus helped them work at city jails, cure hexes on race-horses, or intercede for other souls through prayer. And although monks were never satisfied with their accomplishments, when it came to concentration they offered an example for others—if not to emulate exactly, then at least to take as proof that cognition was morally significant.

There are signs of wider audiences embracing the monastic mode of thinking about thinking in the first millennium CE. We have seen it in the emperors who were thrilled that they could not dis-tract the monks they patronized at St. Gall; in Tsie, whose brother Frange pursued solitude in his pharaonic tomb while relying on her own pious commitment to supporting him; and in the widow of Alexandria who impressed the desert elders by maintaining her composure despite her abusive houseguest. But imperial bene-factors, family members, and wealthy widows with time on their hands were not the only ones to be inspired by monastic cogni-tive models. Rabbis in the Sasanian Empire incorporated concerns about distraction into the Babylonian Talmud, repurposing what they'd read in monastic literature for their Jewish communities in western Persia. And (to take another example) a Christian layper-son asked Anastasios of Sinai in the seventh century how someone who lived in the world, a person who had a house and kids to think about, could pray without ceasing. The ethics of cognition was not on monks' minds alone. Anastasios insisted that the techniques were not monks' alone, either. You didn't have to become a monk to pray without ceasing, he said: acting with an attentive heart during the course of a regular day would have a similar effect.[5]

Monks who were more concerned about the minutiae of cog-nitive practice debated its practical and ethical dimensions in nearly every particular, from meditation methods to schedules to blankets. The result was a staggering array of strategies, some of them standard but many of them customized, like the anonymous monk's two baskets of thought-rocks, Mar Yawnan's conversion in the middle of a medical field trip out of his parents' sight, Gislild-is's manuscript annotations, and Theophilos's walls painted to look like the pages of a codex.

We could try out some of these strategies ourselves, and although monks found that many of them also risked being distracting, they might work better than trying nothing at all. We could review our day to determine when we got distracted, or watch our thoughts as they arise to discern whether they're worth our time. We could be mindful of our mortality, to bring the important things into focus—or at least set goals to give ourselves direction. We could construct meaningful images in our memories, or attach ideas to images that already exist, or meditate by linking and layering concepts into something larger. We could read things that matter to us, in formats that help hold our attention. We could form new technological habits. We could train our bodies to better support our minds, and although we probably wouldn't cut back on our sleep or showers to do that, the monks' emphasis on moderation might still ring true. We could set schedules that strike a balance between variation and consistency, or regularly report our distractions to someone we respect. We could think less about ourselves. We could even keep two baskets of thought-rocks!

The monks would have argued, however, that these individual strategies would have more traction if we also saw things more structurally. Distraction was not just a personal problem, they knew; it was part of the warp of the world. Confronting distraction meant confronting the competing demands of family, work, government, and public—which is why so many monks abandoned that world, to the extent they could, and created alternative social networks and communities that were dedicated to divine concentration.

In the end, it may be the monks' systemic view of distraction that is most useful to consider today. They did agree, if only roughly, on some general principles. Most fundamentally, to tackle distraction it was crucial to identify something worthy of total concentration. It had to be worth the war. Attention would not have been morally necessary, would not have been the objective of their culture of conflict and control, were it not for the fact that it centered on the divine order. And because monks framed ethical cognition as a relationship between the self and the system (or as they put it, between the soul and God), they saw attention as a paradox of states and scales. It sought stability through motion. It widened its vistas by narrowing its focus.

It also fused the personal and the ecological. Hence a more technical feature of monks' cognitive ethics: the mind had to be evaluated in the context of its environment, social groups, physical embodiment, media, memories, emotions, and metacognitive maneuvers. This was why there needed to be multiple and overlapping strategies for concentration, rather than a single sure fix. Abandoning the world for the wilderness was an admirable if optional start. But "the world" was really just a monastic euphemism for the physical and mental distractions that pulled a person away from God, and so—as one monk put it to another in the seventh century—it was the *tropos* that made a monk, not the *topos*. It was *how* rather than *where* a monk lived that mattered. Anastasios's advice to the harried parent was in line with this way of thinking.[6]

Finally, the work of concentrating was supposed to be continuous, because the mind was always moving and the universe to which it was tied was in flux. Challenges would keep arising and monks would find new reasons to feel frustrated. So even the professionals needed encouragement. That might mean celebrating small victories or recognizing that even saints struggled sometimes. It might also mean acknowledging the very persistence of the problem. This was the point of a story recorded in the eleventh century by the Persian biographer Abu Nu'aym: An ascetic Muslim once asked a Christian monk for a lesson, and although the encounter was not all that unusual, the ascetic (and Abu Nu'aym) thought that the monk's response was worth repeating. The monk said that because the world and the bodies that inhabited it were constantly changing, "there remain plenty of lessons for you and for us, even if we follow all lessons."[7] And like so many monastic lessons, this one was both blunt and circular. Monks knew how to keep each other in the fight. They were so optimistic about the mind's capacity to change that they kept looking for lessons—even when they followed all lessons, even when distraction never seemed to die.

ACKNOWLEDGMENTS

Two of my friends are especially good at distracting me from work but also keeping me interested in it, and I wrote this book because Henry Cowles and Claudio Saunt kept telling me to try something different—and Henry even read the whole thing, too. I was able to publish it because Dan Gerstle (my editor) and Lisa Adams (my agent) took premodern history seriously. The students in Medieval Mind Games at the University of Georgia test-drove some of the more complicated cognitive techniques in this book; and the Interlibrary Loan staff at UGA have been a lifeline. Chris Shannon laughed at my monk stories—but only the good ones. Peter Brown gave the manuscript such a warm reading that it felt as though we weren't living in separate states during a pandemic. Many historians and archaeologists helped me along the way, and I owe special thanks to Betsy Bolman, Ina Eichner, Dar Hedstrom, Andreas Kostopoulos, Michel Lauwers, Étienne Louis, Maria Mossakowska-Gaubert, and Joseph Patrich for their help in tracking down images. And finally I'm grateful to Dan Silver, who was my clarinet professor for four years at the University of Colorado at Boulder. I had to work a lot in college and didn't have as much time for the practice rooms as I'd wanted. Dan taught me that two hours could go a long way, with some discipline. That is my conversion story. It changed my life.

Notes

Abbreviations

AP = *Apophthegmata patrum*

AP/G = *Apophthegmata patrum*, Alphabetical Collection

AP/GN = *Apophthegmata patrum*, Anonymous Collection

AP/GS = *Apophthegmata patrum*, Systematic Collection

AP/PJ = *Apophthegmata patrum*, Pelagius and John's Latin Collection

AP/S = *Apophthegmata patrum*, 'Enanisho''s Syriac Collection

CCCM = Corpus Christianorum Continuatio Mediaevalis

CCSL = Corpus Christianorum Series Latina

CSCO = Corpus Scriptorum Christianorum Orientalium

CSEL = Corpus Scriptorum Ecclesiasticorum Latinorum

MGH = Monumenta Germaniae Historica

PL = Patrologia Latina

PO = Patrologia Orientalis

RB = *Regula Benedicti*

RM = *Regula magistri*

SC = Sources Chrétiennes

Introduction

1. Philipp-Lorenz Spreen, Bjarke Mørch Mønsted, Philipp Hövel, and Sune Lehmann, "Accelerating Dynamics of Collective Attention," *Nature Communications* 10 (2019); Johann Hari, *Stolen Focus: Why You Can't Pay Attention—and How to Think Deeply Again* (New York: Crown, 2022), poll

noted at 171–72. Nineteenth century: Caleb Smith, "Disciplines of Attention in a Secular Age," *Critical Inquiry* 45 (2019): 884–909.

2. Consequences of distraction: Adam Gazzaley and Larry D. Rosen, *The Distracted Mind: Ancient Brains in a High-Tech World* (Cambridge, MA: MIT Press, 2016), 123–41; Cal Newport, *A World without Email: Reimagining Work in an Age of Communication Overload* (New York: Portfolio/Penguin, 2021); James Danckert and John D. Eastwood, *Out of My Skull: The Psychology of Boredom* (Cambridge, MA: Harvard University Press, 2020), 42–43, 148–57; James M. Lang, *Distracted: Why Students Can't Focus and What You Can Do about It* (New York: Basic, 2020); Joshua Cohen, *Attention: Dispatches from a Land of Distraction* (New York: Random House, 2018), 5–8; Hari, *Stolen Focus*, esp. 13–14.

3. E.g., Hari, *Stolen Focus*, 10; more subtle is Danièle Cybulski, *How to Live Like a Monk: Medieval Wisdom for Modern Life* (New York: Abbeville, 2021), 73.

4. Stretch/reach: Isaac of Nineveh, *Discourses* 1.22, in Brock, *Syriac Fathers*, p. 261. Fire: Cassian, *Collationes* 9.18. Clarity: Cassian, *Collationes* 9.2. Construction: Cassian, *Collationes* 9.2–3; see also chap. 5. Love: Hildemar, *Expositio* 52. Fish: Ephrem the Syrian, *Hymns on Faith* 20.5, in Brock, *Syriac Fathers*, p. 34; John of Dalyatha, *Letters* 15.7. Ship: Cassian, *Collationes* 10.8; Shem'on d-Ṭaybutheh, *On the Consecration of the Cell* 19. Pottery: Rufinus, *Regula Basilii* 58.3. Cat: John Climacus, *Klimax* 27. Incubation: Shem'on d-Ṭaybutheh, *On the Consecration of the Cell* 4.

5. *AP/S* 1.8.254 (Hor); *AP/G* Sarah 3; Gregory the Great, *Dialogi* 3.16.4 (Martin); Gregory of Tours, *Liber vitae patrum* 11.1 (Caluppa); *Vita Landiberti* 6; Theodoret, *Historia religiosa* 21.13 (James); *Bohairic Life of Pachomius* 21, in *Pachomian Koinonia* 1:44–45. Statues: *AP/G* Anoub 1 (likewise Isaiah, *Asketikon* 6.2); Gerontius, *Vita Melaniae* 44; Theodoret, *Historia religiosa* 5.6.

6. John of Dalyatha, *Letters* 10.1, trans. Hansbury, p. 46.

7. *AP/PJ* 11.14 (John); *AP/GS* 11.39 (John Colobos).

8. Gregory, *Dialogi* prol.5 ("in naui mentis tempestatis ualidae procellis inlidor").

9. Antony of Choziba, *Bios Georgiou* 8.35, trans. Vivian and Athanassakis, p. 65.

10. Basil, *Great Asketikon*, LR 5.1.74, trans. Silvas, p. 174; ibid., SR 295 (Basil's definition of distraction).

11. Snakeskin: Isaac of Nineveh, *Discourses* 2.8.16. Flies: Leander, *De institutione virginum*, lines 6–7. Meat market: John Climacus, *Klimax* 1. Dust cloud: Athanasius, *Vita Antonii* 5, trans. Gregg, p. 33. Hair: John Climacus, *Klimax* 27. Mice: *AP/GN*, N 535. Forest: Pseudo-Macarius, *Logoi* 6.3 (collection 2); *RM* 7.12; Eugippius, *Regula* 18.12. Swamp: Pseudo-Macarius, *Logoi* 4.2–4 (collection 2). Channel: Isaac of Nineveh, *Discourses* 1.37.288. Bandits: Barsanuphius and John, *Letters* 448. Storm: Philoxenus of Mabbug, *Excerpt on Prayer*, in Brock, *Sryiac Fathers*, p. 128. Cargo:

AP/G Syncletica 24. Usurper: Isaiah, *Asketikon* 7.11. Horses: Cassian, *Collationes* 24.5. Thieves: John of Apamea, *Letter to Hesychius* 7, in Brock, *Syriac Fathers*; Babai, *Letter to Cyriacus* 40, in ibid.; Dadishoʿ Qaṭraya, *Commentaire* 3.12; Shemʿon d-Ṭaybutheh, *Book of Medicine* 181a. Fish: John of Dalyatha, *Memre* 1.7. Abortifacients: Isaac of Nineveh, *Discourses* 1.18, trans. Brock, *Syriac Fathers*, p. 250; Shemʿon d-Ṭaybutheh, *Book of Medicine* 194a.

12. *AP/S* 1.8.370, trans. Budge, p. 108 (and variations attested in Arabic and Georgian versions; plus *AP/GS* 2.24; *AP/PJ* 2.12, attributed to Pastor rather than Poemen); *AP/G* Poemen 14 (bodyguard), 20 (clothes), 21 (bottle), 111 (cooking pot). This book only selectively cites the overlapping and variable versions of the *AP* narratives, but see the *Monastica* database hosted by Lund University for a comprehensive picture: https://monastica.ht.lu.se/.

13. The metaphors of sports and war were ubiquitous: see for example Kate Cooper, *The Fall of the Roman Household* (Cambridge: Cambridge University Press, 2007), 17–19, 30–37; Michel Foucault, *Les aveux de la chair*, ed. Frédéric Gros, vol. 4 of *Histoire de la sexualité* (Paris: Gallimard, 2018), 224–30. Former wrestler: Anthony of Choziba, *Bios Georgiou* 4.15–19. Former soldiers: Sulpicius Severus, *Vita Martini* 4; more examples in Daniel Caner, *The Rich and the Pure: Philanthropy and the Making of Christian Society in Early Byzantium* (Oakland: University of California Press, 2021), 17, 246 n. 25. But note the case of the emperor Valens, who had no use for such metaphors and forced monks into the military and the mines in the 370s: Noel Lenski, "Valens and the Monks: Cudgeling and Conscription as a Means of Social Control," *Dumbarton Oaks Papers* 58 (2004): 93–117.

14. Metaphors: Matthew Cobb, *The Idea of the Brain: The Past and Future of Neuroscience* (New York: Basic Books, 2020), esp. 207–365; Henry Cowles, "Peak Brain: The Metaphors of Neuroscience," *Los Angeles Review of Books*, November 30, 2020. On the resonance of monks' approaches to the mind with modern research on neuroplasticity, see Inbar Graiver, *Asceticism of the Mind: Forms of Attention and Self-Transformation in Late Antique Monasticism* (Toronto: Pontifical Institute of Mediaeval Studies, 2018), 177–83.

15. Gazzaley and Rosen, *The Distracted Mind*, esp. 1–98. Yogic, Daoist, and Buddhist comparators: Halvor Eifring, "Spontaneous Thoughts in Meditative Traditions," in *Meditation and Culture: The Interplay of Practice and Context*, ed. Eifring (London: Bloomsbury, 2017), 200–215; Livia Kohn, "Guarding the One: Concentrative Meditation in Taoism," in *Taoist Meditation and Longevity Techniques*, ed. Kohn with Yoshinobu Sakade (Ann Arbor: Center for Chinese Studies at the University of Michigan, 1989), 125–58; Nobuyoshi Yamabe, "An Examination of the Mural Paintings of Visualizing Monks in Toyok Cave 42: In Conjunction with the Origin of Some Chinese Texts on Meditation," in *Turfan Revisited: The First Century of Research into the Arts and Cultures of*

the *Silk Road*, ed. Desmond Durkin-Meisterernst et al. (Berlin: Reimer, 2004), 401–7; Yamabe, "Practice of Visualization and the *Visualization Sūtra*: An Examination of the Mural Paintings at Toyok, Turfan," *Pacific World: Journal of the Institute of Buddhist Studies*, 3rd ser., vol. 4 (2002): 123–43, at 130–34; see also Eric M. Greene, *Chan before Chan: Meditation, Repentance, and Visionary Experience in Chinese Buddhism* (Honolulu: Kuroda Institute and University of Hawai'i Press, 2021), 181–82 (on demonic interruption in the *Great Vaipulya Dahāraṇī Scripture*). East Syrian Christianity at Turfan: Scott Fitzgerald Johnson, "The Languages of Christianity on the Silk Roads and the Transmission of Mediterranean Culture into Central Asia," in *Empires and Exchanges in Eurasian Late Antiquity: Rome, China, Iran, and the Steppe, ca. 250–750*, ed. Nicola Di Cosmo and Michael Maas (Cambridge: Cambridge University Press, 2018), 206–19. On the evolution of the Christian ethics of attentiveness in the early modern and modern periods see Daniel Jütte, "Sleeping in Church: Preaching, Boredom, and the Struggle for Attention in Medieval and Early Modern Europe," *American Historical Review* 125 (2020): 1147–74; David Marno, *Death Be Not Proud: The Art of Holy Attention* (Chicago: University of Chicago Press, 2016); Smith, "Disciplines of Attention in a Secular Age."

16. See especially Richard Sorabji, *Emotion and Peace of Mind: From Stoic Agitation to Christian Temptation* (Oxford: Oxford University Press, 2000); but also Brad Inwood, *Ethics and Human Action in Early Stoicism* (Oxford: Clarendon, 1985), 42–101, 127–81; Foucault, *Les aveux de la chair*, 106–45; Pierre Hadot, "Exercices spirituels," *Exercices spirituels et philosophie antique*, 2nd ed. (Paris: Études Augustiniennes, 1987), 13–58; Graiver, *Asceticism of the Mind*, 52–57, 83–89; and on the technical Stoic understanding of being undistracted/*aperispastos* see David L. Balch, "1 Cor. 7:32–35 and Stoic Debates about Marriage, Anxiety, and Distraction," *Journal of Biblical Literature* 102 (1983): 429–39.

17. Plutarch, *Peri polypragmosynes* 11, 12, 15; Lieve Van Hoof, *Plutarch's Practical Ethics: The Social Dynamics of Philosophy* (Oxford: Oxford University Press, 2010), esp. 176–210.

18. Cassian, *De institutis coenobiorum* 10.6–16. Cassian's concept of acedia was indebted to Evagrius of Pontus: Gabriel Bunge, *Akedia: Die geistliche Lehre des Evagrios Pontikos vom Überdruß* (Cologne: Luthe, 1989). Similarity of this condition to boredom in modern research: James Danckert and John D. Eastwood, *Out of My Skull: The Psychology of Boredom* (Cambridge, MA: Harvard University Press, 2020), 7–8. For variations on the diagnosis see Andrew Crislip, "The Sin of Sloth or the Illness of the Demons? The Demon of Acedia in Early Christian Monasticism," *Harvard Theological Review* 98 (2005): 143–69. For a critique of the Stoic dismissal of inner conflict: Inwood, *Ethics and Human Action in Early Stoicism*, 132–39.

19. Cassian, *Collationes* 7.7–15; likewise Evagrius, *Peri logismon* 37; Shenoute, "A Beloved Asked Me Years Ago," in *Discourses*, p. 181; quotation

from Evagrius, *On Thoughts* 33, trans. Sinkewicz, p. 176; David Brakke, *Demons and the Making of the Monk: Spiritual Combat in Early Christianity* (Cambridge, MA: Harvard University Press, 2006); Graiver, *Asceticism of the Mind*; Columba Stewart, "Evagrius Ponticus and the 'Eight Generic Logismoi,'" in *In the Garden of Evil: The Vices and Culture in the Middle Ages*, ed. Richard Newhauser (Toronto: Pontifical Institute of Mediaeval Studies, 2005), 3–34.

20. Cassian, *De institutis coenobiorum* 7.3–4 (*carnis motus, detorquere*), still with some debts to Evagrius: Columba Stewart, "Evagrius Ponticus and the Eastern Monastic Tradition on the Intellect and Passions," *Modern Theology* 27 (2011): 263–75, at 269–71; and more generally Stewart, *Cassian the Monk* (New York: Oxford University Press, 1998). Density of Evagrius's social networks: Elizabeth A. Clark, *The Origenist Controversy: The Cultural Construction of an Early Christian Debate* (Princeton: Princeton University Press, 1992), 20–38, 60–61, 188–91. Illuminator: Isaac of Nineveh, *Discourses* 2.3.3.92 (= *Centuries on Knowledge* 3.92). Examiner: Brouria Bitton-Ashkelony, "Pure Prayer and Ignorance: Dadisho' Qaṭraya and the Greek Ascetic Legacy," *Studi e materiali di storia delle religioni* 78, 1 (2012): 200–26, quoting a letter of Dadisho' at 202. For a fine-grained analysis of the ways a seemingly traditional monastic text can radically depart from its influences, see Albrecht Diem, *The Pursuit of Salvation: Community, Space, and Discipline in Early Medieval Monasticism* (Turnhout, Belgium: Brepols, 2021), esp. 243–345.

21. Dadisho' Qaṭraya, *Shelya* 32a–34a; Barsanuphius and John, *Letters* 250 (among many others); Peter Brown, *The Body and Society: Men, Women, and Sexual Renunciation in Early Christianity* (New York: Columbia University Press, 1988), 224–35; Brouria Bitton-Ashkelony and Aryeh Kofsky, *The Monastic School of Gaza* (Leiden: Brill, 2006), 152–53; Jonathan L. Zecher, *The Role of Death in* The Ladder of Divine Ascent *and the Greek Ascetic Tradition* (Oxford: Oxford University Press, 2015), 167–72.

22. Pseudo-Macarius, *Logoi* 15.25 (collection 2), trans. Maloney, p. 118; Brakke, *Demons*, esp. 21–22; Graiver, *Asceticism of the Mind*, 45–47. On the varying interpretations of which selfish impulse, exactly, kickstarted the Fall: Brown, *Body and Society*, 220, 326–27, 408–27; Shaw, *Burden of the Flesh*, 175–76. These views departed from Evagrius's controversial position that the Fall had already taken place when intellects had separated from God, before material creation: Clark, *Origenist Controversy*, 71–74.

23. Patricia Cox Miller, *The Corporeal Imagination: Signifying the Holy in Late Ancient Christianity* (Philadelphia: University of Pennsylvania Press, 2009), 19, 24–27, 31; Luke Dysinger, *Psalmody and Prayer in the Writings of Evagrius Ponticus* (Oxford: Oxford University Press, 2005), 27–31, 172–95; Columba Stewart, "Imageless Prayer and the Theological Vision of Evagrius Ponticus," *JECS* 9 (2001): 173–204, at 176.

24. *AP/GS* 16.25; *AP/PJ* 16.16; *AP/S* 1.6.185 (no mention of the first monk's clothing in this version). In the Greek and Syriac versions, the second

monk is styled as a Libyan—someone born beyond the Roman Empire. In the Latin version, the term of choice is *rusticus genere*, "country boy." On the continuities between classical and monastic self-discipline see Zachary B. Smith, *Philosopher-Monks, Episcopal Authority, and the Care of the Self: The Apophthegmata Patrum in Fifth-Century Palestine* (Turnhout, Belgium: Brepols, 2017), 171–280.

25. *Consultationes Zacchei* 3.4. Diversity: *Cambridge History of Medieval Monasticism in the Latin West*, ed. Alison I. Beach and Isabelle Cochelin (Cambridge: Cambridge University Press, 2020), esp. Claudio Rapp and Albrecht Diem, "The Monastic Laboratory: Perspectives of Research in Late Antique and Early Medieval Monasticism," 1:19–39.

26. On the evolution of the Syriac term *iḥidaya* see Sidney H. Griffith, "Monks, 'Singles,' and the 'Sons of the Covenant': Reflections on Syriac Ascetic Terminology," in *Eulogema: Studies in Honor of Robert Taft, S.J.*, ed. E. Carr et al. (Rome: Centro Studi S. Anselmo, 1993), 141–60. The Old English terms are first attested in the tenth century: Sarah Foot, *Veiled Women*, vol. 1, *The Disappearance of Nuns from Anglo-Saxon England* (Aldershot, England: Ashgate, 2000), xiii, 26–30.

27. See the overviews in *Cambridge History of Medieval Monasticism in the Latin West*, ed. Beach and Cochelin, vol. 1; *La vie quotidienne des moines en Orient et en Occident (IVᵉ–Xᵉ siècle)*, vol. 1, *L'état des sources*, ed. Olivier Delouis and Maria Mossakowska-Gaubert (Cairo and Athens: Institut Français d'Archéologie Orientale and École Française d'Athènes, 2015); *Monachismes d'Orient: Images, échanges, influences. Hommage à Antoine Guillaumont*, ed. Florence Jullien and Marie-Joseph Pierre (Turnhout, Belgium: Brepols, 2011).

28. Monastic-lay social networks: Edward J. Watts, *Riot in Alexandria: Tradition and Group Dynamics in Late Antique Pagan and Christian Communities* (Berkeley: University of California Press, 2010), 95–130. Charity, liturgy, endowments: see next chapter. Real estate and finance: Michel Kaplan, "Aumônes, artisanat, domaines fonciers: Les monastères byzantins et la logique économique (Vᵉ–Xᵉ siècle)," in *La vie quotidienne des moines en Orient et en Occident (IVᵉ–Xᵉ siècle)*, vol. 2, *Questions transversales*, ed. Olivier Delouis and Maria Mossakowska-Gaubert (Cairo and Athens: Institut Français d'Archéologie Orientale and École Française d'Athènes, 2019), 2:359–71; *Monastic Estates in Late Antique and Early Islamic Egypt: Ostraca, Papyri, and Essays in Memory of Sarah Clackson*, ed. Anne Boud'hors et al. (Cincinnati: American Society of Papryologists, 2009); Jean-Pierre Devroey, "Monastic Economics in the Carolingian Age," trans. Michael Webb, in *Cambridge History of Medieval Monasticism in the Latin West*, ed. Beach and Cochelin, 1:466–84. Non-Christian donors: Jack Tannous, *The Making of the Medieval Middle East: Religion, Society, and Simple Believers* (Princeton: Princeton University Press, 2018), 381. Intellectual centers: see chaps. 4 and 5. Muslim visitors: Elizabeth Campbell, "A Heaven of Wine: Muslim-Christian Encounters at Monasteries" (PhD diss., Uni-

versity of Washington, 2009); Suleiman A. Mourad, "Christian Monks in Islamic Literature: A Preliminary Report on Some Arabic Apophthegmata Patrum," *Bulletin of the Royal Institute for Inter-Faith Studies* 6 (2004): 81–98; Sabino Chialà, "Les mystiques musulmans lecteurs des écrits chrétiens: Quelques échos d'Apophtegmes," *Proche-Orient Chrétien* 60 (2010): 352–67. Violence: Brent D. Shaw, *Sacred Violence: African Christians and Sectarian Hatred in the Age of Augustine* (Cambridge: Cambridge University Press, 2011), esp. 247, 472, 780; Watts, *Riot in Alexandria*, 19 ("shock troops"); Lenski, "Valens and the Monks," 114. Peacekeeping: Pablo C. Díaz, "Social Plurality and Monastic Diversity in Late Antique Hispania (Sixth to Eighth Century)," trans. Susan González Knowles, in *Cambridge History of Medieval Monasticism in the Latin West*, ed. Beach and Cochelin, 1:195–212, at 197.

CHAPTER 1. THE WORLD

1. Adam: Asterius, *Liber ad Renatum* 3–4. Moses: Claudia Rapp, *Holy Bishops in Late Antiquity: The Nature of Christian Leadership in an Age of Transition* (Berkeley: University of California Press, 2005), 112–14, 128–38; Bitton-Ashkelony and Kofsky, *The Monastic School of Gaza*, 62–81. Acts: Peter Brown, *Through the Eye of a Needle: Wealth, the Fall of Rome, and the Making of Christianity in the West, 350–550 AD* (Princeton: Princeton University Press, 2012), 167–72; Conrad Leyser, *Authority and Asceticism from Augustine to Gregory the Great* (Oxford: Clarendon, 2000), 8–12, 45–47; Christian C. Sahner, "Islamic Legends about the Birth of Monasticism: A Case Study in the Late Antique Milieu of the Qur'ān and Tafsīr," in *The Late Antique World of Early Islam*, ed. Robert G. Hoyland (Princeton: Darwin Press, 2015), 393–435. Multiple origin stories: James E. Goehring, *Ascetics, Society, and the Desert: Studies in Early Egyptian Monasticism* (Harrisburg, PA: Trinity Press International, 1999), esp. 13–35, 137–61; Samuel Rubenson, *The Letters of St. Antony: Monasticism and the Making of a Saint* (Minneapolis: Fortress Press, 1995).

2. Moses: Palladius, *Historia Lausiaca* 19. Apollo: *AP/G* Apollo 2. Bar Sahde: Isho'denaḥ of Basra, *Ktaba d-nakputa* 77. Paul: *Historia monachorum in Aegypto* 24.1; Palladius, *Historia Lausiaca* 22.7.

3. An exception illustrating the rule: the monk Severinus was so cagey about his birthplace and backstory that his hagiographer felt the need to give a lengthy explanation for its absence in his narrative: Eugippius to Paschascius, in *Vita Severini*, pp. 2–3.

4. Goodness of creation: Basil, *Great Asketikon*, SR 92, and for Genesis commentaries on this point see Basil, *Hexaemeron* 4.6–7, 5.4; Ambrose of Milan, *Exameron* 2.5, 3.9; Augustine of Hippo, *De Genesi ad litteram* 2.6, 8.6, 8.13–16; Eucherius, *Instructiones* 1.11; *Intexuimus*, lines 249–51; Bede, *In principium Genesis* 1.18, 2.9, 2.16–17. Sample lists of entangle-

ments: Basil, *Great Asketikon*, LR 8 (family, friends, possessions, work, habits); *AP/GN*, N. 739 (friends, legal disputes, property, farming, livestock); Babai, *Rules* 16 (stories/*aḥādīth* and news/*akhbār*), in Vööbus, *Syriac and Arabic Documents*, p. 181.

5. Basil of Caesarea, *Great Asketikon*, LR 6, quotation 6.1.99, trans. Silvas pp. 178–79; Hildemar, *Expositio*, prologue ("in uno homine duas intentiones esse non posse"); similarly Isaiah, *Asketikon* 11.82. The impossibility of multitasking: Adam Gazzaley and Larry D. Rosen, *The Distracted Mind: Ancient Brains in a High-Tech World* (Cambridge, MA: MIT Press, 2016), 60–62, 72–73, 76–79.

6. See for example Éric Rebillard, *Christians and Their Many Identities in Late Antiquity, North Africa, 200–450 CE* (Ithaca and London: Cornell University Press, 2012); Seth Schwartz, *Were the Jews a Mediterranean Society? Reciprocity and Solidarity in Ancient Judaism* (Princeton: Princeton University Press, 2012); Alan Cameron, *The Last Pagans of Rome* (Oxford: Oxford University Press, 2011); Richard E. Payne, *A State of Mixture: Christians, Zoroastrians, and Iranian Political Culture in Late Antiquity* (Berkeley: University of California Press, 2015); Jason BeDuhn, *Augustine's Manichaean Dilemma*, vol. 1, *Conversion and Apostasy, 373–388 C.E.* (Philadelphia: University of Pennsylvania Press, 2010); Jack Tannous, *The Making of the Medieval Middle East: Religion, Society, and Simple Believers* (Princeton: Princeton University Press, 2018).

7. *History of Mar Yawnan* 3; *Vita Wandregiseli* 4, 7. Contexts: Richard Payne, "Monks, Dinars and Date Palms: Hagiographical Production and the Expansion of Monastic Institutions in the Persian Gulf," *Arabian Archaeology and Epigraphy* 22 (2011): 97–111; Kreiner, *The Social Life of Merovingian Hagiography in the Merovingian Kingdom* (Cambridge: Cambridge University Press, 2014), 67–69, 208–9. On the development of marriage as a Christian ethical commitment: Kate Cooper, *The Fall of the Roman Household* (Cambridge: Cambridge University Press, 2007); Michel Foucault, *Les aveux de la chair*, ed. Frédéric Gros, vol. 4 of *Histoire de la sexualité* (Paris: Gallimard, 2018), esp. 268–80. Policies on married postulants: Basil, *Great Asketikon*, LR 12; Cassian *Collationes* 21.1–10; Fulgentius of Ruspe, *Letters* 1.14 (a married person needs his or her spouse's permission even to give up sex); *So-Called Canons of Maruta* 54.30, 54.32, in Vööbus, *Syriac and Arabic Documents*; Ishoʻ Bar Nūn, *Canons* 16–17, 19, in ibid.; Barsanuphius and John, *Letters* 662. See also the case of Benedicta, whose fiancé hauled her to court for breaking off the engagement (but she won the trial): *Vita Fructuosi* 15.

8. John Moschos, *Pratum spirituale* 60; Leslie Dossey, "The Social Space of North African Asceticism," in *Western Monasticism ante litteram: Spaces of Monastic Observation in Late Antiquity and the Early Middle Ages*, ed. Hendrik Dey and Elizabeth Fentress (Turnhout, Belgium: Brepols, 2011), 137–57, at 140–46 (citing Augustine's *Ep.* 15* at 141); Susanna Elm, *Virgins of God: The Making of Asceticism in Late Antiquity* (Oxford: Claren-

don, 1994), 50–51, 158; Albrecht Diem, "The Gender of the Religious: Wo/Men and the Invention of Monasticism," in *The Oxford Handbook of Women and Gender in Medieval Europe*, ed. Judith Bennett and Ruth Karras (Oxford: Oxford University Press, 2013), 432–46, esp. 437–39; Ville Vuolanto, *Children and Asceticism in Late Antiquity: Continuity, Family Dynamics and the Rise of Christianity* (London: Routledge, 2015), demographics at 95–129; but see also Peter Brown, *The Body and Society: Men, Women, and Sexual Renunciation in Early Christianity* (New York: Columbia University Press, 1988), 266–68 on the genuine pull of *spiritual* companionship between men and women. On the privilege of time and dedication: Samuel Rubenson, "Early Monasticism and the Concept of a 'School,'" in *Monastic Education in Late Antiquity: The Transformation of Classical Paideia*, ed. Lillian I. Larsen and Samuel Rubenson (Cambridge: Cambridge University Press, 2018), 13–32, at 16–20.

9. Households and family members: Shenoute, *Rules* 37–41, 73, 258, 587; *Regula sanctorum patrum* 2.35; Leander, *De institutione virginum* 22; *RB* 69; *Regula monasterii Tarnatensis* 1.14–15, 12.9–11; *Vita Fructuosi* 3; Jonas of Bobbio, *Regula cuiusdam ad virgines* 23; Pablo C. Díaz, "*Regula communis*: Monastic Space and Social Context," in *Western Monasticism ante litteram*, ed. Dey and Fentress, 117–35; Vuolanto, *Children and Asceticism*, 147–76. Children: Mayke de Jong, *In Samuel's Image: Child Oblation in the Early Medieval West* (Leiden: Brill, 1996); Arietta Papaconstantinou, "Notes sur les actes de donation d'enfant au monastère thébain de Saint-Phoibammon," *Journal of Juristic Papyrology* 32 (2002): 83–105; Maria Chiara Giorda, "Children in Monastic Families in Egypt at the End of Antiquity," in *Children in Everyday Life in the Roman and Late Antique World*, ed. Christian Laes and Ville Vuolanto (London: Routledge, 2017), 232–46; Carrie Schroeder, "Children and Egyptian Monasticism," in *Children in Late Ancient Christianity*, ed. Cornelia B. Horn and Robert R. Phenix (Tübingen, Germany: Morh Siebeck, 2009), 317–38. Friends: Claudia Rapp, *Brother-Making in Late Antiquity and Byzantium: Monks, Laymen, and Christian Ritual* (Oxford: Oxford University Press, 2016), 88–179. Dígde: *Aithbe damsa bés mara*; Maeve Callan, "Líadain's *Lament*, Darerca's *Life*, and Íte's *Ísucán*: Evidence for Nuns' Literacies in Early Ireland," in *Nuns' Literacies in Medieval Europe: The Kansis City Dialogue*, ed. Virginia Blanton, Veronica O'Mara, and Patricia Stoop (Turnhout, Belgium: Brepols, 2015), 209–227, at 209–13.

10. Boud'hors and Heurtel, *Les ostraca coptes de la TT 29*. On monks' interest in pharaonic tombs see Elisabeth R. O'Connell, "Transforming Monumental Landscapes in Late Antique Egypt: Monastic Dwellings in Legal Documents from Western Thebes," *Journal of Early Christian Studies* 15 (2007): 239–73; Darlene L. Brooks Hedstrom, *The Monastic Landscape of Late Antique Egypt: An Archaeological Reconstruction* (Cambridge: Cambridge University Press, 2017), 115–16, 237–45, 284–89.

11. John Climacus, *Klimax* 1, trans. Luibheid and Russell, p. 79.

12. Gospels: Jerome, *Vita Hilarionis* 25; *AP/G* Theodore of Pherme 1; *AP/GN*, N. 392, 566; *AP/PJ* 6.5. Augustine: Brown, *Through the Eye of a Needle*, 177–83; Przemysław Nehring, "Disposal of Private Property: Theory and Practice in the Earliest Augustinian Monastic Communities," in *La vie quotidienne des moines en Orient et en Occident (IVᵉ–Xᵉ siècle)*, vol. 2, *Questions transversales*, ed. Olivier Delouis and Maria Mossakowska-Gaubert (Cairo and Athens: Institut Français d'Archéologie Orientale and École Française d'Athènes, 2019), 393–411; similar concerns in Barsanuphius and John, *Letters* 571–72. Curial property: Avshalom Laniado, "The Early Byzantine State and the Christian Ideal of Voluntary Poverty," in *Charity and Giving in Monotheistic Religions*, ed. Mariam Frankel and Yaacov Lev (Berlin: De Gruyter, 2009), 15–43. Cession by charter: Shenoute, *Rules* 243, 593, 595; Caesarius of Arles, *Regula ad virgines* 6; Caesarius, *Regula ad monachos* 1; Aurelian of Arles, *Regula ad virgines* 2; Aurelian, *Regula ad monachos* 3–4, 47; Donatus, *Regula* 7; cf. the Galician *Consensoria monachorum* 9, where monks are required to sign the book containing the monastery's policies about ownership!

13. Private property: Martin Krause, "Die koptischen Kaufurkunden von Klosterzellen des Apollo-Klosters von Bawit aus abbasidischer Zeit," in *Monastic Estates in Late Antique and Early Islamic Egypt: Ostraca, Papyri, and Essays in Memory of Sarah Clackson*, ed. Anne Boud'hors et al. (Cincinnati: American Society of Papyrologists, 2009), 159–69; Ewa Wipszycka, "Les ressources économiques des communautés monastiques en Égypte aux IVᵉ–VIIIᵉ siècles," in *La vie quotidienne des moines*, ed. Delouis and Mossakowska-Gaubert, 2:347–58, at 348–49; Hedstrom, *Monastic Landscape of Late Antique Egypt*, 133–37. Side gigs: Cassian, *De institutis coenobiorum* 7.7, 7.14; see also Shenoute, *Rules* 14, 17, 88, 288–89, 294, 376, 592; *Rule of Naqlun* 32; Donatus, *Regula* 9; Typikon of Pantelleria 16, in Thomas and Hero, *Byzantine Monastic Foundation Documents*.

14. Pseudo-Macarius, *Logoi* 14.3, trans. Maloney, p. 106 (my emphasis), similar is *Logoi* 45.1 and Cassian, *Collationes* 10.11.1 (the mind's renunciation of "the riches and vast resources of all its thoughts"). See also Sebastian P. Brock, "Radical Renunciation: The Ideal of Msarrqûtâ," in *To Train His Soul in Books: Syriac Asceticism in Early Christianity*, ed. Robin Darling Young and Monica J. Blanchard (Washington, DC: Catholic University of America Press, 2011), 122–33.

15. Possessive pronouns: Cassian, *De institutis coenobiorum* 4.13; Shenoute, *Rules* 472; Aurelian of Arles, *Regula ad monachos* 25; *RB* 33; Fructuosus of Braga, *Regula* 11. Clothes: Augustine, *Praeceptum* 5.1 (shared closet); Eugippius, *Regula* 1.99 (assigned clothes on rotation); *RB* 55.1–12 (assigned clothes); *Regula Pauli et Stephani* 27 (assigned clothes); *So-Called Canons of Maruta* 54.22, in Vööbus, *Syriac and Arabic Documents* (names in clothes); Babai, *Rules* 14, in ibid. (clothes on loan). Aughilde's cup: Étienne Louis, "Espaces monastiques sacrés et profanes à Hamage (Nord), VIIᵉ–

IXe siècles," in *Monastères et espace social: Genèse et transformation d'un sys-tème de lieux dans l'occident médiéval* (Turnhout, Belgium: Brepols, 2014), 435–72, at 462.

16. Locks: *Precepts* 107, in *Pachomian Koinonia* 2:162; Cassian, *De institutis coenobiorum* 4.15.1; Caesarius of Arles, *Regula ad virgines* 9, 51; Caesarius, *Regula ad monachos* 3; Aurelian of Arles, *Regula ad virgines* 6; Aurelian, *Regula ad monachos* 6; *Regula monasterii Tarnatensis* 2.1; Donatus, *Regula* 11.1; Isidore, *Regula* 19; Francesca Sogliani, "Proposte di ricostruzione dell'arredo di alcuni ambienti monastici fra IX e XI secolo sulla base dei nuovi risulatati di scavo nel monastero volturnense," in *Monasteri in Europa occidentale (secoli VIII–XI): topografia e strutture*, ed. Flavia de Rubeis and Federico Marazzi (Rome: Viella, 2008), 523–50, at 335–38 (locks and keys at San Vincenzo). Hiding things in beds: *RB* 55.16–19. Separate beds: see chap. 3.

17. Vuolanto, *Children and Asceticism*, 45–80. Parents' house: Evagrius, *Antir-rhetikos* 3.22. Thinking of friends: Hildemar, *Expositio* 19.7. Nightmares: John Climacus, *Klimax* 3. Relatives in the same monastery: e.g., Gregory, *Life of Theodora of Thessalonike* 25–30, in Talbot, *Holy Women in Byzantium*.

18. Cassian, *De institutis coenobiorum* 4.16.2; Shenoute, *Rules* 597; Caesarius of Arles, *Regula ad virgines* 25; Caesarius, *Regula ad monachos* 15; Aurelian of Arles, *Regula ad virgines* 3–4; Aurelian, *Regula ad monachos* 6; *RB* 54; *Regula monasterii Tarnatensis* 19.1–4; Donatus, *Regula* 53; *Rules for Nuns* 9, in Vööbus, *Syriac and Arabic Documents*.

19. Parties: *Canons which are necessary for the monks* 8, in Vööbus, *Syriac and Arabic Documents*; *Rules attributed to Rabbula* 28, in ibid.; *Rule of Naqlun* 30; Donatus, *Regula* 53.3; Jacob of Edessa to Joḥannan the Stylite 49.14, in Vööbus, *Synodicon* 1:231. Weddings: *Regula monasterii Tarnatensis* 13.1–3. Baptisms and godparenting: Caesarius of Arles, *Regula ad virgines* 11; Caesarius, *Regula ad monachos* 10; Aurelian of Arles, *Regula ad virgines* 16; Aurelian, *Regula ad monachos* 20; Ferreolus of Uzès, *Regula* 15; Dona-tus, *Regula* 54.1; *Rules for Nuns* 8, in Vööbus, *Syriac and Arabic Documents*; *Canons which are necessary for the monks* 6; *Rules attributed to Rabbula* 28; Jacob of Edessa to Joḥannan the Stylite 49.14; Theodore Studites, *Testa-ment* 8, in Thomas and Hero, *Byzantine Monastic Foundation Documents*. But see John Moschos, *Pratum spirituale* 3 (baptisms at a Chalcedonian monastery). Saints' feasts: *Rules for the Nuns* 2; Jacob of Edessa to Joḥan-nan the Stylite 49.14; Jacob of Edessa, *Canons* 8, in Vööbus, *Syriac and Arabic Documents*.

20. No visits: Rabbula, *Admonitions for the Monks* 13, in Vööbus, *Syriac and Arabic Documents*; *Rule of Naqlun* 9, 11. Visits: Boud'hors and Heurtel, *Les ostraca coptes*, no. 252 (Frange); Gregory the Great, *Dialogi* 2.33–34 (Benedict); Palladius, *Historia Lausiaca* 39.1–2 (Piôr); Jonas of Bobbio, *Vita Columbani* 2.5.

21. Misgivings and restrictions regarding travel or leaving the cell: Rabbula of Edessa, *Admonitions for the Monks* 2–3, in Vööbus, *Syriac and Arabic*

Documents; Evagrius, *Ad monachos* 55; Cassian, *De institutis coenobiorum* 10.3, 10.6, 10.17–25; Cassian, *Collationes* 1.20.5; *AP/G* Arsenius 11; Isaiah, *Asketikon* 10.4, 10.75–80; Canons of Mar Mattai 1, in Vööbus, *History of Asceticism in the Syrian Orient* 3:173; Shenoute, *Rules* 215, 290; *RM* 57.7–12 (tablets); *RB* 67.7; *Regula monasterii Tarnatensis* 2.2, 3.1; Ferreolus of Uzès, *Regula* 20; Columbanus, *Regula coenobialis*, 219B; Donatus, *Regula* 31.4; John of Dalyatha, *Memre* 5. Heads of monasteries: see, e.g., Christina Harrington, *Women in a Celtic Church: Ireland 450–1150* (Oxford: Oxford University Press, 2002), 54–63; Albrecht Diem, "Gregory's Chess Board: Monastic Conflict and Competition in Early Medieval Gaul," in *Compétition et sacré au haut Moyen Âge: Entre médiation et exclusion*, ed. Philippe Depreux, François Bougard, and Régine Le Jan (Turnhout, Belgium: Brepols, 2015), 165–91, at 169. Traveling scribes: *Lebenswelten des frühen Mittelalters in 36 Kapiteln*, ed. Peter Erhart (St. Gallen, Switzerland: Stiftsarchiv, 2019), 37. Talking about trips: *Statuta patrum* 15–16; *RB* 67.5. People-watching: *AP/GN*, N. 161; Augustine, *Praeceptum* 4 (checking out members of the opposite sex); Hildemar, *Expositio* 67 (eavesdropping on inappropriate conversations). Sex and the marketplace: *AP/GN*, N. 179 (= *AP/GS* 5.31; *AP/PJ* 5.27).

22. Paradise: *Regula sancti Macharii* 6. Downcast eyes: e.g., John of Ephesus, *Lives of the Eastern Saints* 21, at 2:563; Sabino Chialà, "Les mystiques musulmans lecteurs des écrits chrétiens: Quelques échos d'Apophtegmes," *Proche-Orient Chrétien* 60 (2010): 352–67, at 365. See also chap. 3 on monks' obligations to guard their gaze even at home. Eyes-on-the-prize metaphor: Cassian, *Collationes* 1.5.1.

23. Macrina: Elm, *Virgins of God*, 39–47, 78–91. Sons and Daughters of the Covenant (or Resurrection): Rabbula of Edessa, *Commands and Admonitions to the Priests and the Benai Qeiāmā*, in Vööbus, *Syriac and Arabic Documents*; Arthur Vööbus, "The Institution of the Benai Qeiama and Benet Qeiama in the Ancient Syrian Church," *Church History* 3 (1961): 19–27; Brown, *Body and Society*, 101–2, 204, 329; Sidney H. Griffith, "Monks, 'Singles,' and the 'Sons of the Covenant': Reflections on Syriac Ascetic Terminology," in *Eulogema: Studies in Honor of Robert Taft, S.J.*, ed. E. Carr et al. (Rome: Centro Studi S. Anselmo, 1993), 141–60. Papyri: Caroline T. Schroeder, "Women in Anchoritic and Semi-Anchoritic Monasticism in Egypt: Rethinking the Landscape," *Church History* 83 (2014): 1–17.

24. *RM* 1, 7.22–45; *RB* 1; Leander of Seville, *De institutione virginum* 26. ("Pro lege eis est desideriorum uoluntas, cum quicquid putauerint vel elegerint" appears in *RM* 1.8–9 and *RB* 1.8–9.) *Apotaktikoi*: James E. Goehring, *Ascetics, Society, and the Desert: Studies in Early Egyptian Monasticism* (Harrisburg, PA: Trinity Press International, 1999), 53–72; Wipszycka, *Moines et communautés monastiques*, 308–16. Nilus: Daniel Folger Caner, *Wandering, Begging Monks: Spiritual Authority and the Promotion of Monasticism in Late Antiquity* (Berkeley: University of California Press, 2002), 177–90. On the term "Sarabaite," which the *RM* and *RB* used—following

Cassian—to describe monks who did "whatever they wanted": Béatrice Caseau, "L'image du mauvais moine: Les remnuoths et les sarabaïtes de Jérôme et de Cassien," *Zbornik Radova Vizantološkog Instituta/Recueil des Travaux de l'Institut d'Études Byzantines* 46 (2009): 11–25. "Monk" as a term of validation: David Brakke, "Heterodoxy and Monasticism around the Mediterranean Sea," in *The Cambridge History of Medieval Monasticism in the Latin West*, ed. Alison I. Beach and Isabelle Cochelin (Cambridge: Cambridge University Press, 2020), 1:128–43, at 132.

25. Itinerant monks: Caner, *Wandering, Begging Monks*, esp. 199–205. Women as domestic ascetics: Goehring, *Ascetics, Society, and the Desert*, 53–72; Schroeder, "Women in Anchoritic and Semi-Anchoritic Monasticism"; Elm, *Virgins of God*; Brown, *Body and Society*, 259–84; Eliana Magnani, "Female House Ascetics from the Fourth to the Twelfth Century," trans. Lochin Brouillard, in *Cambridge History of Medieval Monasticism in the Latin West*, ed. Beach and Cochelin, 1:213–31; Kim Bowes, *Private Worship, Public Values, and Religious Change in Late Antiquity* (Cambridge: Cambridge University Press, 2008), 71–99, 152–57; Lisa Kaaren Bailey, *The Religious Worlds of the Laity in Late Antique Gaul* (London: Bloomsbury, 2016), 38–42; Harrington, *Women in a Celtic Church*, 35–36, 112–18. Jerome: Andrew Cain, "The Letter Collections of Jerome of Stridon," in *Late Antique Letter Collections: A Critical Introduction and Reference Guide*, ed. Cristiana Sogno, Bradley K. Storin, and Edward J. Watts (Oakland: University of California Press, 2017), 221–38; Caseau, "L'image du mauvais moine." Later monks continued to pick up on the gendered connotations of these criticisms: e.g., Lynda L. Coon, *Dark Age Bodies: Gender and Monastic Practice in the Early Medieval West* (Philadelphia: University of Pennsylvania Press, 2010), 77–79, 111–12.

26. John Rufus, *Vita Petri* 11, trans. Horn and Phenix, p. 13; John of Ephesus, *Lives* 31; Cassian, *Collationes* 18.14 (Piamun).

27. Caseau, "L'image du mauvais moine." On monks' habits of criticizing alternative models see Diem, "Gregory's Chess Board," esp. 165–69. On the fantasy of total detachment see, e.g., *Historia monachorum* 1.36, 1.44. For a critique see Cassian, *Collationes* 24 (which nevertheless argues *against* domestic monasticism).

28. Darlene L. Brooks Hedstrom and Hendrik Dey, "The Archaeology of the Earliest Monasteries," in *Cambridge History of Medieval Monasticism in the Latin West*, ed. Beach and Cochelin, 1:73–96; Brooks Hedstrom, *The Monastic Landscape of Late Antique Egypt*, 198–273; *Western Monasticism ante litteram*, ed. Dey and Fentress; *Monasteri in Europa occidentale*, ed. De Rubeis and Marazzi; Luis Caballero Zoreda, "El conjunto monástico de Santa María de Melque (Toledo). Siglos VII–IX (Criterios seguidos para identificar monasterios hispánicos tardo antiguos)," in *Monjes y monasterios hispanos an la Alta Edad Media*, ed. José Angel García de Cortázar and Ramón Teja (Aguilar de Campoo: Fundación Santa María le Real—Centro de Estudios del Románico, 2006), 99–144; Eleonora Destefanis,

"Archeologia dei monasteri altomedievali tra acquisizioni raggiunte e nuove prospettive di ricerca," *Post-Classical Archaeologies* 1 (2011): 349–82; Slobodan Ćurčić, *Architecture in the Balkans: From Diocletian to Süleyman the Magnificent* (New Haven: Yale University Press, 2010), 142–46; Joseph Patrich, "Recent Archaeological Research on Monasteries in *Palæstina Byzantina*: An Update on Distribution," in *La vie quotidienne des moines*, ed. Delouis and Mossakowska-Gaubert, 2:77–106, cisterns with graffiti at 83–84; O'Connell, "Transforming Monumental Landscapes in Late Antique Egypt," wall paint at p. 251. Macedonius: Theodoret, *Historia religiosa* 13.2.

29. Saint Sabas: Joseph Patrich, "Monastic Landscapes," in *Recent Research in the Late Antique Countryside*, ed. William Boden, Luke Lavan, and Carlos Machado (Leiden: Brill, 2003), 413–45, at 428. Kharg: Marie-Joseph Steve, *L'Île de Khãrg: Une page de l'histoire du Golfe Persique et du monachisme oriental* (Neuchâtel: Recherches et Publications, 2003), 85–153. Hamage: Louis, "Espaces monastiques sacrés et profanes." Punta de l'Illa: epitaph of Justinian in *Inscriptiones Hispaniae Christianae*, ed. Emil Hübner, Supplement (Berlin: Reimer, 1900), no. 409 ("Hic miro maris insolam munimine saepsit / In qua maris circumfluentibus undis").

30. Patrich, "Monastic Landscapes," 428–33; Goehring, *Ascetics, Society, and the Desert*, 89–109; Brooks Hedstrom, *The Monastic Landscape of Late Antique Egypt*, 157–64; Jakob Ashkenazi, "Holy Man versus Monk—Village and Monastery in the Late Antique Levant: Between Hagiography and Archaeology," *Journal of the Economic and Social History of the Orient* 57 (2014): 745–65; Olivier Delouis, "Portée et limites de l'archéologie monastique dans les Balkans et en Asie Mineure jusqu'au Xe siècle," in *Vie quotidienne des moines*, vol. 1, *L'état des sources*, ed. Olivier Delouis and Maria Mossakowska-Gaubert (Cairo and Athens: Institut Français d'Archéologie Orientale and École Française d'Athènes, 2015), 251–74, at 257 (baths).

31. Richard E. Payne, *A State of Mixture: Christians, Zoroastrians, and Iranian Political Culture in Late Antiquity* (Berkeley: University of California Press, 2015), 59–92 (Yazdin and Pethion); Mateu Riera Rullan, "El monasterio de la isla de Cabrera (Islas aleares, siglos V–VIII D.C.). Testimonios arqueológicos de los monjes reprobados por el pap Gregorio Magno," *Hortus Artium Medievalium* 19 (2013): 47–61; Miquel Rosselló, "El conjunto monástico de la Punta de l'Illa de Cullera," in *Los orígenes del cristianismo en Valencia y su entorno*, ed. Albert Ribera i Lacomba (Valencia: Ajuntamenta de València, 2000), 143–50.

32. Palladius, *Historia Lausiaca* 34.4, trans. Wortley, p. 79; *AP/G* Syncletica 19, trans. Ward, p. 234; Darlene L. Brooks Hedstrom, "The Geography of the Monastic Cell in Early Egyptian Monastic Literature," *Church History* 78 (2009): 756–91, esp. 762–63, 779–91 ("cell of the heart").

33. *So-Called Canons of Maruta* 47, in Vööbus, *Syriac and Arabic Documents*.

34. Jerome, *Vita Hilarionis* 11.

35. The pioneering article is Peter Brown, "The Rise and Function of the Holy Man in Late Antiquity," *Journal of Roman Studies* 61 (1971): 80–101; see also Brown, *Treasure in Heaven: The Holy Poor in Early Christianity* (Charlottesville: University of Virginia Press, 2016), 51–70 (quotation at 51); John of Ephesus, *Lives of the Eastern Saints* 4; *Syriac Life of Saint Simeon Stylites* 59. But note Jacob of Edessa's opinion in the seventh century: stylites should do less talking in order not to be distracted from their prayers. If they wanted to get involved in people's lives, they should come down from their columns! (49.5 in Vööbus, *The Synodicon in the West Syrian Tradition*.)

36. Dossey, "The Social Space of North African Asceticism," 148–52; Brown, *Treasure in Heaven*, 71–108. Women visitors: *Historia monachorum* 1.4–9, 1.12; *AP/G* Arsenius 28. Shenoute of Atripe, always a standout abbot, much more aggressively inserted himself into the politics of labor and landholding, not unlike his Syrian colleagues: Ariel G. López, *Shenoute of Atripe and the Uses of Poverty: Rural Patronage, Religious Conflict, and Monasticism in Late Antique Egypt* (Berkeley: University of California Press, 2013), esp. 37–66, 96–127.

37. Cassian, *Collationes* 9.2–3 (Abba Isaac); Vööbus, *History of Asceticism in the Syrian Orient*, 3:39, quoting Ephrem's memra "On Solitaries and Mourners."

38. Daniel Caner, *The Rich and the Pure: Philanthropy and the Making of Christian Society in Early Byzantium* (Oakland: University of California Press, 2021), 24 (Justinian) and 180 (Simeon); Ferreolus, *Regula*, prologue; Ferrandus, *Vita Fulgentii* 10 ("distracted" trans. Eno, p. 26). Donations *pro anima* and prayer professionals: Brown, *Ransom of the Soul*, 149–211 (*remedium* as "protection" at 166); Caner, *The Rich and the Pure*, 192–228; Anne-Marie Helvétius, "Le sexe des anges," in *De la différence des sexes: Le genre en histoire*, ed. Michèle Riot-Sarcey (Paris: Larousse, 2010), esp. 110–21; Albrecht Diem, *Das monastische Experiment: Die Rolle der Keuschheit bei der Entstehung des westlichen Klosterwesens* (Münster: LIT, 2004), 173–85, 200–202, 208–14, 310–21; Gisela Muschiol, *Famula dei: Zur Liturgie in merowingischen Frauenklöstern* (Münster: Aschendorff, 1994), esp. 178–91; Philippe Jobert, *La notion de donation: Convergences, 630–750* (Paris: Belles Lettres, 1977), 205–25.

39. Churches closed to public: Barbara Rosenwein, *Negotiating Space: Power, Restraint, and the Privileges of Immunity* (Ithaca, NY: Cornell University Press, 1997), 59–73; Mayke de Jong, "Monastic Prisoners or Opting Out? Political Coercion and Honour in the Frankish Kingdoms," in *Topographies of Power in the Early Middle Ages*, ed. Jong and Franz Theuws (Leiden: Brill, 2001), 291–328; Diem, *Das monastische Experiment*, esp. 191–93, 255–57, 314–16; Kreiner, *Social Life*, 220–22; Albrecht Diem, *The Pursuit of Salvation: Community, Space, and Discipline in Early Medieval Monasticism* (Turnhout, Belgium: Brepols, 2021), 265–331, 376–77. Qasr el-Banat: Beat Brenk, "La progettazione dei monasteri nel Vicino Ori-

ente, ovvero quello che i testi non dicono," in *Monasteri in Europa occidentale*, ed. de Rubeis and Marazzi, 21–37, at 25–26. Graffiti: Silviu Anghel, "Early Rock-Carved Monasteries in the Northwestern Balkans," in *Western Monasticism ante litteram*, ed. Dey and Fentress, 239–72. Medical and social services: Brown, *Treasure in Heaven*, 89–108; López, *Shenoute*; Andrew T. Crislip, *From Monastery to Hospital: Christian Monasticism and the Transformation of Health Care in Late Antiquity* (Ann Arbor: University of Michigan Press, 2005), 100–42; Heidi Marx-Wolf, "Religion, Medicine, and Health," in *A Companion to Religion in Late Antiquity*, ed. Josef Lössl and Nicholas J. Baker-Brian (Hoboken: Wiley, 2018), 511–28; Daniel Caner, *The Rich and the Pure*, 35–70. Penance: Guy Geltner, "*Detrusio*, Penal Cloistering in the Middle Ages," *Révue Bénédictine* 118 (2008): 89–108.

40. Guests' luggage: *So-Called Canons of Maruta* 51.10, in Vööbus, *Syriac and Arabic Documents*. Showing off: John Climacus, *Klimax* 4, 22. Questions, conversation: Isaiah, *Asketikon* 12.9; Barsanuphius and John, *Letters* 309–12. Carolingian nostalgia: Coon, *Dark Age Bodies*, 128. Carolingian obligations: e.g., Janneke Raaijmakers, *The Making of the Monastic Community of Fulda, c. 744–c. 900* (Cambridge: Cambridge University Press, 2012), 53. Bad thoughts and travelers: Sims-Williams, *An Ascetic Miscellany*, E28/66, p. 169.

41. Elizabeth S. Bolman, "'The Possessions of Our Poverty': Beauty, Wealth, and Asceticism in the Shenoutean Federation," in *The Red Monastery Church: Beauty and Asceticism in Upper Egypt*, ed. Bolman (New Haven: Yale University Press, 2016), 17–25; López, *Shenoute*, 67–95.

42. Gregory, *Dialogi* 3.14.2–5; Brown, *Treasure in Heaven*, 72, citing Zosimos, *Historia nova* 5.23; more generally Brown, *Through the Eye of a Needle*; Ian Wood, *The Transformation of the Roman West* (Leeds: ARC Humanities Press, 2018), 91–108; Lukas Amadeus Schachner, "Economic Production in the Monasteries of Egypt and *Oriens*, AD 320–800" (PhD diss., Oxford University, 2005–6), 84–99; Charanis, "The Monks as an Element in Byzantine Society," 83, with reference to the work of V. G. Vasilievsky; and on the minimal recirculation of this wealth see Brent Shaw, "Charity and the Poor in Roman Imperial Society," *Religion in the Roman Empire* 6 (2020): 229–67, at 257–63. Because donations were always made locally (there were no centralized donations to "the Church"), some monasteries were not at all well endowed or long-lived: e.g., Michel Kaplan, "Aumônes, artisanat, domaines fonciers: Les monastères byzantins et la logique économique (V^e–Xe siècle)," in *La vie quotidienne des moines*, ed. Delouis and Mossakowska-Gaubert, 2:359–71.

43. Shenoute, *Rules* 247, 250, 267, 316–17, 323, 378, 404, quotation no. 522, trans. Layton at p. 315. See also Rabbula, *Admonitions for the Monks* 25, in Vööbus, *Syriac and Arabic Documents*; Augustine, *Ordo monasterii* 8; Isaiah, *Asketikon* 11.52–53. On Shenoute's presentation of himself see López, *Shenoute*, 37–66.

44. Ekkehard IV, *Casus sancti Galli* 14 (Conrad I, who tried to turn the heads of young monks with the enticement of apples), 146 (Otto I, who purposefully dropped his staff in a quiet church); *So-Called Canons of Maruta* 50.6, in Vööbus, *Syriac and Arabic Documents*, p. 131.

45. Bishops: Claudia Rapp, *Holy Bishops in Late Antiquity: The Nature of Christian Leadership in an Age of Transition* (Berkeley: University of California Press, 2005), 100–152; Brown, *Through the Eye of a Needle*, 423–28. Exile: Judith Herrin, "Changing Functions of Monasteries for Women during Byzantine Iconoclasm," in *Byzantine Women: Varieties of Experience, 800–1200*, ed. Lynda Carland (Aldershot, England: Ashgate, 2006), 1–15; Jong, "Monastic Prisoners"; and for wider context see Julia Hillner, *Prison, Punishment and Penance in Late Antiquity* (Cambridge: Cambridge University Press, 2015), 194–274.

46. *Vita patrum Iurensium* 1.10–12; see also Gregory of Tours, *Liber vitae patrum* 1.3 (where the same abbot, Romanus, expresses a similar concern).

CHAPTER 2. COMMUNITY

1. Fortunatus, *Vita Paterni*, esp. 9.29.

2. John Climacus, *Klimax* 8. Different abilities: Basil, *Great Asketikon*, LR 7; Cassian, *De institutis coenobiorum* 5.4; Columbanus, *Regula Columbani* 10; John Moschos, preface to *Pratum spirituale*. On the modern attention economy in need of collective action: Johann Hari, *Stolen Focus: Why You Can't Pay Attention—and How to Think Deeply Again* (New York: Crown, 2022), esp. 143–70.

3. Basil, *Great Asketikon*, LR 7. Wild animals: e.g., *AP/GN*, N. 516. Ephrem: Arthur Vööbus, *History of Asceticism in the Syrian Orient: A Contribution to the History of Culture in the Near East* (Leuven: CSCO, 1960), 2:94–95.

4. John Climacus, *Klimax* 25, trans. Luibheid and Russell, p. 222; Joseph Ḥazzaya, *Lettre sur les trois étapes de la vie monastique* 3.66. Advanced prayer in isolation: Brouria Bitton-Ashkelony, *The Ladder of Prayer and the Ship of Stirrings: The Praying Self in Late Antique East Syrian Christianity* (Leuven: Peeters, 2019), 168–69 (Evagrius of Pontus and John of Dalyatha on dolphins); Shemʿon d-Ṭaybutheh, *Book of Medicine* 186b, trans. Mingana, p. 46 ("When the waters are quiet and clear, the dolphins fly"). Attention-seeking: Cassian, *De institutis coenobiorum* 1.2.1, 1.2.3–4; *Regula monasterii Tarnatensis* 1.25; Isidore, *Regula* 19.

5. Cassian, *Collationes* 19.4–6. On desert tourism and pilgrimage literature: David Brakke, *Demons and the Making of the Monk: Spiritual Combat in Early Christianity* (Cambridge, MA: Harvard University Press, 2006), 127–56; Georgia Frank, *The Memory of the Eyes: Pilgrimages to Living Saints in Christian Late Antiquity* (Berkeley: University of California Press, 2000).

6. Joseph Patrich, "Monastic Landscapes," in *Recent Research in the Late*

Antique Countryside, ed. William Boden, Luke Lavan, and Carlos Machado (Leiden: Brill, 2003), 413–45; Rosemary Cramp, "Monastic Settlements in Britain in the 7th–11th Centuries," in *Monasteri in Europe occidentale (secoli VIII–XI): Topografia e strutture*, ed. Flavia de Rubeis and Federico Marazzi (Rome: Viella, 2008), 113–33, Lindisfarne at 117; Kathryn M. Ringrose, "Monks and Society in Iconoclastic Byzantium," *Byzantine Studies / Études Byzantines* 6 (1979): 130–51. Izla: Dadisho', *Canons* 13, in Vööbus, *Syriac and Arabic Documents*; Babai, *Rules* 7, in ibid. Kellia: Nessim Henry Henein and Michel Wuttmann, *Kellia: L'ermitage copte QR 195*, vol. 1, *Archéologie et architecture* (Cairo: Institute Français d'Archéologie Orientale, 2000); Rodolphe Kasser, *Le site monastique des Kellia (Basse-Égypte): Recherches des années 1981–1983* (Louvain: Peeters, 1984).

7. Outsiders' impressions: Cassian, *De institutis coenobiorum* 7.13; *RM* 24.20–25. For a sense of the variation of rules as they are transmitted in Latin manuscripts, see Albrecht Diem's Monastic Manuscript Project, earlymedievalmonasticism.org. On the diversity of early monastic normative literature: Roberto Alciati, "The Invention of Western Monastic Literature: Texts and Communities," in *The Cambridge History of Medieval Monasticism in the Latin West*, ed. Alison I. Beach and Isabelle Cochelin (Cambridge: Cambridge University Press, 2020), 1:144–62; Albrecht Diem and Philip Rousseau, "Monastic Rules (Fourth to Ninth Century)," in ibid., 162–94; Anne Boud'hors, "Production, Diffusion et usage de la norme monastique: Les sources coptes," in *La vie quotidienne des moines en Orient et en Occident (IVᵉ–Xᵉ siècle)*, vol. 1, *L'état des sources*, ed. Olivier Delouis and Maria Mossakowska-Gaubert (Cairo and Athens: Institut Français d'Archéologie Orientale and École Française d'Athènes, 2015), 69–79; Diem, "Monastic Rules"; Diem, "Inventing the Holy Rule: Observations on the History of Monastic Observance in the Early Medieval West," in *Western Monasticism ante litteram: Spaces of Monastic Observation in Late Antiquity and the Early Middle Ages*, ed. Hendrik Dey and Elizabeth Fentress (Turnhout, Belgium: Brepols, 2011), 53–84.

8. *Vita Ceolfridi* 5–6; Bede, *Vita abbatum* 11; Bede, *Vita Cuthberti* 16 (and compare to the anonymous *Life* in Plummer's edition or Webb's translation); Ferreolus, *Regula*, preface ("mentium cervices" p. 126).

9. Zacharias Scholasticus, *History of Severus*, p. 52 (Zacharias was the other student); Hildemar, *Expositio* 48; Augustine, *De opere monachorum* 14.15; see further Sabine MacCormack, "The Virtue of Work: An Augustinian Transformation," *Antiquité Tardive* 9 (2001): 219–37. *Rule of Benedict*: Albrecht Diem, "Inventing the Holy Rule," 72–76; Diem, *The Pursuit of Salvation: Community, Space, and Discipline in Early Medieval Monasticism* (Turnhout, Belgium: Brepols, 2021), 331–45.

10. Palladius, *Historia Lausiaca* 5.3 (Alexandra), likewise 'Enanisho', *The Book of Paradise*, p. 139; Theodoret, *Historia religiosa* 2.5; Cassian, *De institutis coenobiorum* 3, on which see further Peter Jeffery, "Psalmody and Prayer in

Early Monasticism," in *Cambridge History of Medieval Monasticism in the Latin West*, ed. Beach and Cochelin, 1:112–27.

11. *AP/G* Antony 1; *Pseudo-Matthei Evangelium* 6.2 (Mary's *regula*), 9.1 ("in mente tua deo habitaculum praeparasti"). Modern analogs: Julian Lucas, "Focus Mode: Can 'Distraction-Free' Writing Devices Reconcile Writers and Computers?" *New Yorker*, December 20, 2021.

12. Caesarius, *Regula ad virgines* 19; Caesarius, *Regula ad monachos* 14; Eugippius, *Regula* 1.10–11; Isidore, *Regula* 5.

13. John Climacus, *Klimax* 20. Anchor: Cassian, *De intitutis coenobiorum* 2.14. Body and mind: *Rules of Abraham of Kaškar* 1, in Vööbus, *Syriac and Arabic Documents*. Work helps prayer: Caesarius, *Regula ad virgines* 15; Aurelian of Arles, *Regula ad monachos* 29; *Regula monasterii Tarnatensis* 6.5, see also 10.1–3. Prayer helps work: Isidore, *Regula* 5. Emptying: *RM* 50.3–5, 50.38; *Regula Pauli et Stephani* 34. On monastic manual labor more generally Caner, *Wandering, Begging Monks*, 38–47.

14. Peter Brown, *Treasure in Heaven: The Holy Poor in Early Christianity* (Charlottesville: University of Virginia Press, 2016), esp. 51–108; some qualifications in Daniel Caner, *The Rich and the Pure: Philanthropy and the Making of Christian Society in Early Byzantium* (Oakland: University of California Press, 2021), 167–71.

15. Ferreolus, *Regula* 28 (work assignments), 34 (dog). Basil anticipated similar excuses: Basil, *Great Asketikon*, SR 69.

16. *Regulations of Horsiesios* 15, in *Pachomian Koinonia* 2:202; Shenoute, *Rules* 52, 554; *AP/GN*, N. 118 (wildfire); Isaiah, *Asketikon* 8.18–19, 8.24; *Statuta patrum* 11–16 (demolition); *Regula orientalis* 5, 22 (also the metaphor of demolishing/ *destruere*); *Regula sanctorum patrum* (both recensions) 5.4; *RM* 9.42; Caesarius, *Regula ad virgines* 10; *Regula monasterii Tarnatensis* 8.6–7, 9.4, 13.4, 24 (immaturity), 29; *Canons which are necessary for the monks* 15, in Vööbus, *Syriac and Arabic Documents*; Columbanus, *Regula coenobialis*, 217D; John Climacus, *Klimax* 12, 28; Jonas, *Regula cuiusdam ad virgines* 9 (unbridling the mind); Fructuosus, *Regula* 5, 6; Donatus, *Regula* 28; Isaac of Nineveh, *Discourses* 1.16 (late frost *and* fire). See also Albrecht Diem, "On Opening and Closing the Body: Techniques of Discipline in Early Monasticism," in *Körper er-fassen*, ed. Kordula Schnegg and Elisabeth Grabner-Niel (Innsbruck: StudienVerlag, 2010), 89–112, esp. 96–103; Conrad Leyser, *Authority and Asceticism from Augustine to Gregory the Great* (Oxford: Clarendon, 2000), esp. 95–128; and on monastic acoustics more generally Kim Haines-Eitzen, *Sonorous Desert: What Deep Listening Taught Early Christian Monks—and What It Can Teach Us* (Princeton: Princeton University Press, 2022).

17. Tabennesi: *The Story of Anastasia* 3, in Brock and Harvey, *Holy Women of the Syrian Orient*, 144. Sadalberga: *Vita Sadalbergae* 25 ("alacris in colloquio"). Cluny: Scott G. Bruce, *Silence and Sign Language in Medieval Monasticism: The Clunaic Tradition, c. 900–1200* (Cambridge: Cambridge University Press, 2007), esp. 71–72 on limiting the potential for "talkative" signaling.

18. Rabbula of Edessa, *Admonitions for the Monks* 16, in Vööbus, *Syriac and Arabic Documents*; Isidore, *Regula* 5 ("Nihilque operis aput fratrem remaneat, ne sollicitudinis eius cura mentem ab intentione contemplationis auertat"). Stopping work immediately: Cassian, *De institutis coenobiorum* 4.12; *Statuta patrum* 31; *Regula sancti Macharii abbatis* 14; *Regula orientalis* 12; *Regula et instituta patrum* 6; *RM* 7, 55.1–4; *RB* 43.1–3; Aurelian, *Regula ad virgines* 24; Aurelian, *Regula ad monachos* 30; Donatus, *Regula* 12.1–3; Hildemar, *Expositio* 43 (including exceptions). Students distracted by transitions: James M. Lang, *Distracted: Why Students Can't Focus and What You Can Do about It* (New York: Basic, 2020), 228–31.

19. John Climacus, *Klimax* 19, trans. Luibheid and Russell, p. 195; Palladius, *Historia Lausiaca* 48.2.

20. *Tota mentis intentione*: *Regula communis* 10. Spacing out (*vacare*) during the office: Isidore, *Regula* 17. Staring: Pachomian *Precepts* 7 and *Regulations of Horsiesios* 11, 20, both in *Pachomian Koinonia* 2:146, 200, 204; Columbanus, *Regula coenobialis*, 217C; Sahdona, *Book of Perfection* 2.8.27, in Brock, *Syriac Fathers*. Racing: *RM* 55.9–14; Eugippius, *Regula* 20. Chatting: *Canons which are necessary for the monks* 9, in Vööbus, *Syriac and Arabic Documents*; *Precepts* 8, in *Pachomian Koinonia* 2:146; *Rules attributed to Rabbula* 25, in Vööbus, *Syriac and Arabic Documents*; John of Apamea, *Letter to Hesychius* 35, in Brock, *Syriac Fathers*; Caesarius, *Regula ad virgines* 10; *Regula monasterii Tarnatensis* 6.3; *Regula Pauli et Stephani* 9; Columbanus, *Regula coenobialis*, 222B; Sahdona, *Book of Perfection* 2.8.31; *Rule of Naqlun* 25; Donatus, *Regula* 17.8. Giggling: *Precepts* 8, in *Pachomian Koinonia* 2:146; Columbanus, *Regula coenobialis*, 217C; Isidore, *Regula* 17; Donatus, *Regula* 17.10. Noises: *RM* 47.21–24, 48.6–9; Columbanus, *Regula coenobialis*, 217C, 222B; Sahdona, *Book of Perfection* 2.8.32. Loud praying: Cassian, *Collationes* 9.35.3; *RB* 52.4; Caesarius, Letter to Caesaria 7.5; Donatus, *Regula* 16.4. Inconsiderate bowing: Typikon of Pantelleria 12, in Thomas and Hero, *Byzantine Monastic Foundation Documents*. Hurrying: Cassian, *De institutis coenobiorum* 2.7.1, 2.11.1, 3.5.1; Sahdona, *Book of Perfection* 2.8.29–35. Fidgeting, sitting, leaving early: Shenoute, *Rules* 447; *Statuta patrum* 32; *Vita patrum Iurensium* 3.6 (praise for a monk who *doesn't* leave prayers early); *Regula monasterii Tarnatensis* 6.1–2; *Regula Pauli et Stephani* 4; Gregory, *Dialogi* 2.4; Sahdona, *Book of Perfection* 2.8.29, 32–34. Dawdling: Cassian, *De institutis coenobiorum* 4.16; Shenoute, *Rules* 328; Eugippius, *Regula* 1.25, 37.11. Loud exits: *RB* 52.2–3; Donatus, *Regula* 16.2–3.

21. Latecomers denied entry: Cassian, *De institutis coenobiorum* 3.7.1; *Statuta patrum* 31; *Regula sancti Macharii abbatis* 14; *Regula monasterii Tarnatensis* 5.1; Typikon of Pantelleria 8, in Thomas and Hero, *Byzantine Monastic Foundation Documents*. Latecomers allowed in: *RB* 43.4–6; Donatus, *Regula* 13.4–6; Jonas, *Regula* 8. Simultaneous entry: Ferreolus, *Regula* 13. Sleeping in services: *So-Called Canons of Maruta* 51.16, in Vööbus, *Syriac and Arabic Documents*; *Statuta patrum* 37; *Regula Pauli et Stephani* 8; Sahdona, *Book of Perfection* 2.8.31, 33; Aurelian of Arles, *Regula*

ad monachos 29; Aurelian of Arles, *Regula ad virgines* 23. Other texts on lateness: Caesarius, *Regula ad virgines* 12; Caesarius, *Regula ad monachos* 11.2; Columbanus, *Regula coenobialis*, 222B; John Climacus, *Klimax* 19. Sleeping before dawn (or not): *Bohairic Life of Pachomius* 59, in *Pachomian Koinonia* 1:79 (split); *RM* 33.15–26 (in favor, based on an elaborate psychosomatic rationale); Aurelian, *Regula ad monachos* 28 (against). Short services: Cassian, *De institutis coenobiorum* 2 (including diversity at 2.2.1); Jonas of Bobbio, *De accedendo ad Deum* 26. Bedtime: *Regula monasterii Tarnatensis* 4.7–8. Sleeping in clothes: *RM* 11.120; similar are *RB* 22.5; Donatus, *Regula* 65.5. Cf. *Vita Landiberti vetustissima* 6, where the abbot of Stavelot-Malmedy is furious at the sound of a shoe hitting the ground in the middle of the night.

22. Cassian, *Collationes* 2.11–15 (counsel); Cassian, *De institutis coenobiorum* 4.8 (*mortificare*). Obedience and amputation: Zechner, *The Role of Death*, 128–35, 167–72.

23. Novatus, *Sententia* 64–81 (72: "non cogitas unde uiuas, quia nec debes cogitare"); *AP/G* Mark 2; Cassian, *Collationes* 4.24 (John of Lycopolis).

24. Work assignments: Basil, *Great Asketikon*, LR 38, 41 and SR 117; Shenoute, *Rules* 287, 389–90, 399, 465–66, 547–48; *Regula sanctorum patrum* 3.16–17; Caesarius, *Regula ad virgines* 8; Caesarius, *Regula ad monachos* 8; Aurelian, *Regula ad virgines* 19; Aurelian, *Regula ad monachos* 23; *Regula monasterii Tarnatensis* 9.4, 10.4–5, 12.7–8; *The Canons of the Persians* 2, in Vööbus, *Syriac and Arabic Documents*; Dadisho', *Canons* 19, in ibid.; Babai, *Rules* 25, in ibid.; Columbanus, *Regula Columbani* 10; Fructuosus, *Regula* 5. Following orders: Basil, *Great Asketikon*, LR 52; *Statuta patrum* 40–45; *RM* 7; Caesarius, *Regula ad monachos* 11.2; Aurelian, *Regula ad virgines* 28; Aurelian, *Regula ad monachos* 38; *Regula monasterii Tarnatensis* 5.2–3; Ferreolus, *Regula* 7; *The Canons of the Persians* 15, in Vööbus, *Syriac and Arabic Documents*; Columbanus, *Regula Columbani* 1; Columbanus, *Paenitentiale* A9; *Regula communis* 5.

25. Paul C. Dilley, *Monasteries and the Care of Souls in Late Antique Christianity: Cognition and Discipline* (Cambridge: Cambridge University Press, 2017), 98–105 (on Pachomius); Columbanus, *Regula Columbani* 6 (*cogitationes*); Columbanus, *Paenitentiale* A2 (*per cogitationem peccaverit*); Columbanus, *Paenitentiale* B30 (*commotiones animi*); John Climacus, *Klimax* 4. Right away: Cassian, *De institutis coenobiorum* 4.9, 4.37; *RM* 15, 61–65; *RB* 4.50, 7.44–48. Periodic: Gerontius, *Life of Melania the Younger* 23; Isidore, *Regula* 7; Fructuosus, *Regula* 2, 12; Donatus, *Regula* 23.1–3; *Regula communis* 5; Jonas, *Regula* 6.20–22 (three times a day!). Sharing thoughts with elders in a less structured environment: Isaiah, *Asketikon* 5.11, 8.27, 11.63, 15.76.

26. Eugippius, *Regula* 18.49–52, 18.55 (martyrdom), 25, 32—and see the next chapter for the evident concerns that Eugippius's monks had about their clothes; *RB* 2.6–7, 2.26–35; Valerius, *De genere monachorum* 8–9; also *RM* 2.6–9, 2.32–40. For similar if more subdued notions of accountability see

Caesarius, *Regula ad virgines* 35.10; Ferreolus, *Regula* 2; Donatus, *Regula* 4.4; Jonas, *Regula* 1.18–19. Mentorship and disclosure: Brown, *Body and Society*, 224–35; Foucault, *Les aveux de la chair*, 106–45.

27. Disregarding former social status: *RM* 2.16–22; *RB* 2.16–22; Donatus, *Regula* 1.15–18. Personalized prescriptions: Ferreolus, *Regula* 37; see also John Climacus, *Klimax* 26. Effects on community: *Regula monasterii Tarnatensis* 8.1–4; John Climacus, *Klimax* 4.

28. Gregory, *Dialogi* 2.3.4, 2.3.10.

29. *RM* 11.40–68, 11.75–84. Love: Albrecht Diem, "Disimpassioned Monks and Flying Nuns: Emotion Management in Early Medieval Rules," in *Funktionsräume, Wahrnehmungsräume, Gefühlsräume: Mittelalterliche Lebensformen zwischen Kloster und Hof*, ed. Christina Lutter (Vienna: Böhlau, 2011), 17–39; Diem, *The Pursuit of Salvation*, 399–406, 538–54. Pachomian hierarchies: Edward J. Watts, *Riot in Alexandria: Tradition and Group Dynamics in Late Antique Pagan and Christian Communities* (Berkeley: University of California Press, 2010), 100–103. White Monastery: Rebecca Krawiec, *Shenoute and the Women of the White Monastery: Egyptian Monasticism in Late Antiquity* (Oxford: Oxford University Press, 2002).

30. Reporting fellow monks: Basil, *Great Asketikon*, LR 46; Shenoute, *Rules* 108, 116, 134–36, 139–40, 142–45, 147, 455; Columbanus, *Regula coenobialis*, 218B–C; Donatus, *Regula* 29.2. Pointing out fellow monks' mistakes to them personally: Novatus, *Sententia* 82–90 ("debetis et uos uobis abbates esse"); Shenoute, *Rules* 552; *AP/GN*, N. 478; Eugippius, *Regula* 1.84–90; Columbanus, *Regula coenobialis*, 222D; *Consensoria monachorum* 6. Defending: *Testament of Horseisios* 24, in *Pachomian Koinonia* 3:188–89; Shenoute, *Rules* 405; *RB* 69; Donatus, *Regula* 74; Jonas, *Regula* 23. Different degrees of emphasis on rules vs. abbatial authority vs. mutual support: Diem, "Disimpassioned Monks and Flying Nuns."

31. Barsanuphius and John, *Letters* 301, 331–33—and compare the more socially sensitive advice that Dorotheus later gave to his own monks, as an abbot (*Didaskalia* 4.54, 9.97–100); Augustine, *Praeceptum* 4.8 (and see Leyser, *Authority and Asceticism*, 26–32), echoed in Caesarius, *Regula ad virgines* 24.5–6 and Donatus, *Regula* 51.4–7; Columbanus, *Regula coenobialis*, 218A.

32. Columbanian conflicts: Yaniv Fox, *Power and Religion in Merovingian Gaul: Columbanian Monasticism and the Frankish Elites* (Cambridge: Cambridge University Press, 2014), esp. 219–51. Resentment of brothers' intervention: Basil, *Great Asketikon*, SR 43–44. Eating: see next chapter. Competitiveness: Palladius, *Historia Lausiaca* 18.12–16; Theodoret of Cyrrhus, *Saint Simeon Stylites* 5; Antonius, *The Life and Daily Mode of Living of the Blessed Simeon the Stylite* 6–8; *The Syriac Life of Saint Simeon Stylites* 17–22, 25; Cyril of Scythopolis, *Life of Euthymius* 9, in *Bioi*. Unauthorized physical discipline: Shenoute, *Rules* 400, 582; *RB* 80; Aurelian of Arles, *Regula ad virgines* 11; Aurelian of Arles, *Regula ad monachos* 13; Ferreolus, *Regula* 21; John Climacus, *Klimax* 8. Against peer correction:

Mark the Monk, *Peri ton oiomenon ex ergon dikaiousthai* 166, in *Traités* (= 4.166 in Vivian and Casiday's translation); *The Canons of the Persians* 15, in Vööbus, *Syriac and Arabic Documents*; *Rules of Abraham of Kaškar* 12, in ibid.; Babai, *Rules* 17, in ibid.; Isaac of Nineveh, *Discourses* 2.3.2.39 (= *Centuries on Knowledge* 2.39).

33. Evagrius, *Antirrhetikos* 5.6 (saying mean things), 5.10 (suspicion), 5.11 (slander), 5.14, 5.35 (resentment), 8.37 (elitism); Shenoute, *Rules* 141 (devil), 276 (stupid servant), 403 (impressions); *Rules for Nuns* 12, in Vööbus, *Syriac and Arabic Documents* (name-calling); *Rules attributed to Rabbula* 10, in ibid. (making fun of a monk); *Rule of Naqlun* 23 (insults); *Regula cuiusdam patris ad monachos* 10 (saying bad things about a monk behind his back); Cassian, *Collationes* 16.18 (passive aggression).

34. Basil, *Great Asketikon*, LR 7.4.30; Evagrius, *Ad monachos* 13–15; Cassian, *Collationes* 16.15–19. Eph. 4:26: Theodoret, *Historia religiosa* 4.11; Aurelian, *Regula ad virgines* 10; Aurelian, *Regula ad monachos* 12; Ferreolus, *Regula* 39.34–47.

35. E.g., *Regula sanctorum patrum* 5.2–3; *RB* 23–30, 44; Aurelian, *Regula ad monachos* 34; *Regula monasterii Tarnatensis* 5.4; Isidore, *Regula* 18; *Regula communis* 14. On the culture of companionship see Derek Krueger, "Between Monks: Tales of Monastic Companionship in Early Byzantium," *Journal of the History of Sexuality* 20 (2011): 28–61; Claudia Rapp, *Brother-Making in Late Antiquity and Byzantium: Monks, Laymen, and Christian Ritual* (Oxford: Oxford University Press, 2016), 88–179.

36. Shenoute, *Rules* 340, similar is 364. Authorities: Basil, *Great Asketikon*, LR 36; Isho' Bar Nun, *Canons* 74, in Vööbus, *Syriac and Arabic Documents*. Food and clothes: Aurelian, *Regula ad virgines* 29; Aurelian, *Regula ad monachos* 54; *So-Called Canons of Maruta* 48.3, in Vööbus, *Syriac and Arabic Documents*. On the counterproductivity of bad food at collective meals, see the example of China's Great Leap Forward: James L. Watson, "Feeding the Revolution: Public Mess Halls and Coercive Commensality in Maoist China," in *Handbook of Food and Anthropology*, ed. Jakob A. Klein and Watson (London: Bloomsbury, 2016), 308–20.

37. Palladius, *Historia Lausiaca* 33, repeated in 'Enanisho''s Syriac compilation, *The Book of Paradise*, pp. 218–19; for other unfavorable portraits of the federation see Palladius, *Historia Lausiaca* 18.12–16 (resentment against Macarius), 32 (keeping pigs). Dadisho', *Canons* 26 and preface, in Vööbus, *Syriac and Arabic Documents* (quotation p. 167); on Dadisho''s *Canons* see Sabino Chialà, "Les règles monastiques syro-orientales et leurs caractère spécifique," in *Le monachisme syriaque*, ed. Florence Jullien (Paris: Geuthner, 2010), 107–22, at 118–19. Ishodenah of Basra, *Book of Chastity* 22, 27–29, 32 mentions the conflict and defections at Izla after the death of its founding father.

38. Radegund's life is unusually well documented by early medieval standards: see Caesaria of Arles's letter to Richild and Radegund; Gregory of Tours, *Historiae* 3.4, 3.7, 6.34, 9.2, 9.39–40, 9.42 (quoting in full one of

Radegund's letters); Fortunatus, *Carmina* 8.5–10; Fortunatus, *Vita Radegundis*; Gregory of Tours, *Liber in gloria confessorum* 104; Baudonivia, *Vita Radegundis*. Chrodield and Basina were the granddaughters of Clothar I, Radegund's husband. Their mothers were sisters and also Radegund's first cousins: Clothar had married all three of them (Gregory, *Historiae* 3.4, 4.3).

39. Gregory of Tours, *Historiae* 9.39–43 (quotation 9.39), 10.15–17, 10.20. On the bishops' apparent disinterest in Leubovera's violations of strict enclosure: E. T. Dailey, *Queens, Consorts, Concubines: Gregory of Tours and Women of the Merovingian Elite* (Leiden: Brill, 2015), 64–79. On Caesarius's distinctive concept of enclosure see Diem, *Das monastische Experiment*, 173–85. For a schema of the leading causes of monastic revolts in the Latin world (including elite monks' sense of entitlement): Steffen Patzold, "Les révolts dans la vie monastique médiévale," in *Revolte und Sozialstatus von der Spätantike bis zur Frühen Neuzeit*, ed. Philippe Depreux (Munich: Oldenbourg, 2008), 75–92.

40. Gregory of Tours, *Historiae* 10.16. See Caesarius, *Regula ad virgines* 23 (no checking out men), 36–37 (no men in the monastery). "Unsafe space": Diem, *The Pursuit of Salvation*, 297–303 (on Jonas of Bobbio's critiques of the Caesarean model).

41. Baudonivia, *Vita Radegundis* 2, 5, 8, 9, 13, 16, 19.

CHAPTER 3. BODY

1. See for example Jonas of Bobbio, *Vita Columbani abbatis discipulorumque eius* 2.13, 2.14, 2.16, 2.17, 2.20. Angelic contemplation: Kreiner, *Legions of Pigs in the Early Medieval West* (New Haven: Yale, 2020), 69–76.

2. Anastasios of Sinai, *Eratopokriseis* 19, trans. Munitiz, p. 89.

3. Leslie Lockett, *Anglo-Saxon Psychologies in the Vernacular and Latin Traditions* (Toronto: University of Toronto Press, 2011), 54–109, 179–227; Vittorio Berti, *L'Au-delà l'âme et l'en-deça du corps: Approches d'anthropologie chrétienne de la mort dans l'Église syro-orientale* (Fribourg: Academic Press Fribourg, 2015), 47–109; Winfried Büttner, *"Gottheit in uns": Die monastische und psychologische Grundlegung der Mystik nach einer überlieferten Textkollektion aus Werk des Šem'on d-Ṭaibuṭeh* (Wiesbaden: Harrassowitz, 2017), 234–54, 277–98; Christoph Markschies, *God's Body: Jewish, Christian, and Pagan Images of God*, trans. Alexander Johannes Edmonds (Waco: Baylor University Press, 2019), 100–126, quoting Faustus's *Epistula* 3 at p. 108.

4. Gregory, *Dialogi* 4.38.5 (*nebula, obscurat*); *Rules of Abraham of Kaškar* 1 (crediting the quip to Mark the Monk), trans. Vööbus, in *Syriac and Arabic Documents*, p. 155.

5. Palladius, *Historia Lausiaca* 2.2 (Dorotheus), trans. Wortley, p. 10. Debates about self-torture: Theodoret of Chyrrhus, *Historia religiosa* 26.5; Antonius, *Bios Symeon* 4–8; *Syriac Life of Saint Simeon Stylites* 21 (rope);

Fortunatus, *Vita Radegundis* 25 (manacles and chains), 26 (branding); compare Baudonivia, *Vita Radegundis* 8, which only obliquely alludes to these practices; Susan Ashbrook Harvey, *Asceticism and Society in Crisis: John of Ephesus and* The Lives of the Eastern Saints (Berkeley: University of California Press, 1990), 16–17, 45–46; Arthur Vööbus, *History of Asceticism in the Syrian Orient: A Contribution to the History of Culture in the Near East*, vol. 2 (Louvain: CSCO, 1960), 97–100, 277–78 (including a suspended cage), 292–300.

6. John Climacus, *Klimax* 14, trans. Luibheid and Russell, p. 169. Body-mind training: Peter Brown, *The Body and Society: Men, Women, and Sexual Renunciation in Early Christianity* (New York: Columbia University Press, 1988), 213–40; Michel Foucault, *Les aveux de la chair*, ed. Frédéric Gros, vol. 4 of *Histoire de la sexualité* (Paris: Gallimard, 2018), 106–45, 206–45; Niki Kasumi Clements, *Sites of the Ascetic Self: John Cassian and Christian Ethical Formation* (Notre Dame: University of Notre Dame Press, 2020).

7. Teresa M. Shaw, *The Burden of the Flesh: Fasting and Sexuality in Early Christianity* (Minneapolis: Fortress, 1998), 27–78; Brown, *Body and Society*; Pierre Hadot, "Exercices spirituels antiques et 'philosophie chrétienne,'" *Exercices spirituels et philosophie antique*, 2nd ed. (Paris: Études Augustiniennes, 1987), 59–74; Daniele Pevarello, *The Sentences of Sextus and the Origins of Christian Asceticism* (Tübingen: Mohr Siebeck, 2013), esp. 192–200; Yvan Koenig, "Place et rôle de l'Écriture dans la prière individuelle des moines d'Égypte (IVᵉ–Vᵉ siècle)," in *La vie quotidienne des moines en Orient et en Occident (IVᵉ–Xᵉ siècle)*, vol. 2, *Questions transversales*, ed. Olivier Delouis and Maria Mossakowska-Gaubert (Cairo and Athens: Institut Français d'Archéologie Orientale and École Française d'Athènes, 2019), 239–52, esp. 239–40. For the point that "asceticism" was not a single ethic or practice: Albrecht Diem, "The Limitations of Asceticism," *Medieval Worlds* 9 (2019): 112–38.

8. Gregory, *Dialogi* 1.5.4 (Constantius), 2.1.8 (Benedict), 3.6 (Cassius).

9. Shaw, *Burden of the Flesh*, 39–40 (Stoics); Miller, *Corporeal Imagination*, 32–35, quoting Proclus's *Eclogae de Philosophia Chaldaica* 5.10–11 (I have modified Rappe's translation of *eikones* to "images"); Maud W. Gleason, *Making Men: Sophists and Self-Presentation in Ancient Rome* (Princeton: Princeton University Press, 1995), 55–102 (body language and voice); Brown, *Through the Eye of a Needle*, 197–99 (baths).

10. Palladius, *Historia Lausiaca* 55.2 (Silvania), trans. Wortley, p. 122; Vööbus, *History of Asceticism in the Syrian Orient*, 2:275–76 (Ephrem and Severus, quotation at 275); Ferrandus, *Vita Fulgentii* 2, 28. Other bathing restrictions: Shenoute, *Rules* 70–71.

11. Chrysostom, *Adversus oppugnatores vitae monasticae* 2.6, trans. Hunter, p. 108. "Dried-up": John of Ephesus, *Lives of the Eastern Saints* 42, trans. Brooks, 2:656; see also Dorotheus, *Didaskalia* 10.10, on baths as a means to rehydrate his overworked body in his student days.

12. Young vs. mature monks: Isaiah, *Asketikon* 10.63–65; *RB* 36.8. Cologne: Ferreolus of Uzès, *Regula* 32. Baths for reasons of health: Eugippius, *Regula* 1.114–16; *RB* 36.8; Leander, *De institutione virginum* 20; Donatus, *Regula* 12.12.

13. Attempts to "donate" clothing: Eugippius, *Regula* 8. Restrictions on washing clothes and bedding: Augustine, *Praeceptum* 5.4; *Regula Pauli et Stephani* 28; Eugippius, *Regula* 1.113. *Habitus* pun: Eugippius, *Regula* 1.105 ("hinc uos probate quantum uobis desit in illo interiore sancto habitu cordis ornatus, qui pro habitu corporis litigatis"). Necessary laundering actually served as a metaphor for spiritual maintenance: Susan Ashbrook Harvey, "Housekeeping: An Ascetic Theme in Late Antiquity," in *To Train His Soul in Books: Syriac Asceticism in Early Christianity*, ed. Robin Darling Young and Monica J. Blanchard (Washington, DC: Catholic University of America Press, 2011), 134–54, at 143–45.

14. Livia Kohn, *Monastic Life in Medieval Daoism: A Cross-Cultural Perspective* (Honolulu: University of Hawai'i Press, 2003), 189–90; Ann Heirman and Mathieu Torck, *A Pure Mind in a Clean Body: Bodily Care in Buddhist Monasteries of Ancient India and China* (Ghent: Academia Press, 2012), 137–64; Eric M. Greene, *Chan before Chan: Meditation, Repentance, and Visionary Experience in Chinese Buddhism* (Honolulu: Kuroda Institute and University of Hawai'i Press, 2021), 198–99; Maria E. Doerfler, "'Hair!': Remnants of Ascetic Exegesis in Augustine's *De opere monachorum*," *Journal of Early Christian Studies* 22, no. 1 (2014): 79–111; Daniel Oltean, "Les origines de la tonsure monastique: Les sources grecques," *Byzantion* 82 (2017): 259–97, at 267–81; Susanna Elm, *Virgins of God: The Making of Asceticism in Late Antiquity* (Oxford: Clarendon, 1994), 108–10, 219; *AP/GN*, N. 418 (the monk who never cut his hair).

15. Philipp von Rummel, *Habitus barbarus: Kleidung und Repräsentation spätantiker Eliten im 4. und 5. Jahrhundert* (Berlin: De Gruyter, 2007), 160–63, 215–25; on "barbarian" trendiness in the Roman army see Guy Halsall, *Barbarian Migrations and the Roman West, 376–568* (Cambridge: Cambridge University Press, 2007), 101–10.

16. No long hair, except for recluses: Rabbula, *Admonitions for the Monks* 5, in Vööbus, *Syriac and Arabic Documents*. Shaved heads: *So-Called Canons of Maruta* 59.5, in ibid. Tonsure: Aurelian, *Regula ad monachos* 4. No shaving anything without permission: Shenoute, *Rules* 91, 452, 509. Regular haircuts and beard trims: Gregory of Tours, *Liber vitae patrum* 20.3; Canons of Qyriaqos 52.26, in Vööbus, *The Synodicon in the West Syrian Tradition*, 2:27 (short haircuts for women). Prohibited beard trimming: *Regula monasterii Tarnatensis* 4.6. Hair tied up: Caesarius, *Regula ad virgines* 56 (including manuscript variants of precise measurements), repeated in Donatus, *Regula* 64. See also Isidore, *Regula* 12: everyone should have the same haircut! Debates about tonsure: Edward James, "Bede and the Tonsure Question," *Peritia* 3 (1984): 85–98; Florence Jullien, *Monachisme en Perse: La réforme d'Abraham le Grand, père des moines de l'Orient* (Lou-

vain: Peeters, 2008), 119–24; Maria Mossakowska-Gaubert, "Official Garb of Egyptian Monks and Nuns (4th–8th Century AD): Appearance, Production and Role as a Social Marker," *Orientalia Christiana Periodica* 87 (2021): 71–128, at 98–101; Daniel McCarthy, "Representations of Tonsure in the Book of Kells," *Studia Celtica* 51 (2017): 89–103, discussing the crown-tonsured portrait at 100–102.

17. *AP/G* Poemen 184, trans. Ward, p. 193.

18. See generally Charles J. Metteer, "Distraction or Spiritual Discipline: The Role of Sleep in Early Egyptian Monasticism," *St Vladimir's Theological Quarterly* 51 (2008): 5–43; Leslie Dossey, "Watchful Greeks and Lazy Romans: Disciplining Sleep in Late Antiquity," *Journal of Early Christian Studies* 21 (2013): 209–39; Albrecht Diem, *The Pursuit of Salvation: Community, Space, and Discipline in Early Medieval Monasticism* (Turnhout, Belgium: Brepols, 2021), 478–98.

19. *Instructions of Horsiesios* 6.3, trans. Veilleux, in *Pachomian Koinonia* 3:144; Shenoute, "A Beloved Asked Me Years Ago," in *Discourses*, 180; *RB* 19.7, repeated in Donatus, *Regula* 17.7; *Syriac Life of Saint Simeon Stylites* 44, trans. Doran, p. 128; Theodoret of Cyrrhus, *Historia religiosa* 26.23; Jacob of Sarug, *Homily on Simeon the Stylite*, trans. Susan Ashbrook Harvey, in Wimbush, *Ascetic Behavior in Greco-Roman Antiquity*, 20–23. See also Shenoute, *Rules* 236–37; Isaac of Nineveh, *Discourses* 2.14.12–26; Dadisho' Qaṭraya, *Shelya*, 54a–55a; Dadisho', *Compendious Commentary* 46–49. Cf. guidance on kneeling in Columbanus, *Regula coenobialis*, 221A; Donatus, *Regula* 34; Shem'on d-Ṭaybutheh, *On the Consecration of the Cell* 11, 14. Portrait of Askla: Jean Clédat, *Le monastère et la nécropole de Baouît*, ed. Dominique Bénazeth and Marie-Hélène Rutschowscaya (Cairo: Institut Français d'Archéologie Orientale du Caire, 1999).

20. *AP/G* Arsenius 15, 30, quotation trans. Ward, p. 11; *AP/GS* 12.1; *AP/PJ* 12.1; *AP/S* 1.6.105; and for other *AP* variants see the *Monastica* database at https://monastica.ht.lu.se/; Cyril of Scythopolis, *Life of Euthymius* 21, in *Bioi*. See also Isaac of Nineveh, *Discourses* 1.80.562–63; Dadisho', *Compendious Commentary* 169.

21. Pachomian monasteries: *Greek Life of Pachomius* 14, in *Pachomian Koinonia* 1:307; *Precepts* 87, in *Pachomian Koinonia* 2:160. Amida: John of Ephesus, *Lives of the Eastern Saints* 35, 2:642. Qartamin: Vööbus, *History of Asceticism in the Syrian Orient*, 2:265. Sisoes: *AP/G* Sisoes 33.

22. Macarius: Palladius, *Historia Lausiaca* 18.3, trans. Wortley, p. 39. Other critiques: Metteer, "Distraction or Spiritual Discipline," 13–16. Moderate advice: John of Apamea, *Letter to Hesychius* 61, in Brock, *Syriac Fathers*; Cassian, *Collationes* 14.10; Babai, *Letter to Syriacus* 39, in Brock, *Syriac Fathers*; Columbanus, *Regula Columbani* 10; Isidore, *Regula* 13; John Climacus, *Klimax* 20; Shem'on d-Ṭaybutheh, *On the Consecration of the Cell* 13.

23. *Rule* 37 of St. John Stoudios of Constantinople, no. 4 in Thomas and Hero, *Byzantine Monastic Foundation Documents*; Maria Mossakowska-Gaubert,

"Alimentation, hygiène, vêtements et sommeil chez les moines égyptiens (IVᵉ–VIIIᵉ siècle): L'état des sources archéologiques et écrites," in *La vie quotidienne des moines en Orient et en Occident (IVᵉ–Xᵉ siècle)*, vol. 1, *L'état des sources*, ed. Olivier Delouis and Maria Mossakowska-Gaubert (Cairo and Athens: Institut Français d'Archéologie Orientale and École Française d'Athènes, 2015), 23–55, at 32–33; Ina Eichner, "The Archaeological Evidence of Domestic Life in the Monasteries of Western Thebes: The Example of Deir el-Bakhit," in *La vie quotidienne des moines*, ed. Delouis and Mossakowska-Gaubert, 2:25–36, at 30–31.

24. No bedding: e.g., Fortunatus, *Vita Paterni* 9.28; Antony of Choziba, *Bios Georgiou* 4.19. Shenoute: Ariel G. López, *Shenoute of Atripe and the Uses of Poverty: Rural Patronage, Religious Conflict, and Monasticism in Late Antique Egypt* (Berkeley: University of California Press, 2013), 97. Proscriptions against pillows and other luxe bedding: *Precepts* 81, in *Pachomian Koinonia* 2:159; Caesarius of Arles, *Regula ad virgines* 44–45; Dorotheus of Gaza, *Didaskalia* 3.45; Aurelian of Arles, *Regula ad monachos* 27; Isidore, *Regula* 13; Fructuosus, *Regula* 11; Donatus, *Regula* 53.5. Augustine: *Praeceptum* 1.5–7, 3.3–4, echoed in *Regula Eugippii* 1.59–63; Peter Brown, *Through the Eye of a Needle*, 175–77.

25. Barsanuphius and John, *Letters* 452.

26. *Consultationes Zacchei* 3.10–16.

27. Anne-Marie Helvétius, "Le sexe des anges," in *De la différence des sexes: Le genre en histoire*, ed. Michèle Riot-Sarcey (Paris: Larousse, 2010), 101–30, 246–51; Roland Betancourt, *Byzantine Intersectionality: Sexuality, Gender, and Race in the Middle Ages* (Princeton: Princeton University Press, 2020), 96–106; Doerfler, "Hair!," 98–101; Albrecht Diem, "The Gender of the Religious: Wo/Men and the Invention of Monasticism," in *The Oxford Handbook of Women and Gender in Medieval Europe*, ed. Judith Bennett and Ruth Karras (Oxford: Oxford University Press, 2013), 432–46, esp. 437–40; Diem, *The Pursuit of Salvation*, 191–94; Rebecca Krawiec, *Shenoute and the Women of the White Monastery: Egyptian Monasticism in Late Antiquity* (Oxford: Oxford University Press, 2002), 92–119; Isabelle Réal, "Tâches et gestes quotidiens des moniales en Gaule franque (VIᵉ–Xᵉ siècle): Fragments de vie domestique," in *La vie quotidienne des moines*, ed. Delouis and Mossakowska-Gaubert, 2:203–36, esp. 224–26; Shaw, *Burden of the Flesh*, 235–46; Foucault, *Les aveux de la chair*, 188–89; Brown, *Body and Society*, 366–86.

28. Brown, *Body and Society*, 5–209; Foucault, *Les aveux de la chair*, 149–245.

29. Elm, *Virgins of God*, 184–223, 336, 373–83; Markschies, *God's Body*, 182–319; Foucault, *Les aveux de la chair*, 228–30; Clements, *Sites of the Ascetic Self*; David Brakke, "The Problematization of Nocturnal Emissions in Early Christian Syria, Egypt, and Gaul," *Journal of Early Christian Studies* 3 (1995): 419–60, at 446–53; on the need for *quies* and *solitudo* to combat the spirit of fornication see Cassian, *De institutis coenobiorum* 6.3, see more generally *De institutis coenobiorum* 6 and *Collationes* 12. Some theorists also thought that women could have wet dreams: Donatus, *Regula* 33.

30. Georges Sidéris, "Ascètes et moines eunuques en Égypte et Palestine byzantines (IVe–VIIe siècle)," in *La vie quotidienne des moines*, ed. Delouis and Mossakowska-Gaubert, 2:301–20; Daniel F. Caner, "The Problem and Practice of Self-Castration in Early Christianity," *Vigiliae Christianae* 51 (1997): 396–415; Pevarello, *The Sentences of Sextus*, 62–67 (quoting Edward and Wild's translation of *Sentences* 13); Doerfler, "Hair!," 84–97; Felix Szabo, "Non-Standard Masculinity and Sainthood in Niketas David's *Life* of Patriarch Ignatios," in *Trans and Genderqueer Subjects in Medieval Hagiography*, ed. Alicia Spencer-Hall and Blake Gutt (Amsterdam: Amsterdam University Press, 2021), 109–29. Cf. Roland Betancourt's more optimistic view of eunuchs as transgender persons who "allow[ed] a space to maneuver for trans monks and other nonbinary persons" by virtue of their own social prominence—not just within monasticism but also at the imperial court: *Byzantine Intersectionality*, 119.

31. John Moschos, *Pratum spirituale* 3; cf. Palladius's positive reading of a very similar incident: *Historia Lausiaca* 29.

32. Hermits avoiding women: Brown, *Body and Society*, 241–48. Prohibiting members of the opposite sex: Rabbula, *Admonitions for the Monks* 1, in Vööbus, *Syriac and Arabic Documents*; *Regula et instituta patrum* 4; Babai, *Letter to Cyriacus* 26, 52, in Brock, *Syriac Fathers*; Caesarius, *Regula ad monachos* 11.1; Aurelian, *Regula ad monachos* 15; Johannan Bar Qursos, *Canons* 11.6, in Vööbus, *Syriac and Arabic Documents*; *Rules for Nuns* 7, in ibid.; *Rules of Jacob of Edessa* 11, in ibid.; *Canons of the Persians* 26, in ibid. Exceptions: Shenoute, *Rules* 425 (emergencies); Caesarius, *Regula ad virgines* 36 (clerics and contractors); Ferreolus, *Regula* 4 (conversations happen outside the walls, with witnesses); *Regula monasterii Tarnatensis* 4.1 (relatives), 20 (oratory and guest house); Aurelian, *Regula ad virgines* 14 (church and receiving room), 15 (suppliers and contractors); Aurelian, *Regula ad monachos* 14 (receiving room), 19 (contractors); *Canons which are necessary for the monks* 4 (mom or sister of a sick monk); Donatus, *Regula* 55 (clerics and contractors), 56–57 (select lay guests at the entryway or receiving room). See more generally Alice-Mary Talbot, "Women's Space in Byzantine Monasteries," *Dumbarton Oaks Papers* 52 (1998): 113–27; Gisela Muschiol, "Time and Space: Liturgy and Rite in Female Monasteries of the Middle Ages," in *Crown and Veil: Female Monasticism from the Fifth to the Fifteenth Centuries*, ed. Jeffrey F. Hamburger and Susan Marti, trans. Dietlinde Hamburger (New York: Columbia University Press, 2008), 191–206; Betancourt, *Byzantine Intersectionality*, 91–96, 102–106; M. W. Bychowski, "The Authentic Lives of Transgender Saints: *Imago Dei* and *imitatio Christi* in the *Life* of St. Marinos the Monk," in *Trans and Genderqueer Subjects in Medieval Hagiography*, ed. Spencer-Hall and Gutt, 245–65.

33. Quotation: *AP/GN*, N. 154, trans. Wortley, p. 105. Guarding the gaze: Augustine, *Praeceptum* 4; Isaiah, *Asketikon* 5.23, 10.14, 10.68; Caesarius of Arles, *Regula ad virgines* 23; Cyril of Scythopolis, *Life of Saba* 47, in *Bioi*;

Regula monasterii Tarnatensis 18.13; *On the Order of the Novice-Brothers* 35, in Arthur Vööbus, *History of Asceticism in the Syrian Orient: A Contribution to the History of Culture in the Near East*, vol. 3 (Leuven: CSCO, 1988), 189; Donatus, *Regula* 50; John of Dalyatha, *Letters* 18.2, 18.17, 18.22, 18.28.

34. Gregory of Tours, *Liber vitae patrum* 1.2, 1.6. For examples of both models in the same text see, e.g., *AP/G* Arsenius 28, Longinus 3; Theodoret, *Historia religiosa* 8.13, 11.4. Gregory, *Dialogi* 2.19, 3.16.5. See also Diem, *Das monastische Experiment*, 86–91.

35. Shenoute, *Rules* 47; on his anxiety about individual sins contaminating the entire monastic community see Caroline T. Schroeder, *Monastic Bodies: Discipline and Salvation in Shenoute of Atripe* (Philadelphia: University of Pennsylvania Press, 2007), 54–89. Children: Isaiah, *Asketikon* 5.2; Shenoute, *Rules* 4, 11, 59, 395–96, 504, 508, 513–16, 563, 566, 574; *Rule of Naqlun* 4, 5, 16; *On the Order of the Novice-Brothers* 39, in Vööbus, *History of Asceticism in the Syrian Orient*, 3:189. Beds: Isaiah, *Asketikon* 5.2 (separate beds with some exceptions), 10.8 (no exceptions); Shenoute, *Rules* 1–2, 94; *RB* 22.1; Ferreolus, *Regula* 33; Isidore, *Regula* 17; Donatus, *Regula* 65.1; Jonas of Bobbio, *Regula cuiusdam ad virgines* 14 (shared beds); John of Dalyatha, *Letters* 18.11, 18.35. Same-sex concerns: Kyle Harper, *From Shame to Sin: The Christian Transformation of Sexual Morality in Late Antiquity* (Cambridge, MA: Harvard University Press, 2013), 22–30, 141–58; Carrie Schroeder, "Children and Egyptian Monasticism," in *Children in Late Ancient Christianity*, ed. Cornelia B. Horn and Robert R. Phenix (Tübingen: Morh Siebeck, 2009), 317–38, at 319–21, 336–37; Maria Chiara Giorda, "Children in Monastic Families in Egypt at the End of Antiquity," in *Children in Everyday Life in the Roman and Late Antique World*, ed. Christian Laes and Ville Vuolanto (London: Routledge, 2017), 232–46, at 237–38; Derek Krueger, "Between Monks: Tales of Monastic Companionship in Early Byzantium," *Journal of the History of Sexuality* 20 (2011): 28–61.

36. Institutional efficacy: Diem, *Das monastische Experiment*, 131–321; with subtle differentiations in Diem, *Pursuit of Salvation*, 265–327. Dual-gender monasteries: Alison I. Beach and Andra Juganaru, "The Double Monastery as a Historiographical Problem (Fourth to Twelfth Century)," in *Cambridge History of Medieval Monasticism in the Latin West*, ed. Beach and Cochelin, 1: 561–78; Jan Gerchow, Katrinette Bodarwé, Susan Marti, and Hedwig Röckelein, "Early Monasteries and Foundations (500–1200): An Introduction," in *Crown and Veil*, ed. Hamburger and Marti, 13–40, with the figure on p. 16 of 115 dual-gender monasteries in Gaul in the Merovingian period.

37. Palladius, *Historica Lausiaca* 18.26.

38. Cassian, *De institutis coenobiorum* 5.6, 6.23; Shem'on d-Ṭaybutheh, *Book of Medicine* 179b, trans. Mingana, pp. 35–36; more generally Shaw, *Burden of the Flesh*, 53–64.

39. Cassian, *De institutis coenobiorum* 5.11–20; Fragment 5.2, trans. Veilleux, in *Pachomian Koinonia* 3:88.

40. Athanasius, *Vita Antonii* 7; Florentius, *Vita Rusticulae* 7; Gregory of Tours, *Liber vitae patrum* 5.1 (Portianus); Antony of Choziba, *Bios Georgiou* 3.12; Anastasios of Sinai, *Diegeseis peri tou Sina* 1.18 (George the Arselaite); Isho'denaḥ of Basra, *Ktaba d-nakputa* 65 (Joseph); *AP/GN*, N. 152 (trans. Wortley, p. 152); Jerome, *Vita Hilarionis* 5.

41. Snacks: Augustine, *Praeceptum* 3.1; Cassian, *De institutis coenobiorum* 4.18; *Canons of Mar Mattai* 14, in Vööbus, *History of Asceticism in the Syrian Orient* 3:174; Eugippius, *Regula* 38; *Rules attributed to Rabbula* 17, in Vööbus, *Syriac and Arabic Documents*; Caesarius, *Regula ad virgines* 30.2–3; Ferreolus, *Regula* 35; Donatus, *Regula* 24. Leftovers: Pachomius, *Precepts* 38, 78, in *Pachomian Koinonia* 2:151, 159; Shenoute, *Rules* 193, 195–97, 242. Takeout/street food: *Rules attributed to Ephrem* 2, in Vööbus, *Syriac and Arabic Documents*; Shenoute, *Rules* 526; Eugippius, *Regula* 1.20; *Regula Tarnatensis* 9.14. Functional vs. tasty food: Cassian, *De institutis coenobiorum* 5.8, 5.23; Columbanus, *Regula Columbani* 3. Against satiety or stuffing: Basil, *Great Asketikon*, LR 19; Cassian, *De institutis coenobiorum* 5.6; Isaiah, *Asketikon* 11.44; *Rule of Naqlun* 52; *On the Order of the Novice-Brothers* 4, 15, in Vööbus, *History of Asceticism in the Syrian Orient*, 3:187–88; Columbanus, *Regula Columbani* 3; Columbanus, *Paenitentiale* A6, B12. Enslaved to the belly: *RM* 53.26–33. Emptied by a full belly: Smaragdus, *Expositio* 4.36. Suffocated: Columbanus, *Regula Columbani* 3.

42. Maria Mossakowska-Gaubert, "Les moines égyptiens el leur nourriture terrestre (IV\u1d49–VIII\u1d49 siècle)," in *La vie quotidienne des moines*, ed. Delouis and Mossakowska-Gaubert, 2:145–83, at 149–56; Alfredo Carannante, Salvatore Chilardi, Girolamo Fiorentino, Alessandra Pecci, and Francesco Solinas, "Le cucine di San Vincenzo al Volturno: Ricostruzione funzionale in base ai dati topografici, strutturali, bioarcheologici e chimici," in *Monasteri in Europa occidentale (secoli VIII–XI): Topografia e strutture*, ed. Flavia de Rubeis and Federico Marazzi (Rome: Viella, 2008), 498–507. No meat: *Canons of the Persians* 23, in Vööbus, *Syriac and Arabic Documents*; *So-Called Canons of Maruta* 59.2, in ibid.; Isho' Bar Nun, *Canons* 16 (Arabic version), in ibid.; *Rule of Naqlun* 20; Caesarius, *Regula ad monachos* 24 (except for the sick); *RM* 53.31–33 (exceptions for Easter and Christmas seasons); *RB* 39.11 (referring to the flesh of quadrupeds, with exceptions for the sick); Caesarius, *Regula ad virgines* 71 (except chicken for the sick); Aurelian, *Regula ad monachos* 51 (except fish on feast days and poultry for the sick); Aurelian, *Regula ad virgines* 34–35 (except fish on special occasions and poultry for the sick); Leander, *De institutione virginum* 24; Isidore, *Regula* 9 (except a little bit on feast days); Jonas, *Regula* 10.4; Fructuosus, *Regula* 3 (except fish, or poultry for distinguished guests and sick or traveling monks); Donatus, *Regula* 12.13–14 (except for the sick); *Rule* 29 of Stoudios, in Thomas and Hero, *Byzantine Monastic Foundation Documents* (fish okay). Cf. Basil, *Great Asketikon*, LR 18 (all foods are good because God made them!).

43. Emmanuelle Raga, "Partage alimentaire et ascétisme dans le monachisme

occidental: Les normes alimentaires aristocratiques en toile de fond de la construction des normes cénobitiques (IVᵉ–VIᵉ siècle)," in *La vie quotidienne des moines*, ed. Delouis and Mossakowska-Gaubert, 2:185–202; Shaw, *Burden of the Flesh*, 161–219. See the next chapter for reading during mealtimes.

44. Shenoute, *Rules* 186; *Regula Pauli et Stephani* 19; Krawiec, *Shenoute and the Women of the White Monastery*, esp. 43–46, 100–106.

45. Augustine, *Praeceptum* 3.3–4; likewise *Regula monasterii Tarnatensis* 16. Age: Shenoute, *Rules* 175. Strenuous manual labor: Shenoute, *Rules* 178; *Regula monasterii Tarnatensis* 9.11; *Typikon* 4 of Pantelleria, in Thomas and Hero, *Byzantine Monastic Foundation Documents*. Sick monks: Shenoute *Rules* 33, 156, 157, 158, 160–61, 176–77, 189 (feigning illness and suspecting other monks of faking it); Eugippius, *Regula* 1.57–58 (resentment); Andrew T. Crislip, *From Monastery to Hospital: Christian Monasticism and the Transformation of Health Care in Late Antiquity* (Ann Arbor: University of Michigan Press, 2005), 68–99.

46. Gallic monks: Sulpicius Severus, *Gallus* 1.8.4. Observing/judging at meals: Cassian, *De institutis coenobiorum* 4.17; Shenoute, *Rules* 500 (quotation trans. Layton, p. 307); Jonas, *Regula* 10.12; Isaac, *Life of Samuel* 42. See also Shenoute's policies against forcing fasting monks to eat: *Rules* 207–8, 331, 498, 501; and chap. 2 on competitive fasting.

47. Barsanuphius and John, *Letters* 151–63 (155 on other forms of moderation); Evagrius, *Peri logismon* 35; Gregory, *Liber vitae patrum* 1.3.

48. *Vita patrum Iurensium* 2.4; John of Dalyatha, *Letters* 20.2; Cassian, *De institutis coenobiorum* 5.9 (*mentis labefacere constantiam*), similiar is *Collationes* 1.21; Johannan Bar Qursos, *Rules for the Monastery of Mār Zakkai* 48, trans. Vööbus, *Syriac and Arabic Documents*, p. 61. Other medical misgivings about excessive fasting: Andrew Crislip, "'I have chosen sickness': The Controversial Function of Sickness in Early Christian Ascetic Practice," in *Asceticism and Its Critics: Historical Accounts and Comparative Perspectives*, ed. Oliver Freiberger (Oxford: Oxford University Press, 2006), 179–209; Shaw, *Burden of the Flesh*, 96–112.

49. *AP/GN*, N. 394 (the benefits of a snack); Basil, *Great Asketikon*, SR 17 (legitimate hunger pangs vs. distracted thoughts about snacks); Cassian, *De institutis coenobiorum* 10.2.2 (snacky feelings as a distraction); Evagrius, *Antirrhetikos* 1.22 (liver and spleen), 1.54 (craving fruit at harvest season), 1.59 (disease); *Vita patrum Iurensium* 1.13 (eating too much at harvest season).

50. *On Hermits and Desert Dwellers*, lines 97–100, trans. Amar, p. 70. On the body-as-building see Ashbrook Harvey, "Housekeeping." On prayers as sacrifices (here signaled by incense and smoke) see Lorenzo Perrone, *La preghiera secondo Origene: L'impossibilità donata* (Brescia: Morcelliana, 2011), 513–45, 571–72.

CHAPTER 4. BOOKS

1. Evagrius, *De octo spiritibus malitiae* 6.15, trans. Sinkewicz, p. 84. Evagrius's backstory was widely publicized in Palladius's *Historia Lausiaca* (38.2–9), an account and travelogue of famous ascetics in Egypt written around 420 CE, about twenty years after Evagrius died.

2. Matthew D. C. Larsen and Mark Letteney, "Christians and the Codex: Generic Materiality and Early Gospel Traditions," *Journal of Early Christian Studies* 27 (2019): 383–413; Anthony Grafton and Megan Williams, *Christianity and the Transformation of the Book: Origen, Eusebius, and the Library of Caesarea* (Cambridge, MA: Belknap, 2006); Caroline Humfress, "Judging by the Book: Christian Codices and Late Antique Legal Culture," in *The Early Christian Book*, ed. William Klingshirn and Linda Safran (Washington, DC: Catholic University of America Press, 2007), 141–58; Harry Y. Gamble, *Books and Readers in the Early Church: A History of Early Christian Texts* (New Haven: Yale University Press, 1995), esp. 42–81; Colin H. Roberts and T. C. Skeat, *The Birth of the Codex* (London: Oxford University Press, 1983).

3. Kim Haines-Eitzen, *Guardians of Letters: Literacy, Power, and the Transmitters of Early Christian Literature* (Oxford: Oxford University Press, 2000); Gamble, *Books and Readers*, 82–143; Hugo Lundhaug and Lance Jenott, "Production, Distribution and Ownership of Books in the Monasteries of Upper Egypt: The Evidence of the Nag Hammadi Colophons," in *Monastic Education in Late Antiquity: The Transformation of Classical Paideia*, ed. Lillian I. Larsen and Samuel Rubenson (Cambridge: Cambridge University Press, 2018), 306–25; Chrysi Kotsifou, "Books and Book Production in the Monastic Communities of Byzantine Egypt," in *The Early Christian Book*, ed. Klingshirn and Safran, 48–66; Arthur Vööbus, *History of Asceticism in the Syrian Orient: A Contribution to the History of Culture in the Near East*, vol. 2 (Leuven: CSCO, 1960), 389–93.

4. Jean-Pierre Mahé, "Les pères syriens et les origines du monachisme géorgien d'après le nouveau manuscrit sinaïtique," in *Monachismes d'Orient: Images, échanges, influences. Hommage à Antoine Guillaumont*, ed. Florence Jullien and Marie-Joseph Pierre (Turnhout, Belgium: Brepols, 2011), 51–64, Zedazadeni at 62 n. 68; Muriel Debié, "Livres et monastères en Syrie-Mésopotamie d'après les sources syriaques," in *Le monachisme syriaque*, ed. Florence Jullien (Paris: Geuthner, 2010), 123–68, Simeon at 155; Michael Lapidge, *The Anglo-Saxon Library* (Oxford: Oxford University Press, 2005), Bede at 36–37; Julia Becker, "Präsenz, Normierung und Transfer von Wissen: Lorsch als 'patristische Zentralbibliothek,'" in *Karolingische Klöster: Wissentransfer und kulturelle Innovation*, ed. Becker, Tino Licht, and Stefan Weinfurter (Berlin: De Gruyter, 2015), 71–87; Tito Orlandi, "The Library of the Monastery of Saint Shenute at Atripe," in *Perspectives on Panopolis: An Egyptian Town from Alexander the Great to the Arab Conquest*, ed. A. Egberts, B. P. Muhs, and J. van der Vliet (Leiden:

Brill, 2002), 211–31; Hugo Lundhaug and Lance Jenott, *The Monastic Origins of the Nag Hammadi Codices* (Tübingen: Mohr Siebeck, 2015), 207–33; Joel T. Walker, "Ascetic Literacy: Books and Readers in East-Syrian Monastic Tradition," in *Commutatio et contentio: Studies in the Late Roman, Sasanian, and Early Islamic Near East*, ed. Henning Börm and Josef Wiesehöfer (Düsseldorf: Wellem, 2010), 307–45; Jack Tannous, *The Making of the Medieval Middle East: Religion, Society, and Simple Believers* (Princeton: Princeton University Press, 2018), 181–98; Marlia Mundell Mango, "The Production of Syriac Manuscripts, 400–700 AD," in *Scritture, libri e testi nelle aree provinciali di Bisanzio*, ed. Guglielmo Cavallo, Giuseppe de Gregorio, and Marilena Maniaci (Spoleto: Centro Italiano di Studi sull'Alto Medioevo, 1991), 161–79; Slyvain Destephen, "Quatre études sur le monachisme asianique (IVᵉ–VIIᵉ siècle)," *Journal des Savants* (2010): 193–264, at 232–33; Garth Fowden, "Alexandria between Antiquity and Islam: Commerce and Concepts in First Millennium Afro-Eurasia," *Millennium-Jahrbuch* 16 (2019): 233–70, at 245–49; Susana Calvo Capilla, "The Reuse of Classical Antiquity in the Palace of Madinat al-Zahra' and Its Role in the Construction of Caliphal Legitimacy," *Muqarnas* 31 (2014): 1–33, at 12–15, 22–23.

5. Shem'on d-Ṭaybutheh, *On the Consecration of the Cell* 8.

6. Henrik Rydell Johnsén, "The Virtue of Being Uneducated: Attitudes towards Classical *Paideia* in Early Monasticism and Ancient Philosophy," in *Monastic Education in Late Antiquity*, ed. Larsen and Rubenson, 219–25.

7. Differences between reading aloud and silently: Heinrich Fichtenau, "Monastisches und scholastisches Lesen," in *Herrschaft, Kirche, Kultur: Beiträge zur Geschichte des Mittelalters. Festschrift für Friedrich Prinz zu seinem 65. Geburtstag*, ed. Georg Jenal (Stuttgart: Hiersemann, 1993), 317–37, at 318; Walker, "Ascetic Literacy," 311–15, 320; and see Barsanuphius of Gaza's advice to a monk to read and meditate aloud to tamp down on distractions (*Letters* 431).

8. Calligraphy as creation: Claudia Rapp, "Holy Texts, Holy Men, and Holy Scribes: Aspects of Scriptural Holiness in Late Antiquity," in *The Early Christian Book*, ed. Klingshirn and Safran, 194–222, at 215. Evagrius's education in context: Blossom Stefaniw, "The School of Didymus the Blind in Light of the Tura Find," in *Monastic Education in Late Antiquity*, ed. Larsen and Rubenson, 153–81. Acedia: Gabriel Bunge, *Akedia: Die geistliche Lehre des Evagrios Pontikos vom Überdruß* (Cologne: Luthe, 1989), esp. 51–68.

9. *AP/GN*, N. 185, trans. Wortley, p. 131 ("becomes iron": an analogy between sexual thoughts/*porneia* and books as both potentially difficult to excise). Curriculum: Stefaniw, "The School of Didymus the Blind"; Catherine M. Chin, *Grammar and Christianity in the Late Roman World* (Philadelphia: University of Pennsylvania Press, 2008); Jean Leclercq, *The Love of Learning and the Desire for God: A Study of Monastic Culture*, trans. Catharine Misrahi (New York: Fordham University Press, 1961),

58–60, 139–84; Rita Copeland and Ineke Sluiter, eds., *Medieval Grammar and Rhetoric: Language Arts and Literary Theory, AD 300–1475* (Oxford: Oxford University Press, 2009).

10. Hugo Lundhaug, "The Dishna Papers and the Nag Hammadi Codices: The Remains of a Single Monastic Library?," in *The Nag Hammadi Codices and Late Antique Egypt*, ed. Lundhaug and Lance Jenott (Tübingen: Mohr Siebeck, 2018), 329–86; Tannous, *The Making of the Medieval Middle East*, 160–80, 187–97, 210–15; Giorgia Vocino, "A Peregrinus's Vade Mecum: MS Bern 363 and the 'Circle of Sedulius Scottus,'" in *The Annotated Book in the Early Middle Ages: Practices of Reading and Writing*, ed. Mariken Teeuwen and Irene van Renswoude (Turnhout, Belgium: Brepols, 2017), 87–123, at 97–100.

11. Isaac's work in Turfan: Sims-Williams, *An Ascetic Miscellany*, E28/12, p. 25, excerpted from Isaac, *Discourses* 2.1. Pontigny: Leclercq, *The Love of Learning and the Desire for God*, 316, citing Auxerre, Bibliothèque municipale 50, fol. 139v; see also Walker, "Ascetic Literacy," 316–24.

12. Ferreolus, *Regula* 19. Administrative aspirations: Roger Bagnall, "The Educational and Cultural Background of Egyptian Monks," in *Monastic Education in Late Antiquity*, ed. Larsen and Rubenson, 75–100. Unread books: *AP/GS* 10.191; *AP/PJ* 10.114; *AP/S* 1.8.250, quotation slightly modifying Budge's translation at p. 73; other *AP* variants in Arabic, Ethiopic, and Slavic noted in the *Monastica* database at https://monastica.ht.lu.se/; see also the Pachomian *Prophecy of Apa Charour* quoted in Lundhaug and Jenott, *Monastic Origins of the Nag Hammadi Codices*, 166.

13. Required reading: *Precepts* 139–40, 142, in *Pachomian Koinonia* 2:166; *Regulations of Horsiesios* 16, in *Pachomian Koinonia* 2:202. For a schema of elementary reading pedagogy see Lillian I. Larsen, "'Excavating the Excavations' of Early Monastic Education," in *Monastic Education in Late Antiquity*, ed. Larsen and Rubenson, 101–24. Text and aurality: Paul C. Dilley, *Monasteries and the Care of Souls in Late Antique Christianity: Cognition and Discipline* (Cambridge: Cambridge University Press, 2017), 110–47; John Wortley, "How the Desert Fathers 'Meditated,'" *Greek, Roman, and Byzantine Studies* 46 (2006): 315–28. Jonas: *Paralipomena* 29–30, in *Pachomian Koinonia* 2:53–55.

14. Dilley, *Monasteries and the Care of Souls*, 144–45; Yvan Koenig, "Place et rôle de l'Écriture dans la prière individuelle des moines d'Égypte (IVᵉ–Vᵉ siècle)," in *La vie quotidienne des moines en Orient et en Occident (IVᵉ–Xᵉ siècle)*, vol. 2, *Questions transversales*, ed. Olivier Delouis and Maria Mossakowska-Gaubert (Cairo and Athens: Institut Français d'Archéologie Orientale and École Française d'Athènes, 2019), 239–52.

15. Pachomian regularization: Brakke, *Demons and the Making of the Monk*, 92, following Armand Veilleux, *La liturgie dans le cénobitisme pachômien au quatrième siècle* (Rome: Herder, 1968), 262–75. Liturgical alternatives: Peter Jeffery, "Psalmody and Prayer in Early Monasticism," in *The Cambridge History of Medieval Monasticism in the Latin West* ed. Alison I.

Beach and Isabelle Cochelin (Cambridge: Cambridge University Press, 2020), 1:112–27. Rich parents' house: Evagrius, *Antirrhetikos* 3.22 (Ps. 83:11/84:11). For Evagrius's approach to shaping the self through scripture: Luke Dysinger, *Psalmody and Prayer in the Writings of Evagrius Ponticus* (Oxford: Oxford University Press, 2005).

16. Stoic thought-management: Robert E. Sinkewicz, *Evagrius of Pontus: The Greek Ascetic Corpus* (Oxford: Oxford University Press, 2003), 145–46; Pierre Hadot, *Exercices spirituels et philosophie antique*, 2nd ed. (Paris: Études Augustiniennes, 1987), 20–27, 66–68. Evagrius's demonology: David Brakke, *Demons and the Making of the Monk: Spiritual Combat in Early Christianity* (Cambridge, MA: Harvard University Press, 2006), 48–77. Manuscript tradition: Brakke, introduction to *Antirrhetikos*, 1–6, 41–44; Hugo Gressmann and W. Lüdtke, "Euagrios Pontikos," *Zeitschrift für Kirchengeschichte* 35 (1914): 86–96; and more generally Paul Géhin, "D'Égypte en Mésopotamie: La réception d'Évagre le Pontique dans les communautés syriaques," in *Monachismes*, ed. Jullien and Pierre, 29–49. A similar (but longer-winded) manual circulated in the Syriac tradition of Isaiah's *Akestikon*: see Logos 16 in Draguet's ed.

17. Barsanuphius, *Letters* 427; Inbar Graiver, "The Paradoxical Effects of Attentiveness," *Journal of Early Christian Studies* 24 (2016): 199–227.

18. Cassian, *Collationes* 1.17 (mind as churning mill), 14.10 (*formet*). Context for Cassian's arguments: Conrad Leyser, "*Lectio divina, oratio pura*: Rhetoric and the Techniques of Asceticism in the *Conferences* of John Cassian," in *Modelli di santità e modelli di comportamento: Contrasti, intersezioni, complementarità*, ed. Giulia Barone, Marina Caffiero, and F. Scorza (Turin: Rosenberg & Sellier, 1994), 79–105; cf. Rebecca Krawiec, "Monastic Literacy in John Cassian: Toward a New Sublimity," *Church History* 81 (2012): 765–95.

19. Peter Jeffery, "Monastic Reading and the Emerging Roman Chant Repertory," in *Western Plainchant in the First Millennium: Studies in the Medieval Liturgy and Its Music*, ed. Sean Gallagher, James Haar, John Nádas, and Timothy Striplin (Aldershot, England: Ashgate, 2003), 45–103, at 53–63; Michaela Puzicha, "*Lectio divina*—Ort der Gottesbegegnung," in *Erbe und Auftrage: Monastische Welt*, ed. Beuron Archabbey (Beuron, Germany: Beuroner Kunstverlag, 2011), 245–63; Ellen Muehlberger, *Moment of Reckoning: Imagined Death and Its Consequences in Late Ancient Christianity* (Oxford: Oxford University Press, 2019), 119–29; Niki Kasumi Clements, *Sites of the Ascetic Self: John Cassian and Christian Ethical Formation* (Notre Dame: University of Notre Dame Press, 2020), 118–22; *AP/GN*, N. 185 (the book "becomes iron"—also cited in n. 9 of this chapter). *In corde/ore*: *RM* 7.71; *RB* 5.17; Baudonivia, *Vita Radegundis* 8, 19 (among many other examples).

20. Fichtenau, "Monastisches und scholastisches Lesen," 325–29; Marie-Joseph Steve, *L'Île de Khārg: Une page de l'histoire du Golfe Persique et du monachisme oriental* (Neuchâtel: Recherches et Publications, 2003), 106–8.

Checking out books: *Precepts* 25, in *Pachomian Koinonia* 2:149; Shenoute, *Rules* 245–46; Augustine, *Praeceptum* 5.9–10; Eugippius, *Regula* 1.123–24; *RB* 48.15–16; *Regula monasterii Tarnatensis* 22.2–3; Isidore, *Regula* 8; monastery of St. John Stoudios, *Rule* 26, in Thomas and Hero, *Byzantine Monastic Foundation Documents*; and the hagiographic example of Bar-'Idta in his time at Izla: Abraham, *History of Rabban Bar-'Idta*, lines 146, 168–93, pp. 173–76. Damage: Isidore, *Regula* 17. See also Cassian, *Collationes* 1.6.2, 4.21 on possessiveness of books.

21. Different reading routines: Augustine, *Ordo monasterii* 3; *Regula orientalis* 24; *Regula et instituta patrum* 5; *RM* 50; Eugippius, *Regula* 1.10; *So-Called Canons of Maruta* 54.23, in Vööbus, *Syriac and Arabic Documents*; Caesarius, *Regula ad virgines* 19; Caesarius, *Regula ad monachos* 14; Aurelian, *Regula ad monachos* 28; *Regula monasterii Tarnatensis* 9.5, 9.7; Ferreolus, *Regula* 19, 26; Isidore, *Regula* 5; Fructuosus, *Regula* 4; Donatus, *Regula* 20.1; *Regula communis* 10; Shem'on d-Taybutheh, *On the Consecration of the Cell* 11; Joseph Ḥazzaya, *Lettre sur les trois étapes de la vie monastique* 3.74–76, 3.83. Reading during matins: Hildemar, *Expositio* 10, whose recommendations are based on the percentage of monks who are tired! Switching between reading and work/praying: Leander of Seville, *De institutione virginum* 15; Fructuosus, *Regula* 6. Sundays: *RM* 75; *RB* 48. Assigned reading: *RM* 15.28–37. Reading to prevent chatting: *Rules of Abraham of Kaškar* 8, in Vööbus, *Syriac and Arabic Documents*. Substitute for work: Ferreolus, *Regula* 28. Reading during work: Caesarius of Arles, *Regula ad virgines* 20; Leander of Seville, *De institutione virginum* 15; Donatus, *Regula* 20.7. Meals: Augustine, *Ordo monasterii* 7; Augustine, *Praeceptum* 3.2; Cassian, *De institutis coenobiorum* 4.17; *RM* 24; Eugippius, *Regula* 1.16; *RB* 38; Caesarius, *Regula ad virgines* 18; Caesarius, *Regula ad monachos* 9; Aurelian, *Regula ad virgines* 32; Aurelian, *Regula ad monachos* 48–49; *Regula monasterii Tarnatensis* 8.10–12; *Regula Pauli et Stephani* 18; Isidore, *Regula* 9; Fructuosus, *Regula* 3; Donatus, *Regula* 33.1–5; Jonas of Bobbio, *Regula cuiusdam ad virgines* 9.13–14; *The Canons of the Persians* 13, in Vööbus, *Syriac and Arabic Documents*; Dadisho', *Canons* 4, in ibid.; Babai, *Rules* 6, in ibid.; monastery of St. John Stoudios, *Rule* 28, in Thomas and Hero, *Byzantine Monastic Foundation Documents*.

22. Isidore of Seville, *Regula* 5; similarly Columbanus, *Regula coenobialis*, 223D, on not reading when you were supposed to be doing something else; Joseph Ḥazzaya, *Lettre sur les trois étapes de la vie monastique* 3.68.

23. *AP/G*, Epiphanius of Cyprus 8, trans. Ward, p. 58; Leander of Seville, *Regula* 15 (lines 542–45 in the Latin ed. of Campos Ruiz).

24. *Regula communis* 10 (lines 315–18 in the Latin ed. of Campos Ruiz). For the context to this text see Pablo C. Díaz, "*Regula communis*: Monastic Space and Social Context," in *Western Monasticism ante litteram: Spaces of Monastic Observation in Late Antiquity and the Early Middle Ages*, ed. Hendrik Dey and Elizabeth Fentress (Turnhout, Belgium: Brepols, 2011), 117–35.

25. Annotations: Evina Steinová, *Notam superponere studui: The Use of Annotation Symbols in the Early Middle Ages* (Turnhout, Belgium: Brepols, 2019); Teeuwen and Renswoude, eds., *The Annotated Book in the Early Middle Ages*; Kallirroe Linardou, "An Exercise in Extravagance and Abundance: Some Thoughts on the *marginalia decorata* in the Codex Parasinus graecus 216," in *Graphic Devices and the Early Decorated Book*, ed. Michelle P. Brown, Ildar H. Garipzanov, and Benjamin C. Tilghman (Woodbridge, UK: Boydell, 2017), 218–42. Sedulius: Vocino, "A *Peregrinus*'s Vade Mecum," 94–97. On figures 11–12: Charles Plummer, "On the Colophons and Marginalia of Irish Scribes," *Proceedings of the British Academy* 12 (1926): 11–44; Damian McManus, *A Guide to Ogam* (Maynooth, Ireland: An Sagart, 1997), 133 (hangover); Martin Hellmann, "Tironische Tituli: Die Verwendung stenographischer Marginalien zur inhaltichen Erschließung von Texten des frühen Mittelalters," in *The Annotated Book*, ed. Teeuwen and Renswoude, 263–83, at 271 (Tironian shorthand example).

26. Saba: Mango, "The Production of Syriac Manuscripts," 178; William Wright, *Catalogue of Syriac Manuscripts in the British Museum Acquired since the Year 1838* (London: Gilbert and Rivington, 1870), 1:15–17. Gislildis: Henry Mayr-Harting, "Augustinus von Hippo, Chelles und die karolingische Renaissance: Beobachtungen zu Cod. 63 der Kölner Dombibliothek," in *Mittelalterliche Handschriften der Kölner Dombibliothek: Drittes Symposion* (Cologne: Erzbischöfliche Diözesan- und Dombibliothek, 2010), 25–36; see also Bernhard Bischoff, "Die Kölner Nonnenhandschriften und das Skriptorium von Chelles," in *Mittelalterliche Studien: Ausgewählte Aufsätze zur Schriftkunde und Literaturegeschichte* (Stuttgart: Hiersemann, 1961), 1:16–34; Rosamond McKitterick, "Nuns' Scriptoria in England and Francia in the Eighth Century," *Francia* 19, no. 1 (1989): 1–35, at 2–4.

27. M. B. Parkes, *Pause and Effect: An Introduction to the History of Punctuation in the West* (Berkeley: University of California Press, 1993), esp. 9–29; Nicholas Everett, "Literacy from Late Antiquity to the Early Middle Ages, c. 300–800 AD," in *The Cambridge Handbook of Literacy*, ed. David Olson and Nancy Torrance (Cambridge: Cambridge University Press, 2008), 362–85; Gamble, *Books and Readers in the Early Church*, 48, 74, 203–4; George E. Kiraz, "Dots in the Writing Systems of the Middle East," in *Near and Middle Eastern Studies at the Institute for Advanced Study, Princeton: 1935–2018*, ed. Sabine Schmidtke (Princeton: Gorgias Press, 2018), 265–75, esp. 268–71. Pompeius: Parkes, *Pause and Effect*, 10.

28. Cassiodorus, *Institutiones* 1.15.12 ("quaedam viae sunt sensuum et lumina dictionum"). The linguistic situation in the early medieval West: Roger Wright, *A Sociophilological Study of Late Latin* (Turnhout, Belgium: Brepols, 2002); Julia M. H. Smith, *Europe after Rome: A New Cultural History, 500–1000* (Cambridge: Cambridge University Press, 2005), 13–50.

29. *AP/G*, trans. Ward, xxxvi.

30. Breaks, rubrication, standout letters: Parkes, *Pause and Effect*; *Comparative Oriental Manuscript Studies: An Introduction*, ed. Alessandro Bausi et al. (Hamburg: Comparative Oriental Manuscript Studies, 2015), esp. 84–85, 148, 168–69, 202–5, 259–62. Script changes and rhetoric: Kreiner, *The Social Life of Hagiography in the Merovingian Kingdom* (Cambridge: Cambridge University Press, 2014), 282–86. Obelus: Irene van Renswoude, "The Censor's Rod: Textual Criticism, Judgment, and Canon Formation in Late Antiquity in the Early Middle Ages," in *The Annotated Book*, ed. Teeuwen and Renswoude, 555–95. Crosses: Cynthia Hahn, "The Graphic Cross as Salvific Mark and Organizing Principle: Making, Marking, Shaping," in *Graphic Devices*, ed. Brown et al., 100–126. Activating portraits: Éric Palazzo, "Graphic Visualization in Liturgical Manuscripts in the Early Middle Ages: The Initial 'O' in the Sacramentary of Gellone," in ibid., 63–79.

31. Too much to read: Braulio of Saragossa, *Vita Aemiliani* 1; Bede, prefatory letter to Acca, *In principium Genesis*, lines 18–24 (p. 66 in Kendall's translation); Hrabanus Maurus, preface to *De rerum naturis*, cols. 11–12; and more generally Ann M. Blair, *Too Much to Know: Managing Scholarly Information before the Digital Age* (New Haven: Yale University Press, 2010), 11–61. Biblical compilations: Matthias M. Tischler, "Bibliotheca: Die Bibel als transkulturelle Bibliothek von Geschichte und Geschichten," in *Die Bibliothek—The Library—La Bibliothèque*, ed. Andreas Speer and Lars Reuke (Berlin: De Gruyter, 2020), 559–80. Otfrid and columnar commentaries: Cinzia Grifoni, "Reading the Catholic Epistles: Glossing Practices in Early Medieval Wissembourg," in *The Annotated Book*, ed. Teeuwen and Renswoude, 705–42.

32. Grafton and Williams, *Christianity and the Transformation of the Book*, 22–132; Matthew R. Crawford, *The Eusebian Canon Tables: Ordering Textual Knowledge in Late Antiquity* (Oxford: Oxford University Press, 2019), 57–74.

33. Timothy M. Law, "La version syro-hexaplaire et la transmission textuelle de la Bible grecque," in *L'ancien Testament en syriaque*, ed. Fr. Briquel Chatonnet and P. Le Moigne (Paris: Geuthner, 2008), 101–20; Timothy's comments appear in Ep. 71*, trans. Brock, in *A Brief Outline of Syriac Literature*, 246.

34. Grafton and Williams, *Christianity and the Book*, 132–77; R. W. Burgess and Michael Kulikowski, *Mosaics of Time: The Latin Chronicle Traditions from the First Century BC to the Sixth Century AD*, vol. 1, *A Historical Introduction to the Chronicle Genre from Its Origins to the High Middle Ages* (Turnhout, Belgium: Brepols, 2013), 119–26.

35. Helmut Reimitz, *History, Frankish Identity and the Framing of Western Ethnicity, 550–850* (Cambridge: Cambridge University Press, 2015), 222–31.

36. Crawford, *Eusebian Canon Tables*; Carruthers, *The Book of Memory*, 174; Judith McKenzie and Francis Watson, *The Garima Gospels: Early Illuminated Gospel Books from Ethiopia* (Oxford: Mana al-Athar, 2016), 145–86.

37. Lawrence Nees, "Graphic Quire Marks and Qur'anic Verse Markers in Frankish and Islamic Manuscripts from the Seventh and Eighth Centuries," in *Graphic Devices*, ed. Brown et al., 80–99, at 91–99; Nees, "'Merovingian' Illuminated Manuscripts and Their Links with the Eastern Mediterranean World," in *East and West in the Early Middle Ages: The Merovingian Kingdoms in Mediterranean Perspective*, ed. Stefan Esders, Yaniv Fox, Yitzhak Hen, and Laury Sarti (Cambridge: Cambridge University Press, 2019), 297–317; Claude Gilliot, "Creation of a Fixed Text," in *The Cambridge Companion to the Qur'ān*, ed. Jane Dammen McAuliffe (Cambridge: Cambridge University Press, 2006), 41–57, at 47–48.

38. Unpopular technical innovations: Renswoude, "The Censor's Rod," 578; Mango, "The Production of Syriac Mansucripts," 172. Kinks: Reimitz, *History, Frankish Identity and the Framing of Western Ethnicity*, 226.

39. TV shows: Johann Hari, *Stolen Focus: Why You Can't Pay Attention—and How to Think Deeply Again* (New York: Crown, 2022), 89. Video games: Adam Gazzaley and Larry D. Rosen, *The Distracted Mind: Ancient Brains in a High-Tech World* (Cambridge, MA: MIT Press, 2016), 89–92, 194–99.

40. Sinéad O'Sullivan, "Reading and the Lemma in Early Medieval Textual Culture," in *The Annotated Book*, ed. Teeuwen and Renswoude, 37–196.

CHAPTER 5. MEMORY

1. Cassian, *Collationes* 14.9–13, quotation 14.12 ("nunc mens mea poeticis illis uelut infecta carminibus illas fabularum nugas historiasque bellorum"). See also ibid. 7.4.2 (Serenus on anchoring the mind with a carefully stocked memory). Nesteros designed this space based on the description in Hebrews 9:4–5 of the ark of the covenant and its contents; this text in turn was an adaptation of descriptions in the Hebrew Bible (e.g., Exodus 16:18, 25:18; 3 Kings 6:23–28).

2. Mary Carruthers, *The Book of Memory: A Study of Memory in Medieval Culture*, 2nd ed. (Cambridge: Cambridge University Press, 2008), esp. 217–27 (on ethics and memory); Carruthers, *The Craft of Thought: Meditation, Rhetoric, and the Making of Images, 400–1200* (Cambridge: Cambridge University Press, 1998) (on monks' role in developing the arts of memory in the early Middle Ages).

3. Carruthers, *Book of Memory*, 153–94, quotation 153; Scott Fitzgerald Johnson, *Literary Territories: Cartographical Thinking in Late Antiquity* (Oxford: Oxford University Press, 2016); Andy Merrills, "Geography and Memory in Isidore's *Etymologies*," in *Mapping Medieval Geographies: Geographical Encounters in the Latin West and Beyond*, ed. Keith D. Liley and Daniel Birkholz (Cambridge: Cambridge University Press, 2013), 45–64;

Darlene L. Brooks Hedstrom, "The Geography of the Monastic Cell in Early Egyptian Monastic Literature," *Church History* 78, no. 4 (2009): 756–91; Antonio Sennis, "Narrating Places: Memory and Space in Medieval Monasteries," in *People and Space in the Middle Ages, 300–1300*, ed. Wendy Davies, Guy Halsall, and Andrew Reynolds (Turnhout, Belgium: Brepols, 2006); Carruthers, *Craft of Thought*, 6–59, 272–76; Michel Lauwers, "Constructing Monastic Space in the Early and Central Medieval West (Fifth to Twelfth Century)," trans. Matthew Mattingly, in *The Cambridge History of Medieval Monasticism in the Latin West*, ed. Alison I. Beach and Isabelle Cochelin (Cambridge: Cambridge University Press, 2020), 1:317–39, esp. 330; Adam S. Cohen, "Monastic Art and Architecture, c. 700–1100: Material and Immaterial Worlds," in ibid., 519–541, at 525–33.

4. Elizabeth S. Bolman, "Late Antique Aesthetics, Chromophobia, and the Red Monastery, Sohag, Egypt," *Eastern Christian Art* 3 (2006): 1–24, quotation at 20; Bolman, ed., *The Red Monastery Church: Beauty and Asceticism in Upper Egypt* (New Haven and London: Yale University Press, 2016), esp. Bolman, "A Staggering Spectacle: Early Byzantine Aesthetics in the Triconch," 119–27, at 122 (Paul Silentiarios, "irresistible force").

5. Yizhar Hirschfeld, "The Early Byzantine Monastery at Khirbet ed-Deir in the Judean Desert: The Excavations in 1981–1987," *Qedem* 38 (1999): i–xii, 1–180, at plate IV and pp. 107–12, 133–34; Rosemary Cramp, *Wearmouth and Jarrow Monastic Sites*, vol. 2 (Swindon: English Heritage, 2006), esp. 163–66; Luis Caballero Zoreda, "El conjunto monástico de Santa María de Melque (Toledo): Siglos VII–IX (Criterios seguidos para identificar monasterios hispánicos tardo antiguos)," in *Monjes y monasterios hispanos an la Alta Edad Media*, ed. José Angel García de Cortázar and Ramón Teja (Aguilar de Campoo, Spain: Fundación Santa María le Real—Centro de Estudios del Románico, 2006), 99–144, at 121–38; Caballero, "Un canal de transmission de lo clásico en la alta Edad Media española: Arquitectura y escultura de influjo omeya en la península ibérica entre mediados del siglo VIII e inicios del siglo X (1)," *al-Qantara* 15 (1994): 321–48, at 339–42. Varying attitudes toward elaborate monastic spaces: Beat Brenk, "Klosterbaukunst des ersten Jahrtausends: Rhetorik versus Realität," *Annali della Scuola Normale Superiore di Pisa: Classe di Littere e Filosofia*, ser. 4, vol. 5 (2000): 317–42, esp. 330–36. Pachomius: *Paralipomena* 32, in *Pachomian Koinonia* 2:55–56, trans. Vieilleux at p. 56. Cistercians: Carruthers, *Craft of Thought*, 84–87, 257–61.

6. Éric Palazzo, *L'invention chrétienne des cinq sens dans la liturgie et l'art au Moyen Âge* (Paris: Cerf, 2014); Bissera V. Pentcheva, *Hagia Sophia: Sound, Space, and Spirit in Byzantium* (University Park: Pennsylvania State University Press, 2017); Mary Carruthers, *The Experience of Beauty in the Middle Ages* (Cambridge: Cambridge University Press, 2013); Carruthers, *Craft of Thought*, 116–70.

7. Anagogy: Peter Dronke, *Imagination in the Late Pagan and Early Chris-

tian World: The First Nine Centuries A.D. (Florence: SISMEL/Edizioni del Galluzzo, 2003), 5–24.

8. Patricia Cox Miller, *The Corporeal Imagination: Signifying the Holy in Late Ancient Christianity* (Philadelphia: University of Pennsylvania Press, 2009), esp. 81–115 ("visceral seeing" drawing on James Elkins at p. 104); Kreiner, "A Generic Mediterranean: Hagiography in the Early Middle Ages," in *East and West in the Early Middle Ages: The Merovingian Kingdoms in Mediterranean Perspective*, ed. Stefan Esders, Yaniv Fox, Yitzhak Hen, and Laury Sarti (Cambridge: Cambridge University Press, 2019), 202–17; Joaquin Martínez Pizarro, *A Rhetoric of the Scene: Dramatic Narrative in the Early Middle Ages* (Toronto: University of Toronto Press, 1989).

9. *Life of St. Mary of Egypt* 10–12, trans. Maria Kouli, in Talbot, *Holy Women of Byzantium*, pp. 76–77. See also Irina Dumitrescu's analysis of the Latin and Old English versions of this text: *The Experience of Education in Anglo-Saxon Literature* (Cambridge: Cambridge University Press, 2018), 129–56.

10. See especially Roland Betancourt, *Byzantine Intersectionality: Sexuality, Gender, and Race in the Middle Ages* (Princeton: Princeton University Press, 2020), 1–14.

11. For example: Beatrice Kitzinger, *The Cross, the Gospels, and the Work of Art in the Carolingian Age* (Cambridge: Cambridge University Press, 2019), 99–196; Laura E. McCloskey, "Exploring *meditatio* and *memoria* in Ireland through the *Book of Durrow*: Manuscript Illumination as the Intersection of Theological and Artistic Traditions," *Eolas: The Journal of the American Society of Irish Medieval Studies* 11 (2018): 32–59; Coon, *Dark Age Bodies*, 216–46. Overviews: Kurt Weitzmann, *Late Antique and Early Christian Book Illumination* (New York: George Braziller, 1977), 15–24, 73–127; Lawrence Nees, *Early Medieval Art* (Oxford: Oxford University Press, 2002), 153–71, 195–211.

12. Benjamin C. Tilghman, "Patterns of Meaning in Insular Manuscripts: Folio 183r in the Book of Kells," in *Graphic Devices and the Early Decorated Book*, ed. Michelle P. Brown, Ildar H. Garipzanov, and Benjamin C. Tilghman (Woodbridge, UK: Boydell, 2017), 163–78.

13. *RM* 10; Eugippius, *Regula* 28; *RB* 7; John Climacus, *Ladder of Divine Ascent*. The first three texts refer in passing to Jacob's ladder in Gen. 28:12; John adds to this the image of ascending by steps in Ps. 83:6 (*Ladder* 30). See also Jonathan L. Zecher, *The Role of Death in* The Ladder of Divine Ascent *and the Greek Ascetic Tradition* (Oxford: Oxford University Press, 2015), 36–48. Medieval principle of *divisio*: Carruthers, *Book of Memory*, 99–152.

14. Palazzo, *L'invention chrétienne des cinq sens*, quotation at 42; Mary J. Carruthers, "*Ars oblivionialis, ars inveniendi*: The Cherub Figure and the Arts of Memory," *Gesta* 48 (2009): 99–117; Lina Bolzoni, *The Web of Images: Vernacular Preaching from Its Origins to St Bernardino da Siena*, trans. Carole Preston and Lisa Chien (Aldershot, England: Ashgate, 2004), 126–35. *The Six Wings* was translated by Bridget Balint in *The Medieval Craft*

of Memory, ed. Carruthers and Ziolkowski, 82–102 (where the text is attributed to Alan of Lille).

15. Arts of memory in the high Middle Ages: Carruthers, *Book of Memory*, 153–94, 274–337.

16. Foer, *Moonwalking with Einstein: The Art and Science of Remembering Everything* (New York: Penguin, 2011); Joshua Foer, "How I Learned a Language in 22 Hours," *The Guardian*, November 9, 2012, https://www.theguardian .com/education/2012/nov/09/learn-language-in-three-months.

17. Carruthers, *Craft of Thought*, esp. 77–81, 116–33; Rachel Fulton, "Praying with Anselm at Admont: A Meditation on Practice," *Speculum* 81 (2006): 700–733; Michaela Puzicha, "*Lectio divina*—Ort der Gottesbegegnung," in *Erbe und Auftrage: Monastische Welt*, ed. Beuron Archabbey (Beuron, Germany: Beuroner Kunstverlag, 2011), 245–63; Duncan Robertson, *Lectio divina: The Medieval Experience of Reading* (Collegeville, MN: Liturgical Press, 2011). Flowers, medicines, and repurposed memories are all Alcuin's metaphors (though not his exclusively): John C. Cavadini, "A Carolingian Hilary," in *The Study of the Bible in the Carolingian Era*, ed. Celia Chazelle and Burton Van Name Edwards (Turnhout, Belgium: Brepols, 2003), 133–40, at 133; Carruthers, *Craft of Thought*, 117–20.

18. See the taxonomies in Halvor Eifring, "Types of Meditation," in *Asian Traditions of Meditation*, ed. Eifring (Honolulu: University of Hawai'i Press, 2016), 27–47; Halvor Eifring and Are Holen, "The Uses of Attention: Elements of Meditative Practice," in *Hindu, Buddhist, and Daoist Meditation: Cultural Histories*, ed. Eifring (Oslo: Heremes Academic Publishing, 2014), 1–26. Buddhist meditation ca. 400–700 CE: Eric M. Greene, *Chan before Chan: Meditation, Repentance, and Visionary Experience in Chinese Buddhism* (Honolulu: Kuroda Institute and University of Hawai'i Press, 2021), esp. 110–58.

19. See the late antique commentaries inflected with this reading of 2 Cor. 10:13: Ambrosiaster, *In epistulas ad Corinthios*, pp. 276–77; Pelagius, *Ad Corinthios II*, pp. 287–88. On the possibility of a seventh-century date for the *RM* see Albrecht Diem, *The Pursuit of Salvation: Community, Space, and Discipline in Early Medieval Monasticism* (Turnhout, Belgium: Brepols, 2021), 273, 326, 331–45.

20. *RM*, prologue, quoting Ps. 2:9, 1 Cor. 4:21, Ps. 44:7–8, Ps. 88:33. The *RM* quotes the psalms of the Vetus Latina version of the Bible, so I have made a few minor changes to the Douay Rheims Challoner translation (which is based on the Vulgate).

21. See especially Hilary of Poitiers, *Tractatus super Psalmos* 2.34–38, pp. 61–63 (a pastoral reading of *virga*); Jerome, *Commentarioli in Psalmos* 2, pp. 181–82 (following God); Augustine, *Enarrationes in psalmos* 44:17–18, pp. 505–6 in Dekkers and Fraipont's Latin ed. (governance as discipline, rod as Christ); Pelagius, *Ad Corinthios II*, p. 150 (with a link to the monastic antiheroes Ananias and Sapphira); Arnobius the Younger, *Commentarii in Psalmos* 44, pp. 62–65 (renunciation); Cassiodorus, *Expositio psalmorum*

2.10, 88.33, vol. 1, pp. 46–47 (power and fairness) and vol. 2, p. 813 (different forms of divine discipline) in Adriaen's Latin ed.

22. Bede, *Vita Cuthberti* 8; Shem'on d-Ṭaybutheh, *Mystical Works* 169b, trans. Mingana, p. 20. Exegetical meditation as a distraction: Brouria Bitton-Ashkelony, "Pure Prayer and Ignorance: Dadisho' Qaṭraya and the Greek Ascetic Legacy," *Studi e materiali di storia delle religioni* 78, 1 (2012): 200–226, at 214–18; Sabina Chialà, "Les mystiques syro-orientaux: Une école ou une époque?" in *Les mystiques syriaques*, ed. Alain Desreumaux (Paris: Geuthner, 2011), 63–78, at 72–76.

23. Erica Weaver, "Premodern and Postcritical: Medieval Enigmata and the Hermeneutic Style," *New Literary History* 50.1 (2019): 43–64, "wandering" at 53; Aldhelm, *Aenigmata* 41 (pillow), 42 (ostrich), 62 (bubble), constellations *passim*.

24. Notes: Markus Schiegg, "Source Marks in Scholia: Evidence from an Early Medieval Gospel Manuscript," in *The Annotated Book in the Early Middle Ages: Practices of Reading and Writing*, ed. Mariken Teeuwen and Irene van Renswoude (Turnhout, Belgium: Brepols, 2017), 237–61, at 238, 243; Alberto Cevolini, "Making *notae* for Scholarly Retrieval: A Franciscan Case Study," in ibid., 343–67, at 351; Carruthers, *Book of Memory*, 3–8, 243–57. More on Hrabanus and his meditational play: Lynda L. Coon, *Dark Age Bodies: Gender and Monastic Practice in the Early Medieval West* (Philadelphia: University of Pennsylvania Press, 2010), 13–41, 216–46. Fulda's library under Hrabanus: Janneke Raaijmakers, *The Making of the Monastic Community of Fulda, c. 744–c. 900* (Cambridge: Cambridge University Press, 2012), 189–98.

25. This excerpt is from Hrabanus Maurus, *De rerum naturis*, 206–207. Hrabanus's source for this paragraph is Isidore, *Etymologiae* 8.1.25–26 (which also embeds a passage from Horace, *Epistles* 1.2.26).

26. Hrabanus's sources for this paragraph: *Clavis sanctae scripturae* 12.2.15 (alluding to Leviticus 11:7); ibid. 12.2.17 (quoting 2 Peter 2:22), with some small differences.

27. Hrabanus's source for this paragraph: Bede, *In epistolas VII catholicas*, pp. 275–76 (itself a condensed version of Gregory the Great, *Regula pastoralis* 1.30).

28. Hrabanus's sources for this paragraph: *Clavis sanctae scripturae* 12.2.16 (Matthew 7:6, 8:31); ibid. 12.2.18 (Luke 15:15); ibid. 12.2.20 (Psalm 16:14); Augustine, *Enarrationes in psalmos* 16 (Psalm 16:14 and Matthew 27:25); Cassiodorus, *Expositio psalmorum* 16.14 (Psalm 16:14 and Matthew 27:25); *Clavis sanctae scripturae* 12.2.19 (Proverbs 11:22); ibid. 12.2.21 (Isaiah 65:4). See also Isaiah Shachar, *The Judensau: A Medieval Anti-Jewish Motif and Its History* (London: Warburg Institute, 1974), 8–10.

29. E.g., "Caueat lector bonus ne suo sensui obtemperet scripturas, sed scripturis sanctis obtemperet sensum suum": *Regula cuiusdam patris ad monachos* 1 (echoing Cassian, *De institutis coenobiorum* 7.16).

30. Hrabanus in the context of Carolingian religious polemic: Jean-Louis Ver-

strepen, "Raban Maur et le Judaïsme dans son commentaire sur le qua-
tre livres des Rois," *Revue Mabillon* 68 (1996): 23–55; Bat-Sheva Albert,
"*Adversus Iudaeos* in the Carolingian Empire," in *Contra Iudaeos: Ancient
and Medieval Polemics between Christians and Jews*, ed. Ora Limor and Guy
Stroumsa (Tübingen: Mohr Siebeck, 1996), 119–42; Bat-Sheva Albert,
"Anti-Jewish Exegesis in the Carolingian Period: The Commentaries on
Lamentations of Hrabanus Maurus and Pascasius Radbertus," in *Bibli-
cal Studies in the Early Middle Ages*, ed. Claudio Leondari and Giovanni
Orlandi (Florence: SISMEL/Edizioni del Galluzzo, 2005), 175–92;
Gerda Heydemann, "The People of God and the Law: Biblical Models in
Carolingian Legislation," *Speculum* 95 (2020): 89–131.

31. Barsanuphius and John, *Letters* 60 (where Euthymius identifies with the
Gadarene swine in the synoptic gospels, to link his thoughts to the demons
that possessed the pigs).

32. Subjectivity: Scott Fitzgerald Johnson, *Literary Territories*, esp. 1–16, 29–
60; Kreiner, *Legions of Pigs in the Early Medieval West* (New Haven: Yale
University Press, 2020), 69–77.

33. Eucherius of Lyon, *Instructionum libri duo*, preface; Anna M. Silvas,
introduction to *The Asketikon of St Basil the Great* (Oxford: Oxford Uni-
versity Press, 2005); Micol Long, "Monastic Practices of Shared Read-
ing as Means of Learning," in *The Annotated Book in the Early Middle
Ages*, ed. Teeuwen and Renswoude, 501–28 (Gregory the Great, Alcuin,
Ruodulfus of Fulda—a student of Hrabanus); Michael Fox, "Alcuin the
Exegete: The Evidence of the *Quaestiones in Genesim*," in *The Study of the
Bible in the Carolingian Era*, ed. Chazelle and Edwards, 39–60; Hugo
Lundhaug, "Memory and Early Monastic Literary Practices: A Cogni-
tive Perspective," *Journal of Cognitive Historiography* 1 (2014): 98–120.
Teaching moments: Ferrandus, *Vita Fulgentii* 24; Isidore, *Regula* 8; *Vita
Geretrudis* 3.

34. "Meditatio sancta de corde non cesset": Caesaerius of Arles, *Regula ad vir-
gines* 18; repeated by Aurelian of Arles, *Regula ad virgines* 20; Aurelian,
Regula ad monachos 24. Similar sentiments in Isidore, *Regula* 3; Jonas of
Bobbio, *Regula cuiusdam ad virgines* 12.10–11. Theophilos: Włodzimierz
Godlewski, "Monastic Life in Makuria," in *La vie quotidienne des moines
en Orient et en Occident (IVᵉ–Xᵉ siècle)*, vol. 1, *L'état des sources*, ed. Olivier
Delouis and Maria Mossakowska-Gaubert (Cairo and Athens: Institut
Français d'Archéologie Orientale and École Française d'Athènes, 2015),
81–97, at 83–85.

35. Hugh's text: *Libellus de formatione arche*. Victorine historiography: Mar-
shall Crossnoe, "'Devout, Learned, and Virtuous': The History and Histories of the Order of St. Victor," in *A Companion to the Abbey of St. Victor
in Paris*, ed. Hugh Feiss and Juliet Mousseau (Leiden: Brill, 2018), 1–51;
Ursula Vones-Liebenstein, "Similarities and Differences between Monks
and Regular Canons in the Twelfth Century," in *The Cambridge History of
Medieval Monasticism in the Latin West*, ed. Beach and Cochelin, 2:766–

82. For the argument that Hugh's text represents a series of lectures on an actual painting: Conrad Rudolph, *The Mystic Ark: Hugh of St. Victor, Art, and Thought in the Twelfth Century* (New York: Cambridge University Press, 2014). For the argument that the ark was a mental picture: Carruthers, *Craft of Thought*, 243–46; Carruthers, *Book of Memory*, 293–302.

36. Noah: Jean Leclercq, *Otia monastica: Études sur le vocabulaire de la contemplation au Moyen Âge* (Rome: Pontificium Institutum S. Anselmi, 1963), 87–88. On the ark as solution to *instabilitas*: Hugh, *De arca Noe* 1.1—this was a companion text to his *Libellus*.

37. In Rudolph's models (*The Mystic Ark*), only the top story of the structure is covered. But the timbers reaching from the farthest and lowest corners of the ark to the lip of the pillar create planes that resemble slanted walls or a roof: see *Libellus de formatione arche*, pp. 124–26 in Sicard's Latin ed.

38. Hugh of St. Victor, *Didascalion* 3.10: "delectatur enim quodam aperto decurrere spatio."

39. Cassian, *Collationes* 10.8–14 (Ps. 69:2/70:2); see also Conrad Leyser, "*Lectio divina, oratio pura*: Rhetoric and the Techniques of Asceticism in the *Conferences* of John Cassian," in *Modelli di santità e modelli di comportamento: Contrasti, intersezioni, complementarità*, ed. Giulia Barone, Marina Caffiero, and F. Scorza (Turin: Rosenberg & Sellier, 1994), 79–105, at 88; Brouria Bitton-Ashkelony and Aryeh Kofsky, *The Monastic School of Gaza* (Leiden: Brill, 2006), 168–74, 176–82.

40. *Bohairic Life of Pachomius* 105, in *Pachomian Koinonia* 1:146. But see the contrasting attitudes of *AP/G* Theodora 8; *AP/PJ* 11.13 (John the Short).

CHAPTER 6. MIND

1. Gregory, *Dialogi* 2.3.5–9 (*cogitationis lapsum* at 2.3.9); Isaac of Nineveh, *Discourses* 2.3.4.65 (= *Centuries on Knowledge* 4.65), trans. Brock, *Syriac Fathers*, p. 267. Distraction as drunkenness: Cassian, *Collationes* 4.2, 10.13; Isaac of Nineveh, *Discourses* 2.5.4. Elevated concentration as drunkenness: Pseudo-Macarius, *Logoi* 8.4 (collection 2); Isaac of Nineveh, *Discourses* 2.10.35; John of Dalyatha, *Letters* 7.1; Joseph Ḥazzaya, *Lettre sur les trois étapes de la vie monastique* 3.94. The latter metaphor is ubiquitous in east Syrian mystic literature, though the theme of mystical inebriation can be traced back to the Jewish philosopher Philo of Alexandria: see Hans Lewy, *Sobria ebrietas: Untersuchungen zur Geschichte der antiker Mystik* (Giessen, Germany: Töpelmann, 1929).

2. Abraham of Nathpar, *On Prayer* 4, trans. Brock, *Syriac Fathers*, p. 194; likewise Behishoʿ Kamulaya, *Memre* 3, p. 295 (= 54a).

3. Basil, *Great Asketikon*, LR 15.3; Erica Weaver, "Performing (In)Attention," *Representations* 152 (2020): 1–24.

4. 'Enanisho', *Book of Paradise* 2.21, p. 390; Dadisho' Qatraya, *Compendious Commentary* 60–61; likewise the Ge'ez version, *Filekseyus* 30.

5. Tudor Andrei Sala, "Eyes Wide Shut: Surveillance and Its Economy of Ignorance in Late Antique Monasticism," in *La vie quotidienne des moines en Orient et en Occident (IVᵉ–Xᵉ siècle)*, ed. Olivier Delouis and Maria Mossakowska-Gaubert, vol. 2, *Questions transversales* (Cairo and Athens: Institut Français d'Archéologie Orientale and École Française d'Athènes, 2019), 283–300, quoting Shenoute at 289 (= *Canons* 3, ZC 302–3).

6. Dorotheus, *Didaskalia* 11.120; Shem'on d-Taybutheh, *Book of Medicine* 191a, trans. Mingana, p. 54.

7. E.g., *AP/GN*, N. 56, 227; *AP/S* 1.8.249; Kevin Roose, *Futureproof: 9 Rules for Humans in an Age of Automation* (New York: Random House, 2021), e.g., 168, 172–75. On the semantic range of "discernment" see Antony D. Rich, *Discernment in the Desert Fathers: Diakrisis in the Life and Thought of Early Egyptian Monasticism* (Bletchley, England: Paternoster, 2007).

8. Dorotheus, *Didaskalia* 9.99; Cassian, *Collationes* 1.19–21, 2.5 (on the importance of context; see also 21.11–17), 2.7 (Abrahamic delusions).

9. Dorotheus, *Didaskalia* 3.40; Columbanus, *Regula Columbani* 8; Barsanuphius and John, *Letters* 407–8. On uncertainty as an essential part of discernment, see especially Lorenzo Perrone, "'Trembling at the Thought of Shipwreck': The Anxious Self in the Letters of Barsanuphius and John of Gaza," in *Between Personal and Institutional Religion: Self, Doctrine, and Practice in Late Antique Eastern Christianity*, ed. Brouria Bitton-Ashkelony and Perrone (Turnhout, Belgium: Brepols, 2013), 9–36. Mentorship: see chapter 2, and also Rich, *Discernment*, 189–202.

10. The philosopher David J. Chalmers makes this comparison in *Reality+: Virtual Worlds and the Problems of Philosophy* (New York: Norton, 2022), 51–55, 452–53.

11. On the familial resemblance of demonic sieges to modern obsession, see Inbar Graiver, *Asceticism of the Mind: Forms of Attention and Self-Transformation in Late Antique Monasticism* (Toronto: Pontifical Institute of Mediaeval Studies, 2018), 129–62. "Paralysis by analysis": Ethan Kross, *Chatter: The Voice in Our Head, Why It Matters, and How to Harness It* (New York: Crown, 2021), 27.

12. Bouncer: Johann Hari, *Stolen Focus: Why You Can't Pay Attention—and How to Think Deeply Again* (New York: Crown, 2022), interview with Gazzaley at 43–44. Nesting: John of Apamea, *Letter to Hesychius* 41–42, in Brock, *Syriac Fathers*. Germinating: Cassian, *Collationes* 4.3. Pesticide: Ferreolus, *Regula* 9 ("ne in mente sua bonum semen sparsum enecet adulterina permixtio").

13. Hildemar, *Expositio*, prol.28; Dorotheus, *Didasaklia* 3.42.

14. Evagrius, *Peri logismon* 19, trans. Sinkewicz, p. 166; see also Michel Foucault, *Les aveux de la chair*, ed. Frédéric Gros, vol. 4 of *Histoire de la sexualité* (Paris: Gallimard, 2018), 140–42.

15. John of Apamea, *Letter to Hesychius* 41, trans. Brock, p. 91; *AP/G* Poemen 93, trans. Ward, p. 180 (and for Poemen's metaphors see the introduction); Inbar Graiver, "The Paradoxical Effects of Attentiveness," *Journal of Early Christian Studies* 24 (2016): 199–227, at 216–27; Graiver, "'I Think' vs. 'The Thought Tells Me': What Grammar Teaches Us about the Monastic Self," *Journal of Early Christian Studies* 25 (2017): 255–79.

16. *AP/GN*, N. 104, trans. Wortley, pp. 76–77; John Climacus, *Klimax* 4, trans. Luibheid and Russell, p. 113. Crowding: Evagrius, *Ad monachos* 14, 37, 98; Isidore, *Regula* 6; Conrad Leyser, *Authority and Asceticism from Augustine to Gregory the Great* (Oxford: Clarendon, 2000), 95–100.

17. Origen, *Peri euches* 31–32, quotation at 32, trans. Greer, p. 168; Lorenzo Perrone, *La preghiera secondo Origene: L'impossibilità donata* (Brescia: Morcelliana, 2011), esp. 51–122, 321–22, and 530–45 (on Clement of Alexandria's similarly Platonic confidence); Brouria Bitton-Ashkelony, *The Ladder of Prayer and the Ship of Stirrings: The Praying Self in Late Antique East Syrian Christianity* (Leuven: Peeters, 2019), 21–51. Not that Neoplatonists *never* felt distracted: the philosopher Porphyry thought it was exceptional that his teacher Plotinus—the leading exponent of late antique Platonism—didn't get distracted from his inner thoughts during conversations with other people (*Life of Plotinus* 8). But conversations, and other parts of a philosopher's workday that competed with contemplation, were not the same thing as a mind struggling during prayer.

18. Cassian, *Collationes* 11.6–8.

19. Sahdona, *Book of Perfection* 2.8.3, trans. Brock, *Syriac Fathers*, 202; John Climacus, *Klimax* 4, trans. Luibheid and Russell, pp. 104–5 (see Ps. 95:6).

20. Basil, *Great Asketikon*, LR 5.3.82–93; *AP/G* Antony 35, trans. Ward, p. 8; Cassian, *Collationes* 1.4–5; *AP/G* Dioscorus 1; *AP/GN*, N. 92, trans. Wortley, p. 73.

21. Conversation: Sahdona, *Book of Perfection* 2.8.25, in Brock, *Syriac Fathers*. People in power, judges: Basil, *Great Asketikon*, SR 21, 201, 306; Pseudo-Macarius, *Logoi* 15.19 (collection 2); Cassian, *Collationes* 23.6.2; Theodoret, *Historia religiosa* 21.33; Gerontius, *The Life of Melania the Younger* 42; *RB* 20; Donatus, *Regula* 18; *On Prayer*, in Brock, *Syriac Fathers*, p. 175; Hildemar, *Expositio* 52. This strategy may stem from Origen, *Peri euches* 8.2: see Perrone, *La preghiera secondo Origene*, 160–63. Distancing: Kross, *Chatter*, 51–61.

22. Shem'on d-Ṭaybutheh, *Book of Medicine* 171b, trans. Mingana, p. 23; Shem'on, *Profitable Counsels* 20, trans. Kessel and Sims-Williams, p. 293 (and see also 285); *AP/GN*, N. 548 ("graft" trans. Wortley, p. 373); Cassian, *Collationes* 9.27–32; Barsanuphius and John, *Letters* 237.

23. Pierre Hadot, "Exercices spirituels," in *Exercices spirituels et philosophie antique*, 2nd ed. (Paris: Études Augustiniennes, 1987), 13–58, at 37–47; Ellen Muehlberger, *Moment of Reckoning: Imagined Death and Its Consequences in Late Ancient Christianity* (Oxford: Oxford University Press,

2019), classical pedagogy at 129–42, quotation 132 (= Libanius, *Progymnasamata* 24); Jonathan L. Zecher, *The Role of Death in* The Ladder of Divine Ascent *and the Greek Ascetic Tradition* (Oxford: Oxford University Press, 2015), 52–79.

24. Cassian, *Collationes* 23.9; Babai, *Letter to Cyriacus* 55, in Brock, *Syriac Fathers*; Dadishoʿ, *Shelya*, 54a–55a.

25. John Climacus, *Klimax* 6; similarly Anastasios of Sinai, *Eratopokriseis* 17; Zecher, *The Role of Death*, 217; Evagrius, *Praktikos* 29, trans. Sinkewicz, pp. 102–103. See more generally Alan E. Bernstein, *Hell and Its Rivals: Death and Retribution among Christians, Jews, and Muslims in the Early Middle Ages* (Ithaca: Cornell University Press, 2017), 67–98.

26. Angels: *AP/GN*, N. 487, trans. Wortley, p. 319 (likewise Isaiah, *Asketikon* 2.9 and Dadishoʿ Qaṭraya, *Commentaire du livre d'abba Isaïe* 2.10); *Bohairic Life of Pachomius* 114, in *Pachomian Koinonia* 1:167–8; *RM* 10.92–120 (drawing on *Passio Sebastiani* 13, in PL 17:1027). See more generally Jean Leclercq, *The Love of Learning and the Desire for God: A Study of Monastic Culture*, trans. Catharine Misrahi (New York: Fordham University Press, 1961), 65–86.

27. John Climacus, *Klimax* 4 (oven), 7 (beds), trans. Luibheid and Russell, pp. 96, 138; Catherine Jolivet-Lévy, "La vie des moines en Cappadoce (VIᵉ–Xᵉ siècle): Contribution à un inventaire des sources archéologiques," in *La vie quotidienne des moines en Orient et en Occident (IVᵉ–Xᵉ siècle)*, vol. 1, *L'état des sources*, ed. Olivier Delouis and Maria Mossakowska-Gaubert (Cairo and Athens: Institut Français d'Archéologie Orientale and École Française d'Athènes, 2015), 215–49, Simeon at 291–320.

28. *AP/GN*, N. 135. See also Paul C. Dilley, *Monasteries and the Care of Souls in Late Antique Christianity: Cognition and Discipline* (Cambridge: Cambridge University Press, 2017), 148–85; Zecher, *The Role of Death*, 104–9.

29. Isaac of Nineveh, *Discourses* 1.58.407, trans. Wensinck, p. 273; Antony of Choziba, *Bios Georgiou* 1.5, trans. Vivian and Athanassakis, p. 38 (fish hook); John of Apamea, *Letter to Hesychius* 68, trans. Brock, *Syriac Fathers*, 97; John of Ephesus, *Lives of the Eastern Saints* 13, trans. Brooks, 1:202.

30. Oliver Burkeman, *Four Thousand Weeks: Time Management for Mortals* (New York: Farrar, Straus and Giroux, 2021), esp. 57–69.

31. Gregory, *Dialogi* 2.35. On the Stoic and Neoplatonic influences here see Pierre Courcelle, "La vision cosmique de saint Benoît," *Revue d'Études Augustiniennes et Patristiques* 13 (1967): 97–117. On the significance of the time of night see Basilius Steidle, "Intempesta noctis hora: Die mitternächtliche 'kosmische Vision' St. Benedikts (Dial. 2,25.2)," *Benediktinische Monatschrift* 57 (1981): 191–201.

32. *Visio Baronti* 11, 13; Jonas, *Vita Columbani* 2.12; *Vita Sadalbergae* 26; Gregory, *Dialogi* 4.50.6.

33. Boniface, *Letters* 10 (quotation p. 8 in Tangl's Latin ed.). Other calls for discernment in dreams and visions: Rich, *Discernment*, 184–88. Early

medieval China: Eric M. Greene, *Chan before Chan: Meditation, Repentance, and Visionary Experience in Chinese Buddhism* (Honolulu: Kuroda Institute and University of Hawai'i Press, 2021), esp. 57–109.

34. On the surge in visionary literature in the early Middle Ages: Claude Carozzi, *Le voyage de l'âme dans l'Au-delà d'après la littérature latine (V^e–XIIIe siècle)* (Rome: École Française de Rome, 1994), 13–297; Matthew Dal Santo, *Debating the Saints' Cult in the Age of Gregory the Great* (Oxford: Oxford University Press, 2012), esp. 21–148; Kreiner, "Autopsies and Philosophies of a Merovingian Life: Death, Responsibility, Salvation," *Journal of Early Christian Studies* 22 (2014): 113–52; Peter Brown, *The Ransom of the Soul: Afterlife and Wealth in Early Western Christianity* (Cambridge, MA: Harvard University Press, 2015), esp. 65–79, 158–67, 197–204. Late antique precedent: Muehlberger, *Moment of Reckoning*, 147–82.

35. Bitton-Ashkelony, *The Ladder of Prayer*; Brouria Bitton-Ashkelony, "Pure Prayer and Ignorance: Dadishoʻ Qaṭraya and the Greek Ascetic Legacy," *Studi e materiali di storia delle religioni* 78, 1 (2012): 200–226, "undistracted prayer" at 204; Perrone, *La preghiera*, 564–87; Columba Stewart, "Imageless Prayer and the Theological Vision of Evagrius Ponticus," *JECS* 9 (2001): 173–204.

36. Vittorio Berti, *L'Au-delà de l'âme et l'en-deça du corps: Approches d'anthropologie chrétienne de la mort dans l'Église syro-orientale* (Fribourg: Academic Press Fribourg, 2015), 73–135, quotation at 123. Education and networks: Sabina Chialà, "Les mystiques syro-orientaux: Une école ou une époque?" in *Les mystiques syriaques*, ed. Alain Desreumaux (Paris: Geuthner, 2011), 63–78.

37. Dadishoʻ Qaṭraya had a somewhat different opinion about this: Bitton-Ashkelony, "Pure Prayer and Ignorance," 209–14.

38. Isaac of Nineveh, *Discourses* 3.9.9–11, 3.9.15. Gregory and exegetical vision: Conrad Leyser, *Authority and Asceticism from Augustine to Gregory the Great* (Oxford: Clarendon, 2000), 181–85. For similar views in Evagrius and Cassian see Luke Dysinger, *Psalmody and Prayer in the Writings of Evagrius Ponticus* (Oxford: Oxford University Press, 2005), 59–60, 62–103.

39. Asterius, *Liber ad Renatum* 9.19 ("Ut de praemio futurae uitae taceam, quam magnum est huic solo fixis haerere uestigiis, et animum per caelum cum sideribus ambulare!"); *AP/GN*, N. 371, trans. Wortley, p. 241; John of Dalyatha, *Memre* 6.16, 8.8; Joseph Ḥazzaya, *Lettre sur les trois étapes de la vie monastique* 4.140; Shemʻon d-Ṭaybutheh, *Book of Medicine* 166a; Joseph Ḥazzaya, *On Spiritual Prayer*, in Brock, *Syriac Fathers*, 316–17.

40. John of Dalyatha, *Memre* 1.3; Mar Shamli, *Letter* 9; Columbanus, *Sermones* 1.4 ("Qui enim, rogo, terrena ignorat, caelestia cur scrutatur?"); Isaac of Nineveh, *Discourses* 3.5.6, trans. Chialà p. 44 and Hansbury p. 321; Behishoʻ Kamulaya, *Memre* 3, trans. Blanchard, pp. 306–7 (68a); see also Columba Stewart, *Cassian the Monk* (New York: Oxford University Press, 1998), 51–54, on progressive contemplation according to Evagrius

and Cassian. On dating Behisho''s work to the later eighth century, see Sabino Chialà, "La *Lettre* de Mar Šamli à un de ses disciples: Écrit inédit d'un auteur méconnu," *Le Muséon* 125 (2012): 35–54, at 40–45. On the semantic range of *mad'a* in this period: Winfried Büttner, *"Gottheit in uns": Die monastische und psychologische Grundlegung der Mystik nach einer überlieferten Textkollektion aus Werk des Šem'on d-Ṭaibuṭeh* (Wiesbaden: Harrassowitz, 2017), 210–16, 286–98.

41. Behisho' Kamulaya, *Memre* 3, p. 309 (72a); Gregory, *Dialogi* 4.1.1.

42. Evagrius, *Peri logismon* 40, trans. Sinkewicz, p. 180; Evagrius, *Scholia on the Psalms* 8 on Ps. 138:16, trans. Dysinger, in *Psalmody and Prayer*, 175, and see more generally 172–84; Joseph Ḥazzaya, *Lettre sur les trois étapes de la vie monastique* 5.142.

43. Philoxenus of Mabbug, *Excerpt on Prayer*, in Brock, *Syriac Fathers*, p. 129; Barsanuphius and John, *Letters* 207, trans. Chryssavgis, 1:215; Bitton-Ashkelony, *The Ladder of Prayer*, 198 (Joseph Ḥazzaya); John of Dalyatha, *Memre* 6.15; Isaac of Nineveh, *Discourses* 1.22, trans. Brock, in *Syriac Fathers*, p. 257.

44. Stupor (*temha*) and skipping the office: Robert Beulay, *L'enseignement spirituel de Jean de Dalyatha, mystique syro-oriental du VIIIe siècle* (Paris: Beauchesne, 1990), 215–39.

45. Isaac of Nineveh, *Discourse* 2.32.5, trans. Brock, p. 143; Behisho', *Memre* 4, pp. 326–27 (91a); see also Bitton-Ashkelony, *Ladder of Prayer*, 88–101 (Isaac of Nineveh), 174 (John of Dalyatha), 197–203 (Joseph Ḥazzaya); Joseph Ḥazzaya, *Letter* 49, trans. Hansbury, in John of Dalyatha, *Letters*, p. 298. Evagrius had not discussed the mind's limits in pure prayer: Brouria Bitton-Ashkelony, "The Limit of the Mind (*nous*): Pure Prayer according to Evagrius Ponticus and Isaac of Nineveh," *Zeitschrift für antikes Christentum* 15, no. 2 (2011): 291–321, at 312. The concept of flow was first developed by the psychologist Mihaly Csikszentmihalyi: *Beyond Boredom and Anxiety: The Experience of Play in Work and Games* (San Francisco: Jossey-Bass, 1975), with contributions by Isabella Csikszentmihalyi.

46. Cassian, *Collationes* 23.5.7–9 (*labere, decidere, lubricis cogitationibus, conruere, abducere*); Isaac of Nineveh, *Discourses* 2.5.4, trans. Brock, p. 7.

47. Mar Shamli, *Letter* 13; Joseph Ḥazzaya, *Letter* 49, in John of Dalyatha, *Letters*; Shem'on d-Ṭaybutheh, *On the Consecration of the Cell* 17 (see also Isaac of Nineveh, *Discourses* 1.72.495, also citing Macarius).

48. Isaac of Nineveh, *Discourses* 2.3.2.18 (= *Centuries on Knowledge* 2.18); Büttner, *Gottheit in uns*, 132–34, 299–300; Beulay, *L'enseignement spirituel*, 423–64; Khayyat, introduction to John of Dalyatha, *Les homélies I–XV*, pp. 13–23; Bitton-Ashkelony, *The Ladder of Prayer*, 159–88.

49. Basil, *Hexaemeron* 8.2. Augustine: Muehlberger, *Moment of Reckoning*, 65–104 ("simulations of death" at 68). Hairpin: Asen Kirin and Katherine Marsengill, *Modernism Foretold: The Nadler Collection of Late Antique Art from Egypt* (Athens, GA: Georgia Museum of Art, 2020), 59, 194–95

252 NOTES TO PAGES 190-93

(catalog no. 52). On the late antique and early medieval penchant for scalar thinking: Kreiner, *Legions of Pigs in the Early Medieval West* (New Haven: Yale University Press, 2020), 44–77.

50. Peter Brown, *The Body and Society: Men, Women, and Sexual Renunciation in Early Christianity* (New York: Columbia University Press, 1988), 235–40; Foucault, *Les aveux de la chair*, 106–45; Joshua Cohen, *Attention: Dispatches from a Land of Distraction* (New York: Random House, 2018), 558.

CONCLUSION

1. "The Parting of Body and Soul," in *Necrosima*, trans. Burgess, p. 29.
2. Livia Kohn, *Monastic Life in Medieval Daoism: A Cross-Cultural Perspective* (Honolulu: University of Hawai'i Press, 2003), 185 (distracted prayers and liturgies); Eric M. Greene, *Chan before Chan: Meditation, Repentance, and Visionary Experience in Chinese Buddhism* (Honolulu: Kuroda Institute and University of Hawai'i Press, 2021), 159–60, 174–76 (drinking and sex); Greene, *The Secrets of Buddhist Meditation: Visionary Meditation Texts from Early Medieval China* (Honolulu: Kuroda Institute and University of Hawai'i Press, 2021), 61–69, 81–86 (physical and psychic risks). Source proliferation: Kohn, *Monastic Life in Medieval Daoism*, esp. 203–25; Greene, *Chan before Chan*; Ann Heirman and Mathieu Torck, *A Pure Mind in a Clean Body: Bodily Care in Buddhist Monasteries of Ancient India and China* (Ghent: Academia Press, 2012) (monastic rules/vinayas).
3. Moschos, *Pratum spirituale* 130, trans. Wortley, p. 108. Modern diagnoses: see, e.g., Johann Hari, *Stolen Focus: Why You Can't Pay Attention—and How to Think Deeply Again* (New York: Crown, 2022); Adam Gazzaley and Larry D. Rosen, *The Distracted Mind: Ancient Brains in a High-Tech World* (Cambridge, MA: MIT Press, 2016); James Danckert and John D. Eastwood, *Out of My Skull: The Psychology of Boredom* (Cambridge, MA: Harvard University Press, 2020), esp. 42–43, 90–100, 148–57; Cal Newport, *A World without Email: Reimagining Work in an Age of Communication Overload* (New York: Portfolio/Penguin, 2021).
4. Samuel Rubenson, "The Formation and Re-Formation of the Sayings of the Desert Fathers," *Studia Patristica* 55 (2013): 3–22; Zachary B. Smith, *Philosopher-Monks, Episcopal Authority, and the Care of the Self: The Apophthegmata Patrum in Fifth-Century Palestine* (Turnhout, Belgium: Brepols, 2017); Brouria Bitton-Ashkelony and Aryeh Kofsky, *The Monastic School of Gaza* (Leiden: Brill, 2006), 99–100; Sabina Chialà, "Les mystiques syro-orientaux: Une école ou une époque?" in *Les mystiques syriaques*, ed. Alain Desreumaux (Paris: Geuthner, 2011), 63–78, at 70–72; Gianfrancesco Lusini, "Le monachisme en Éthiopie: Esquisse d'une histoire" and Florence Jullien, "Types et topiques de l'Égypte: Réinterpréter les modèles aux VIᵉ–VIIᵉ siècles," both in *Monachismes d'Orient: Images, échanges, influences. Hommage à Antoine Guillaumont*, ed. Jullien and Marie-Joseph Pierre

(Turnhout, Belgium: Brepols, 2011), 133–47, 151–63; Samuel Rubenson, *The Letters of St. Antony: Monasticism and the Making of a Saint* (Minneapolis: Fortress Press, 1995), 14–34; J. Leclerq, "L'ancienne version latine des Sentences d'Évagre pour les moines," *Scriptorium* 5 (1951): 195–213; Sims-Williams, *An Ascetic Miscellany*.

5. Anastasios, *Eratopokriseis* 24. See further John Haldon, "The Works of Anastasius of Sinai: A Key Source for the History of Seventh-Century East Mediterranean Society and Belief," in *The Byzantine and Early Islamic Near East*, vol. 1, *Problems in the Literary Source Material*, ed. Averil Cameron and Lawrence I. Conrad (Princeton: Darwin Press, 1992), 107–47, at 131–32. Rabbis: Michal Bar-Asher Siegal, *Early Christian Monastic Literature and the Babylonian Talmud* (Cambridge: Cambridge University Press, 2013), 77–86.

6. *Topos/tropos:* Anthony of Choziba recounting George of Choziba's comments to him: *Bios Georgiou* 8.33.

7. Abu Nuʿaym, *Ḥilyat al-awliya* 10:136–47, trans. Suleiman A. Mourad, "Christian Monks in Islamic Literature: A Preliminary Report on Some Arabic Apophthegmata Patrum," *Bulletin of the Royal Institute for Inter-Faith Studies* 6 (2004): 81–98, at p. 92. Mind in motion: Cassian, *Collationes* 1.18; John Climacus, *Klimax* 4; Isaac of Nineveh, *Discourses* 2.15; Beh Ishoʿ, *Memre* 6. Small victories: e.g., *AP/GN*, N. 211; Isaac of Nineveh, *Discourses* 2.1.

Ancient and Medieval Sources

For the benefit of nonspecialist readers, I have prioritized English- or other modern-language translations here, though translations in the text are mine unless noted otherwise. Scholars will know where to find the critical editions.

Abraham. *The History of Rabban Bar-'Idta.* Translated by E. A. Wallis Budge. In vol. 2 of *The Histories of Rabban Hormizd the Persian and Rabban Bar-'Idta.* London: Luzac, 1902.

Aithbe damsa bés mara. Edited and translated by Donncha Ó hAodha, "The Lament of the Old Woman of Beare." In *Sages, Saints and Storytellers: Celtic Studies in Honour of Professor James Carney,* edited by Donnchadh Ó Corráin, Liam Breatnach, and Kim McCone. Kildare, Ireland: An Sagart, 1989.

Aldhelm of Malmesbury. *Aenigmata.* Translated by A. M. Juster, *Saint Aldhelm's Riddles.* Toronto: University of Toronto Press, 2015.

Ambrose of Milan. *Exameron.* Translated by John J. Savage, *Saint Ambrose: Hexameron, Paradise, and Cain and Abel.* Washington, DC: Catholic University of America Press, 1961.

Ambrosiaster. *In epistulas ad Corinthios.* Edited by Heinrich Joseph Vogels. CSEL 81.2. Vienna: Hölder-Pichler-Tempsky, 1968.

Anastasios of Sinai. *Diegeseis peri tou Sina* and *Diegemata psychophele.* Edited and translated by André Binggeli, "Anastase le Sinaïte: *Récits sur le Sinaï* et *Récits utiles à l'âme*." PhD diss., University of Paris–Sorbonne, 2001.

———. *Eratopokriseis.* Translated by Joseph A. Munitiz, *Questions and Answers.* Turnhout, Belgium: Brepols, 2011.

Antonius. *Bios kai politeia tou makariou Symeon tou Stylitou.* Translated by Robert Doran, "The Life and Daily Mode of Living of the Blessed Simeon the Stylite." In *The Lives of Simeon Stylites.* Kalamazoo: Cistercian Publications, 1992.

Antony. *Letters.* Edited and translated by Samuel Rubenson, in *The Letters of St. Antony: Monasticism and the Making of a Saint.* Minneapolis: Fortress Press, 1995.

Antony of Choziba. *Bios kai politeia tou en hagiois patros hemon Georgiou.* Translated by Tim Vivian and Apostolos N. Athanassakis, *The Life of Saint George of Choziba and the Miracles of the Most Holy Mother of God at Choziba.* San Francisco: International Scholars Publications, 1994.

Apophthegmata patrum. Alphabetical Collection [*AP/G*]. Translated by Benedicta Ward, *The Sayings of the Desert Fathers.* Rev. ed. Kalamazoo: Cistercian Publications, 1984.

———. Anonymous Collection [*AP/GN*]. Edited and translated by John Wortley, *The Anonymous Sayings of the Desert Fathers: A Select Edition and Complete English Translation.* Cambridge: Cambridge University Press, 2013.

———. Systematic Collection [*AP/GS*]. Edited and translated by Jean-Claude Guy, *Les Apophtegmes des pères: Collection systématique.* 3 vols. SC 387, 474, 498. Paris: Cerf, 1993–2005.

———. Pelagius and John's Latin Collection [*AP/PJ*]. PL 73:851–988. Paris: Migne, 1849.

———. 'Enanisho''s Syriac Collection [*AP/S*]. Translated by Ernest A. Wallis Budge, *The Wit and Wisdom of the Christian Fathers of Egypt: The Syrian Version of the* Apophthegmata patrum *by 'Ânân Îshô' of Bêth 'Âbhe.* London: Oxford University Press, 1934.

Arnobius the Younger. *Commentarii in Psalmos.* Edited by Klaus-D. Daur. CCSL 25. Turnhout, Belgium: Brepols, 1990.

Asterius. *Liber ad Renatum monachum.* Edited by S. Gennaro. In *Scriptores "Illyrici" minores.* CCSL 85. Turnhout, Belgium: Brepols, 1972.

Athanasius of Alexandria. *Vita Antonii / Bios kai politeia tou hosiou patrios hemon Antoniou.* Translated by Robert C. Gregg, *The Life of Saint Antony.* New York: Newman Press, 1980.

Augustine of Hippo. *Enarrationes in psalmos.* Translated by Maria Boulding and edited by John E. Rotelle, *Expositions of the Psalms.* Part 3, vols. 15–20 of *The Works of Saint Augustine: A Translation for the 21st Century.* Hyde Park, NY: New City Press, 2000.

———. *De Genesi ad litteram.* Translated by Edmund Hill, "The Literal Meaning of Genesis." In *On Genesis.* Part 1, vol. 13 of *The Works of Saint Augustine: A Translation for the 21st Century.* Brooklyn, NY: New City Press, 2002.

———. *De opere monachorum.* Translated by Mary Sarah Muldowney, "The Work of Monks." In *Saint Augustine: Treatises on Various Subjects,* edited by Roy J. Defarri. Washington, DC: Catholic University of America Press, 1952.

———. *Ordo monasterii.* Translated by George Lawless. In *Augustine of Hippo and His Monastic Rule.* Oxford: Oxford University Press, 1987.

———. *Praeceptum.* Translated by George Lawless. In *Augustine of Hippo and His Monastic Rule.* Oxford: Oxford University Press, 1987.

Aurelian of Arles. *Regula ad monachos.* PL 68:385–95. Paris: Migne, 1847.

———. *Regula ad virgines.* PL 68:399–406. Paris: Migne, 1847.

Barsanuphius and John of Gaza. *Letters.* Translated by John Chryssavgis. 2 vols. Washington, DC: Catholic University of America Press, 2006–7.

Basil of Caesarea. *Great Asketikon.* Translated by Anna M. Silvas, *The Asketikon of St Basil the Great.* Oxford: Oxford University Press, 2005.

———. *Hexaemeron.* Edited and translated by Stanislas Giet, *Homélies sur l'Hexaéméron.* 2nd ed. SC 26. Paris: Cerf, 1968.

Baudonivia. *Vita Radegundis.* Translated by Jo Ann McNamara and John E. Halborg with E. Gordon Whatley, "Radegund: II." In *Sainted Women of the Dark Ages.* Durham, NC: Duke University Press, 1992.

Bede. *In epistolas VII catholicas.* Edited by M. L. W. Laistner. CCSL 121. Turnhout, Belgium: Brepols, 1983.

———. *In principium Genesis.* Translated by Calvin B. Kendall, *On Genesis.* Liverpool: Liverpool University Press, 2008.

———. *Vita beatorum abbatum Benedicti, Ceolfridi, Eosterwini, Sigfridi, atque Hwaetberhti.* Translated by J. F. Webb, "Lives of the Abbots of Wearmouth and Jarrow." In *The Age of Bede.* London: Penguin, 1998.

———. *Vita Cuthberti.* Translated by Bertram Colgrave. In *Two Lives of Saint Cuthbert.* New York: Greenwood, 1969.

Behisho' Kamulaya. *Memre.* Edited and translated by Monica J. Blanchard, "Discourses on the Monastic Way of Life." PhD diss., Catholic University of America, 2001.

Boniface. *Letters.* Translated by Ephraim Emerton. New York: Columbia University Press, 1940.

Braulio of Saragossa. *Vita Aemiliani.* Translated by A. T. Fear, "The Life of Aemilian the Confessor." In *Lives of the Visigothic Fathers.* Liverpool: Liverpool University Press, 1997.

Brock, Sebastian P. *A Brief Outline of Syriac Literature.* Kottayam, India: St. Ephrem Ecumenical Research Institute, 1997.

———. *The Syriac Fathers on Prayer and the Spiritual Life.* Kalamazoo: Cistercian Publications, 1987.

Brock, Sebastian P., and Susan Ashbrook Harvey, trans. *Holy Women of the Syrian Orient.* Updated ed. Berkeley: University of California Press, 1998.

Boud'hors, Anne, and Chantal Heurtel. *Les ostraca coptes de la TT 29: Autour du moine Frangé.* 2 vols. Brussels: Centre de Recherches en Archéologie et Patrimoine, 2010.

Caesaria of Arles. Letter to Richild and Radegund. Translated by Jo Ann McNamara and John E. Halborg with E. Gordon Whatley. In *Sainted Women of the Dark Ages.* Durham, NC: Duke University Press, 1992.

Caesarius of Arles, Letter to Caesaria. Edited and translated by Adalbert de Vogüé and Joël Courreau. In *Oeuvres pour les moniales.* SC 345. Paris: Cerf, 1988.

———. *Regula ad monachos.* Edited and translated by Adalbert de Vogüé and Joël Courreau, *Oeuvres pour les moines,* SC 398. Paris: Cerf, 1994.

———. *Regula ad virgines.* Edited and translated by Adalbert de Vogüé and Joël Courreau, *Oeuvres pour les moniales.* SC 345. Paris: Cerf, 1988.

Cassian, John. *Collationes.* Translated by Boniface Ramsey, *The Conferences.* New York: Newman Press, 1997.

————. *De institutis coenobiorum*. Translated by Boniface Ramsey, *The Institutes*. New York: Newman Press, 2000.

Cassiodorus, *Expositio psalmorum*. Translated by P. G. Walsh, *Explanation of the Psalms*. 3 vols. New York: Paulist Press, 1990–91.

————. *Institutiones*. Translated by James W. Halporn, *Institutions of Divine and Secular Learning*. Liverpool: Liverpool University Press, 2004.

Chrysostom, John. *Adversus oppugnatores vitae monasticae*. Translated by David G. Hunter, "Against the Opponents of the Monastic Life." In *Two Treatises by John Chrysostom*. Lampeter, Wales: Edwin Mellen Press, 1988.

Clavis sanctae scripturae. Edited by Jean-Baptiste Pitra. In *Patres antenicaeni*. Vol. 2 of *Analecta sacra spicilegio Solesmensi parata*. Paris: Typis Tusculanis, 1884.

Clement of Llanthony. *De sex alis*. Translated by Bridget Balint, "On the Six Wings of the Seraph." In *The Medieval Craft of Memory: An Anthology of Texts and Pictures*, edited by Mary Carruthers and Jan M. Ziolkowski. Philadelphia: University of Pennsylvania Press, 2002.

Columbanus. *Paenitentiale*. Edited and translated by G. S. M. Walker. In *Sancti Columbani Opera*. Dublin: Dublin Institute for Advanced Studies, 1970.

————. *Regula coenobialis*. Edited and translated by G. S. M. Walker. In *Sancti Columbani Opera*. Dublin: Dublin Institute for Advanced Studies, 1970. My endnotes refer to the Latin version found in PL 80:216–224 (Paris: Migne, 1850), which is closer to the manuscript tradition.

————. *Regula Columbani*. Edited and translated by G. S. M. Walker. In *Sancti Columbani Opera*. Dublin: Dublin Institute for Advanced Studies, 1970.

————. *Sermones*. Edited and translated by G. S. M. Walker. In *Sancti Columbani Opera*. Dublin: Dublin Institute for Advanced Studies, 1970.

Consensoria monachorum. Translated by Claude Barlow, "Monastic Agreement." In vol. 2 of *Iberian Fathers*. Washington, DC: Catholic University of America Press, 1969.

Consultationes Zacchei christiani et Apollonii philosophi. Edited and translated by Jean Louis Feiertag with Werner Steinmann, *Questions d'un païen à un chrétien*. SC 401–2. Paris: Cerf, 1994.

Cyril of Scythopolis. *Bioi*. Translated by R. M. Price. In *Lives of the Monks of Palestine*. Kalamazoo: Cistercian Publications, 1991.

Dadisho' Qaṭraya. *Commentaire du livre d'abba Isaïe*. Translated by René Draguet. CSCO 327. Leuven, Belgium: CSCO, 1972.

————. *Compendious Commentary*. Translated by Mario Kozah, Abdulrahim Abu-Husayn, and Suleiman Mourad, *Dadisho' Qaṭraya's Compendious Commentary on the Paradise of the Egyptian Fathers in Garshuni*. Piscataway, NJ: Gorgias Press, 2016.

————. *Filekseyus* [Ge'ez version of the *Compendious Commentary*]. Translated by Robert Kitchen, "Introduction to Selections from the Ge'ez *Filekseyus*: Questions and Answers of the Egyptian Monks." In Kozah et al., *An Anthology of Syriac Writers from Qatar*.

————. *Shelya*. Edited and translated by Alphonse Mingana, "A Treatise on

Solitude." In *Early Christian Mystics* = *Woodbrooke Studies* 7 (1934): 70–143 (ET), 201–47 (Syriac).

Donatus of Besançon. *Regula ad virgines*. Translated by Jo Ann McNamara and John E. Halborg, "The Rule of St. Donatus of Besançon." *Vox Benedictina* 2 (1985): 85–107, 181–203.

Dorotheus of Gaza. *Didaskalia*. Edited and translated by L. Regnault and J. de Préville, *Oeuvres spirituelles*. SC 92. Paris: Cerf, 1963.

Ekkehard IV. *Casus sancti Galli*. Edited and translated by Hans F. Haefele and Ernst Tremp with Franziska Schnoor, *St. Galler Klostergeschichten*. Darmstadt: Wissenschaftliche Buchgesellschaft, 2020.

'Enanisho'. *The Book of Paradise*. Translated by E. A. Wallis Budge. 2 vols. London: Drugulin, 1904.

Eucherius of Lyon. *Instructionum libri duo*. Edited by C. Mandolfo. CCSL 66. Turnhout, Belgium: Brepols, 2004.

Eugippius of Castellum Lucullanum. *Regula*. Edited by Fernando Villegas and Adalbert de Vogüé. CSEL 87. Vienna: Hölder-Pichler-Tempsky, 1976.

———. *Vita Severini*. Translated by George W. Robinson, *The Life of Saint Severinus*. Cambridge, MA: Harvard University Press, 1914.

Evagrius of Pontus. *Ad monachos*. Translated by Robert E. Sinkewicz, "To Monks in Monasteries and Communities." In *Evagrius of Pontus: The Greek Ascetic Corpus*. Oxford: Oxford University Press, 2003.

———. *Antirrhetikos*. Translated by David Brakke, *Talking Back: A Monastic Handbook for Combating Demons*. Collegeville, MN: Liturgical Press, 2009.

———. *De octo spiritibus malitiae / Peri ton okto logismon*. Translated by Robert E. Sinkewicz, "Eight Thoughts." In *Evagrius of Pontus: The Greek Ascetic Corpus*. Oxford: Oxford University Press, 2003.

———. *Praktikos*. Translated by Robert E. Sinkewicz. In *Evagrius of Pontus: The Greek Ascetic Corpus*. Oxford: Oxford University Press, 2003.

———. *Peri logismon*. Translated by Robert E. Sinkewicz, "On Thoughts." In *Evagrius of Pontus: The Greek Ascetic Corpus*. Oxford: Oxford University Press, 2003.

Ferrandus of Carthage. *Vita Fulgentii*. Translated by Robert B. Eno, "Life of the Blessed Bishop Fulgentius." In *Fulgentius: Selected Works*. Washington, DC: Catholic University of America Press, 1997.

Ferreolus of Uzès. *Regula*. Edited by Vincent Desprez, "La *Regula Ferrioli*: Texte critique." *Revue Mabillon* 60 (1982): 117–48.

Florentius. *Vita Rusticulae sive Marcia abbatissae Arelatensis*. Edited by Bruno Krusch. MGH Scriptores rerum Merovingicarum 4. Hanover and Leipzig: Hahn, 1902.

Fortunatus, Venantius. *Carmina*. Edited and translated by Michael Roberts, *Poems*. Cambridge, MA: Harvard University Press, 2017.

———. *Vita Radegundis*. Translated by Jo Ann McNamara and John E. Halborg with E. Gordon Whatley, "Radegund: I." In *Sainted Women of the Dark Ages*. Durham, NC: Duke University Press, 1992.

————. *Vita Paterni*. Edited by Bruno Krusch. MGH Auctores Antiquissimi 4.2. Berlin: Weidmann, 1885.

Fructuosus of Braga. *Regula*. Translated by Claude Barlow, "Rule for the Monastery of Compludo." In vol. 2 of *Iberian Fathers*. Washington, DC: Catholic University of America Press, 1969.

Fulgentius of Ruspe. *Letters*. Translated by Robert B. Eno, in *Fulgentius: Selected Works*. Washington, DC: Catholic University of America Press, 1997.

Gerontius. *Vita Melaniae iunioris*. Translated by Elizabeth A. Clark, *The Life of Melania, the Younger*. New York and Toronto: Edwin Mellen Press, 1985.

Gregory the Great. *Dialogi / De miraculis patrum italicorum*. Translated by Odo John Zimmerman, *Saint Gregory the Great: Dialogues*. New York: Fathers of the Church, 1959.

Gregory of Tours. *Historiae*. Translated by Lewis Thorpe, *The History of the Franks*. New York: Penguin, 1974.

————. *Liber in gloria confessorum*. Translated by Raymond Van Dam, *Glory of the Confessors*. Corr. ed. Liverpool: Liverpool University Press, 2004.

————. *Liber vitae patrum*. Translated by Edward James, *Life of the Fathers*. 2nd ed. Liverpool: Liverpool University Press, 1991.

Hilary of Poitiers. *Tractatus super Psalmos*. Edited by J. Doignon. CCSL 61. Turnhout, Belgium: Brepols, 1997.

Hildemar of Civate. *Expositio in regulam Sancti Benedicti*. Edited and translated by the Hildemar Project. http://hildemar.org.

Historia monachorum in Aegypto. Translated by Norman Russell, *The Lives of the Desert Fathers*. Kalamazoo: Cistercian Publications, 1981.

History of Mar Yawnan. Translated by Sebastian Brock. In Kozah et al., *An Anthology of Syriac Writers from Qatar*.

Hrabanus Maurus. *De rerum naturis/De universo*. PL 111: 9–614. Paris: Migne, 1852.

Hugh of St. Victor. *De arca Noe*. Edited by Patrice Sicard. CCCM 176. Turnhout, Belgium: Brepols, 2001.

————. *Didascalion*. Edited by Charles Henry Buttimer. Washington, DC: Catholic University Press, 1939.

————. *Libellus de formatione arche*. Translated by Conrad Rudolph. In *The Mystic Ark: Hugh of St. Victor, Art, and Thought in the Twelfth Century*. New York: Cambridge University Press, 2014.

Intexuimus. Edited by Michael Gorman, "The Visigothic Commentary on Genesis in Autun 27 (S. 29)." *Recherches Augustiniennes et Patristiques* 30 (1997): 167–277.

Isaac of Kalamun. *The Life of Samuel of Kalamun*. Edited and translated by Anthony Alcock. Warminster, England: Aris & Phillips, 1983.

Isaac of Nineveh. *Discourses* 1. Translated by A. J. Wensinck, *Mystic Treatises by Isaac of Nineveh*. Amsterdam: Koninklijke Akademie van Wetenschappen, 1923.

————. *Discourses* 2.1–2. Translated by Sebastian Brock, "St Isaac the Syrian: Two Unpublished Texts." *Sobornost* 19 (1997): 7–33.

————. *Discourses* 2.3 [= *Centuries on Knowledge/Kephalaia gnostica/Rīšē d-īdaʿtā*]. Translated by Paolo Bettiolo, *Isacco di Ninive: discorsi spirituali*. 2nd ed. Magnano, Italy: Edizioni Qiqajon, 1990.

————. *Discourses* 2.4–41. Translated by Sebastian Brock, *Isaac of Nineveh: "The Second Part," Chapters IV–XLI*. CSCO 555. Louvain: Peeters, 1995.

————. *Discourses* 3. Translated by Mary Hansbury, "Isaac the Syrian: The Third Part." In Kozah et al., *An Anthology of Syriac Writers from Qatar*.

————. *Discourses* 5. Translated by Mary Hansbury, "Two Discourses of the Fifth Part in Isaac the Syrian's Writings." In Kozah et al., *An Anthology of Syriac Writers from Qatar*.

Isaiah of Scetis. *Asketikon*. Translated by René Draguet, *Les cinq recensions de l'Ascéticon syriaque d'Abba Isaïe*. CSCO 293–94. Louvain: CSCO, 1968.

Ishoʿdenaḥ of Basra. *Ktaba d-nakputa*. Edited and translated by J.-B. Chabot, *Le livre de la chastité*. Rome: École Française de Rome, 1896.

Isidore of Seville. *Etymologiae sive origines*. Translated by Stephen A. Barney, W. J. Lewis, J. A. Beach, and Oliver Berghof, *Etymologies*. Cambridge: Cambridge University Press, 2006.

————. *Regula*. Translated by Aaron W. Godfrey, "The Rule of Isidore." *Monastic Studies* 18 (1998): 7–29.

Jerome. *Commentarioli in Psalmos*. Edited by D. Germain Morin. CCSL 72. Turnhout, Belgium: Brepols, 1959.

————. *Vita Hilarionis*. Translated by Carolinne White, "Life of Hilarion." In *Early Christian Lives*. New York: Penguin, 1998.

John Climacus. *Klimax / Plakes pneumatikai*. Translated by Colm Luibheid and Norman Russell, *The Ladder of Divine Ascent*. Mahwah, NJ: Paulist Press, 1982.

John of Dalyatha. *Memre*. Edited and translated by Nadira Khayyat, *Les Homélies I–XV*. Antelias, Lebanon: Centre d'Études et de Recherches Orientales; Hadath, Lebanon: Université Antonine, 2007.

————. *Letters*. Translated by Mary T. Hansbury. Piscataway, NJ: Gorgias Press, 2006.

John of Ephesus. *Lives of the Eastern Saints*. Edited and translated by E. W. Brooks. PO 17–19. Paris: Firmin-Didot, 1923–26.

John Moschos. *Pratum spirituale*. Translated by John Wortley, *The Spiritual Meadow*. Kalamazoo: Cistercian Publications, 1992.

John Rufus. *Vita Petri Iberi*. Edited and translated by Cornelia B. Horn and Robert R. Phenix Jr., *The Life of Peter the Iberian*. Atlanta: Society of Biblical Literature, 2008.

Jonas of Bobbio. *De accedendo ad Deum*. Edited and translated by Albrecht Diem, in *The Pursuit of Salvation: Community, Space, and Discipline in Early Medieval Monasticism, with a Critical Edition and Translation of the* Regula cuiusdam ad uirgines. Turnhout, Belgium: Brepols, 2021.

————. *Vita Columbani abbatis discipulorumque eius*. Translated by Alexander O'Hara and Ian Wood, *Life of Columbanus and His Disciples*. Liverpool: Liverpool University Press, 2017.

————. *Regula cuiusdam ad virgines.* Edited and translated by Albrecht Diem, in *The Pursuit of Salvation.* Turnhout, Belgium: Brepols, 2021.

Joseph Ḥazzaya. *Lettre sur les trois étapes de la vie monastique.* Edited and translated by Paul Harb and François Graffin. PO 45.2. Turnhout, Belgium: Brepols, 1992. The book cites this edition; there is also an English translation by Gunnar Olinder, *A Letter of Philoxenus of Mabbug Sent to a Friend.* Gothenburg: [Wettergren and Kerber], 1950.

Kozah, Mario, Abdulrahim Abu-Husayn, Saif Shaheen Al-Murikhi, and Haya Al Thani, eds. *An Anthology of Syriac Writers from Qatar in the Seventh Century.* Piscataway, NJ: Gorgias Press, 2015.

Leander of Seville. *De institutione virginum.* Translated by Claude Barlow, "The Training of Nuns and the Contempt of the World." In vol. 1 of *Iberian Fathers.* Washington, DC: Catholic University of America Press, 1969.

The Life of Simeon of the Olives. Edited by Robert Hoyland and Kyle Brunner, translated by Sebastian Brock. Piscataway, NJ: Gorgias Press, 2021.

Mark the Monk. *Traités.* Edited and translated by George-Matthieu de Durand. SC 445, 455. Paris: Cerf, 1999–2000. The book cites the section numbers of this edition; there is also an English translation by Tim Vivian and Augustine Casiday, *Counsels on the Spiritual Life.* Crestwood, NY: St Vladimir's Seminary Press, 2009.

Mar Shamli. *Letter.* Edited and translated by Sabino Chialà, "La *Lettre* de Mar Šamli à un de ses disciples: Écrit inédit d'un auteur méconnu." *Le Muséon* 125 (2012): 35–54.

Necrosima. Translated by Henry Burgess. In *Select Metrical Homilies of Ephrem Syrus.* London: Blackader, 1853.

Novatus. *Sententia.* Edited by Fernando Villegas, "Les Sentences pour les moines de Novat le Catholique." *Revue Bénédictine* 86 (1976): 49–74.

Origen. *Peri euches.* Translated by Rowan A. Greer, *On Prayer.* New York: Paulist Press, 1979.

Pachomian Koinonia. Translated by Armand Veilleux. 3 vols. Kalamazoo: Cistercian Publications, 1980–82.

Palladius. *Historia Lausiaca.* Translated by John Wortley, *The Lausiac History.* Collegeville, MN: Liturgical Press, 2015.

Pelagius. *Ad Corinthios II.* Edited by J. Armitage Robinson, in *Expositions of Thirteen Epistles of St. Paul.* Cambridge: Cambridge University Press, 1926.

Plutarch. *Peri polupragmosunes.* Edited and translated by W. C. Helmbold, in *Plutarch's Moralia* 6. Loeb Classical Library. London: Heinemann; Cambridge, MA: Harvard University Press, 1939.

Porphyry. *Life of Plotinus.* Translated by A. H. Armstrong. Loeb Classical Library 440. Cambridge, MA: Harvard University Press, 1969.

Pseudo-Macarius. *Logoi.* Translated by George A. Maloney, *The Fifty Spiritual Homilies and the Great Letter.* New York: Paulist Press, 1992.

Pseudo-Matthei Evangelium. Edited and translated by Jan Gijsel, in *Libri de nativitate Mariae.* Corpus Christianorum Series Apocryphum 9. Turnhout, Belgium: Brepols, 1997.

Regula Benedicti [*RB*]. Translated by Bruce L. Venarde, *The Rule of Benedict*. Cambridge, MA: Harvard University Press, 2011.

Regula communis. Translated by Claude Barlow, "General Rule for Monasteries." In vol. 2 of *Iberian Fathers*. Washington, DC: Catholic University of America Press, 1969.

Regula cuiusdam patris ad monachos. Edited by Fernando Villegas, "La 'Regula cuiusdam Patris ad monachos': Ses sources littéraires et ses rapports avec la 'Regula monachorum' de Colomban." *Revue d'Histoire de la Spiritualité* 49 (1973): 3–36.

Regula et instituta patrum. Edited and translated by Adalbert de Vogüé. In *Les règles des saints pères*. SC 298. Paris: Cerf, 1983.

Regula magistri [*RM*]. Translated by Luke Eberle, *The Rule of the Master*. Kalamazoo: Cistercian Publications, 1977.

Regula monasterii Tarnatensis. Edited by Fernando Villegas, "La 'Regula Monasterii Tarnatensis': Texte, sources et datation." *Revue Bénédictine* 84 (1974): 7–65.

Regula orientalis. Edited and translated by Adalbert de Vogüé. In *Les règles des saints pères*. SC 298. Paris: Cerf, 1983.

Regula Pauli et Stephani. Translated by H. Hagan, "The Rule of Paul and Stephen." *American Benedictine Review* 58, no. 3 (2007): 313–42.

Regula sancti Macharii abbatis. Edited and translated by Adalbert de Vogüé. In *Les règles des saints pères*. SC 297. Paris: Cerf, 1982.

Regula sanctorum patrum Serapionis, Macharii, Pafnutii, et alterius Macharii. Edited and translated by Adalbert de Vogüé. In *Les règles des saints pères*. SC 297. Paris: Cerf, 1982.

Regula sanctorum patrum Serapionis, Macharii, Paunuti, et alii Machari. Edited and translated by Adalbert de Vogüé. In *Les règles des saints pères*. SC 298. Paris: Cerf, 1983.

Rufinus. *Regula Basilii*. Translated by Anna M. Silvas, *The Rule of Saint Basil in Latin and English*. Collegeville, MN: Liturgical Press, 2013.

Rule of Naqlun. Translated by Michel Breydy, "La version de *Règles et préceptes de St. Antoine* vérifiée sur les manuscrits arabes." In *Études sur le christianisme dans l'Égypte de l'antiquité tardive*, edited by Ewa Wipszycka. Rome: Institutum Patristicum Augustinianum, 1996.

Severus, Sulpicius. *Gallus: Dialogi de virtutibus sancti Martini*. Translated by Bernard M. Peebles, *Dialogues*. Fathers of the Church 7. Washington, DC: Catholic University of America Press, 1949.

———. *Vita Martini*. Translated by F. H. Hoare, "Life of Saint Martin of Tours." In *Soldiers of Christ: Saints and Saints' Lives from Late Antiquity and the Early Middle Ages*, edited by Thomas F. X. Noble and Thomas Head. University Park: Pennsylvania State University Press, 1995.

Shem'on d-Ṭaybutheh. *On the Consecration of the Cell*. Translated by André Louf, "Discours sur la cellule de Mar Syméon de Taibouteh." *Collectanea Cisterciensia* 64 (2002): 34–55.

———. *Book of Medicine*. Edited and translated by Alphonse Mingana, "Mystical Works of Simon of Ṭaibutheh." In *Early Christian Mystics = Woodbrooke Studies* 7 (1934): 1–69 (English), 281–320 (Syriac).

————. *Profitable Counsels*. Edited and translated by Grigory Kessel and Nicholas Sims-Williams, "The *Profitable Counsels* of Šemʿōn d-Ṭaibūtēh: The Syriac Original and Its Sogdian Version." *Le Muséon* 124 (2011): 279–302.

Shenoute of Atripe. *Discourses*. Translated by David Brakke and Andrew Crislip. In *Selected Discourses of Shenoute the Great: Community, Theology, and Social Conflict in Late Antique Egypt*. Cambridge: Cambridge University Press, 2015.

————. *Rules*. Edited and translated by Bentley Layton. In *The Canons of Our Fathers: Monastic Rules of Shenoute*. Oxford: Oxford University Press, 2014.

Sims-Williams, Nicholas, ed. *An Ascetic Miscellany: The Christian Sogdian Manuscript E28*. Turnhout, Belgium: Brepols, 2017.

Smaragdus of St. Mihiel. *Expositio in regulam sancti Benedicti*. Translated by David Barry, *Commentary on the Rule of Saint Benedict*. Kalamazoo: Cistercian Publications, 2007.

Statuta patrum. Edited and translated by Adalbert de Vogüé. In *Les règles des saints pères*. SC 297. Paris: Cerf, 1982.

The Syriac Life of Saint Simeon Stylites. Translated by Robert Doran. In *The Lives of Simeon Stylites*. Kalamazoo: Cistercian Publications, 1992.

Talbot, Alice-Mary, ed. *Holy Women of Byzantium: Ten Saints' Lives in English Translation*. Washington, DC: Dumbarton Oaks, 1996.

Theodoret of Cyrrhus. *Historia religiosa / Philotheos historia*. Translated by R. M. Price, *A History of the Monks of Syria*. Kalamazoo: Cistercian Publications, 1985.

Thomas, John Philip, and Angela Constantinides Hero, eds. *Byzantine Monastic Foundation Documents: A Complete Translation of the Surviving Founders' Typika and Testaments*. Vol. 1. Washington, DC: Dumbarton Oaks, 2000.

Valerius of Bierzo. *De genere monachorum*. Edited and translated by Manuel C. Díaz y Díaz. In *Valerio del Bierzo: Su persona, su obra*. León: Caja España de Inversiones; Archivio Histórico Diocesano de León, 2006.

Visio Baronti. Translated by J. N. Hillgarth. In *Christianity and Paganism, 350–750: The Conversion of Western Europe*. Rev. ed. Philadelphia: University of Pennsylvania Press, 1986.

Vita Ceolfridi abbatis. Translated by J. F. Webb, "The Anonymous History of the Life of Ceolfrith." In *The Age of Bede*. London: Penguin, 1998.

Vita Fructuosi. Translated by A. T. Fear, "The Life of Fructuosus of Braga." In *Lives of the Visigothic Fathers*. Liverpool: Liverpool University Press, 1997.

Vita Geretrudis. Translated by Jo Ann McNamara and John E. Halborg with E. Gordon Whatley, "Gertrude, Abbess of Nivelles." In *Sainted Women of the Dark Ages*. Durham, NC: Duke University Press, 1992.

Vita Landiberti vetustissima. Edited by Bruno Krusch and Wilhelm Levison. MGH Scriptores rerum Merovingicarum 6. Hanover and Leipzig: Hahn, 1913.

Vita patrum Iurensium. Translated by Tim Vivian, Kim Vivian, and Jeffery Burton Russell, *The Life of the Jura Fathers*. Kalamazoo: Cistercian Publications, 1999.

Vita Sadalbergae. Translated by Jo Ann McNamara and John E. Halborg with E. Gordon Whatley, "Saint Sadalberga." In *Sainted Women of the Dark Ages*. Durham, NC: Duke University Press, 1992.

Vita Wandregiseli. Edited by Bruno Krusch and Wilhelm Levison. MGH Scriptores rerum Merovingicarum 5. Hanover and Leipzig: Hahn, 1910.

Vööbus, Arthur, ed. and trans. *The Synodicon in the West Syrian Tradition*. 4 vols. CSCO 367–68, 375–76. Louvain: CSCO, 1975–76.

———, ed. and trans. *Syriac and Arabic Documents Regarding Legislation Relative to Syrian Asceticism*. Stockholm: ETSE, 1960.

Wimbush, Vincent L., ed. *Ascetic Behavior in Greco-Roman Antiquity: A Sourcebook*. Minneapolis: Fortress Press, 1990.

Zacharias Scholasticus. *History of Severus*. Edited and translated by M.-A. Kugener, *Vie de Sévère, par Zacharie le Scholastique*. PO 2.1. Paris: Firmin-Didot, 1903. The book cites the page numbers from this edition; there is also an English translation by Lena Ambjörn, *The Life of Severus by Zachariah of Mytilene*. Piscataway, NJ: Gorgias Press, 2008.

CREDITS

Map: Lindsay Holman / Ancient World Mapping Center.

Fig. 1: Jacek Pochanke / Alamy Stock Photo.

Fig. 2: Photograph taken in 1959 or 1960 during a survey by the Mission archéologique française, directed by Roman Ghirshman. Reproduced from Marie-Joseph Steve, *L'Île de Khārg: Une page de l'histoire du Golfe Persique et du monachisme oriental* (Neuchâtel: Recherches et Publications, 2003), plate 55.1.

Fig. 3: © Etienne Louis.

Figs. 4a/4b: © Elizabeth S. Bolman.

Fig. 5: American Research Center in Egypt, Inc. (ARCE). Photo credit: Arnaldo Vescovo.

Fig. 6: Photo credit: Darlene Brooks Hedstrom.

Fig. 7: Dublin, Trinity College Library, Ms. 58, fol. 32v. The Board of Trinity College Dublin.

Fig. 8: Dublin, Trinity College Library, Ms. 58, fol. 255v. The Board of Trinity College Dublin.

Fig. 9: © Institute français d'archéologie orientale (IFAO).

Fig. 10: © DAIK/LMU. Photo I. Eichner.

Figs. 11a/11b: St. Gallen, Cod. sang. 904, fols. 189, 204 (Ireland, ca. 845 CE).

Fig. 12: Vatican, Ms. Lat. 5758, p. 134. © 2023 Biblioteca Apostolica Vaticana. Reproduced by permission of Biblioteca Apostolica Vaticana, with all rights reserved.

Fig. 13: Cologne, Erzbischöfliche Dioezesan- und Dombibliothek, Cod. 63, fol. 174v.

INDEX

Page number in *italics* indicate illustrations.
Page numbers after 200 refer to notes.

OTHER BOOKS BY JAMIE KREINER

Legions of Pigs in the Early Medieval West

*The Social Life of Hagiography in
the Merovingian Kingdom*

THE WANDERING MIND